STRENGTHENING INDIA'S INTERGOVERNMENTAL FISCAL TRANSFERS

LEARNINGS FROM THE ASIAN EXPERIENCE

Abdul D. Abiad, Çiğdem Akın, Bruno Carrasco, Jurgen Conrad, Shikha Jha,
Navendu Karan, Sonalini Khetrapal, Abhijit Sen Gupta, Rishav Singh, and Lei Lei Song

DECEMBER 2020

ASIAN DEVELOPMENT BANK

 Creative Commons Attribution 3.0 IGO license (CC BY 3.0 IGO)

Notes:
In this report, "$" refers to United States dollars.
ADB recognizes "China" as the People's Republic of China.
The fiscal year (FY) of the Government of India and its agencies ends on 31 March. "FY" before a calendar year denotes the year in which the fiscal year ends, e.g., FY2019 ends on 31 March 2019.
In 2011, the Government of India approved the name change of the State of Orissa to Odisha. This document reflects this change. However, when reference is made to policies that predate the name change, the formal name Orissa is retained.

Cover design by Francis Manio. On the cover: Floral pattern is inspired by the Indian culture and art. Vines represent the growth and paths for distribution from a common source.

Contents

Tables, Figures, and Boxes

Boxes

About the Contributors

Abdul D. Abiad is director of the Macroeconomic Research Division of the Economic Research and Regional Cooperation Department at the Asian Development Bank (ADB), where he oversees ADB's flagship publication, the *Asian Development Outlook*. From 2000 to 2015, he was with the International Monetary Fund in Washington, DC, where he worked on the *World Economic Outlook*. Abiad's research has focused on finance sector development and international financial integration, fiscal policy, exchange rates and trade, economic resilience, and infrastructure. He holds a PhD in economics from the University of Pennsylvania.

Çiğdem Akın is a senior public management economist in ADB's Central and West Asia Department. She held the same position earlier at the South Asia Department. Akın has project management experience in public finance, fiscal decentralization and local governance, tax administration and finance sector development. Prior to ADB, she was an assistant professor of economics at the Johns Hopkins University School of Advanced International Studies in Washington, DC and Bologna, Italy, and a researcher at the International Monetary Fund and the ADB Institute in Japan. She has publications on international economics, business cycles, and housing markets. Akın holds a PhD in economics from the George Washington University.

Bruno Carrasco is chief of the Governance Thematic Group at ADB's Sustainable Development and Climate Change Department. He leads the operational guidance and knowledge solutions work across fiscal management, governance of infrastructure, and related areas. Carrasco's research has focused on applied policy on fiscal and monetary management. Earlier at ADB's South Asia Department, he was director of the Public Management, Financial Sector and Trade Division from 2010 to 2019 and was also director of the Regional Cooperation and Coordination Division from 2008 to 2010. He was a senior economist at the European Central Bank from 2000 to 2003, while on leave from ADB. Carrasco holds a PhD in economics from the University of Essex.

Jurgen Conrad is a financial industry professional. After joining ADB in 2002, he led policy-based lending programs and technical assistance projects on financial and private sector development, and public–private partnerships in Central and West Asia, and South Asia Departments. From 2013 to 2018, Conrad headed ADB's economics team in Beijing. While on leave from ADB, he worked as an advisor for Japan Bank for International Cooperation in Tokyo from 2009 to 2011. Prior to ADB, Conrad worked with Deutsche Bank and a leading German economic think tank. He holds a master of arts in economics and finance from the Goethe University Frankfurt.

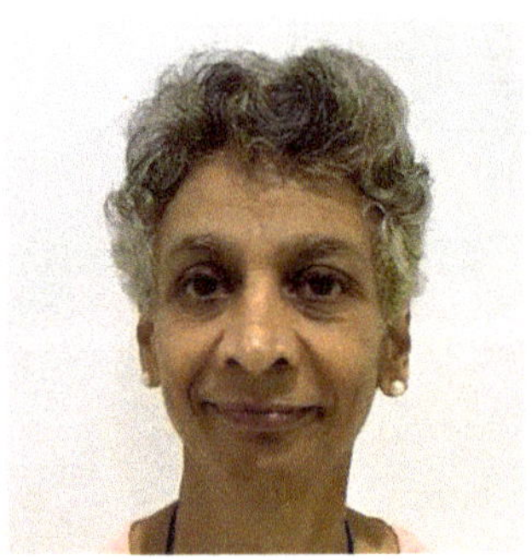

Shikha Jha is a development economics professional. After joining ADB in 2004, she led operational policy work in Central and West Asia Department, and public sector governance research as principal economist at the Economic Research and Regional Cooperation Department. Before ADB, Jha was a professor at the Indira Gandhi Institute of Development Research and an economist at the National Institute of Public Finance and Policy. She also served as a consultant to the World Bank and an advisor to the Twelfth Finance Commission of India. Jha holds a PhD in economics from the Indian Statistical Institute and completed postdoctoral research at the London School of Economics.

Navendu Karan is a senior public management economist in ADB's South Asia Department. He specializes in public sector management reforms. His expertise also includes debt management and sustainability analysis, economic analysis of energy projects, and public–private partnership transaction advisory. Prior to ADB, Karan worked with IL&FS Infrastructure Development Corporation Ltd., the Reserve Bank of India, and PricewaterhouseCoopers Pvt Ltd. India. He also supported the Government of the Lao People's Democratic Republic as a fiscal decentralization advisor and co-authored the study *Fiscal Sustainability of Debt of States* for the Twelfth Finance Commission of India. Karan holds a PhD in economics from the Indian Institute of Management Ahmedabad.

Sonalini Khetrapal is a social sector specialist in ADB's South Asia Department. She specializes in health systems policy, planning and management, health financing, and health insurance. She leads ADB's support to the National Urban Health Mission in India and the Health Sector Development Program in Bhutan. She has published several research articles in international peer-reviewed journals and recently authored a book *Healthcare for India's Poor—The Health Insurance Way*. Prior to ADB, she worked for international development institutions including the World Bank and UNICEF. Khetrapal holds a PhD in health economics and policy from the University of London.

Abhijit Sen Gupta is a senior economist at the Asian Infrastructure Investment Bank, where he leads the research on cost–benefit analysis of infrastructure projects and undertakes studies on infrastructure in South Asia. Prior to this, Sen Gupta was senior economics officer in ADB's South Asia Department, focusing on international financial integration, fiscal decentralization, global value chain participation, and macroeconomic stabilization. He also worked with the World Bank and the International Monetary Fund and was an associate professor at the Jawaharlal Nehru University. He has published widely in international peer-reviewed journals. Sen Gupta holds a PhD in international economics from the University of California, Santa Cruz.

Rishav Singh is a director at the Public Finance Practice of Deloitte Touche Tohmatsu India, LLP. He has advised several state governments in India on designing and implementing funding strategy for the education sector and worked on establishing and strengthening linkages between the sector's key performance indicators and the resource allocation strategy. He has also supported the state governments in development of medium-term expenditure frameworks and undertaking budget reforms. Singh holds a master of arts in economics and a diploma in management from the Indian Institute of Management Calcutta.

Lei Lei Song is a regional economic advisor in ADB's South Asia Department, where he leads and coordinates economic work and development research and conducts policy dialogue with developing member countries on substantive economic, thematic, and sector issues. Song has professional and research experience in applied macroeconomics, international economics, and development economics. Before joining ADB, he was a research fellow at the Melbourne Institute of Applied Economic and Social Research, and a visiting academic at the Australian Treasury in Canberra. Song holds a PhD in economics from the University of Melbourne.

Foreword

Decentralization has played a prominent role in Asia and the Pacific as part of a broader public sector reform agenda. Devolution of more political, administrative, and fiscal powers to the subnational governments has gained momentum, increasingly driven by the motivation to broaden the outreach of high-quality services.

Reforms to fiscal federalism have in many instances driven the decentralization process. A growing body of the literature links diverse outcomes in income distribution, performance of subnational governments, and effectiveness of public service delivery with the features of the intergovernmental fiscal arrangements.

India is a federal republic with a long tradition of decentralization. With an annual economic growth rate averaging over 7% in recent decades and a diverse population of over 1.3 billion people, India is among the world's most dynamic economies with its own emerging challenges.

The Government of India aspires to improve the living standards of its citizens through inclusive and regionally balanced development. For that purpose, it puts greater emphasis on enhancing the governance, institutional capacity, and performance of the public sector at all tiers of the government while maintaining a sound fiscal framework. Across India's decentralized system, these goals have placed the state governments under the spotlight, requiring them to be more accountable in the delivery of this ambitious development agenda.

The Finance Commission of the Government of India is an autonomous constitutional body, established every 5 years, to make recommendations to the President of India on the quantum of tax sharing between the central and state governments, the formula for horizontal devolution, and the allocation of various other grants. In November 2017, the Fifteenth Finance Commission (15th FC) was mandated to design the new contours of India's intergovernmental fiscal transfer system originally for the period of 2020–2025. In November 2019, the period was extended one more year to include 2026.

The 15th FC has pursued a consultative approach, leveraging a broad range of ideas from national and international experts in multilateral development agencies. A request to the Asian Development Bank (ADB) was made for an in-depth assessment of India's fiscal federalism framework and synthesize the learnings from Asia and the Pacific. ADB's assessments focused primarily on the design of intergovernmental fiscal transfer systems and the use of performance-based transfers in promoting (i) subnational governance, and (ii) better outcomes in social sectors such as education and health.

This report covers ADB's policy recommendations to strengthen India's fiscal transfer system based on the comparative learnings from Australia, Indonesia, Japan, the People's Republic of China, and the Republic of Korea. While every country is unique and there is no "one size fits all" system, the report's key conclusion is that an effective intergovernmental fiscal transfer system employs the right mix of unconditional equalization transfers, specific-purpose transfers, and performance-based transfers to achieve the desired outcomes without sacrificing the autonomy of subnational governments.

Good governance is globally recognized as a catalyst for successful development. To help bolster progress in governance standards, this report develops a governance index for the Indian states and proposes a mechanism for the allocation of performance-based grants by the 15th FC, based on the states' periodic improvements in the governance index. The index covers indicators related to each state's (i) transparency and public accountability in local service delivery, (ii) sound fiscal and public financial management practices, (iii) per capita development expenditures, and (iv) improvements in ease of doing business. Similar indices are also proposed for achieving outcomes in the education and health sectors.

The recommendations provided for the consideration of the 15th FC are built upon ADB's globally recognized expertise, knowledge, and successful project implementation experience in public sector management reforms across India as well as in Asia and the Pacific. A close collaboration among a team of diverse regional and sectoral experts has contributed to the report's comprehensive coverage and policy analysis.

ADB's evidence-based research has helped raise the awareness on critical reforms related to fiscal federalism in India and good practices on decentralization among the government officials, policymakers, multilateral development agencies, and academia. ADB shared the learnings at the High-Level Roundtable on Fiscal Relations across Levels of Government, jointly organized by the 15th FC, ADB, Organisation for Economic Co-operation and Development (OECD), and the World Bank in New Delhi on 4 April 2019.

We are confident that this publication will become a key knowledge resource for policymakers and practitioners in public finance to strengthen fiscal decentralization in developing countries and also guide ADB's future operations in governance and public sector management reforms.

Bambang Susantono
*Vice-President for Knowledge Management
  and Sustainable Development*
Asian Development Bank

Shixin Chen
Vice-President for Operations 1
Asian Development Bank

Acknowledgments

This report was prepared in response to an invitation by the Chair of the Fifteenth Finance Commission (15th FC) of the Government of India to the Asian Development Bank (ADB) to assess and share the Asian experiences in fiscal decentralization and recommend findings from this analysis for the 15th FC's consideration. The report was developed based on the original terms of reference of the 15th FC for the period of 2020-2025. Based on the consultations with the 15th FC on 19 March 2018 and the presentation made to the 15th FC on 16 August 2018, the comments received were incorporated into the report. The main findings of the report were presented to the 15th FC on 4 April 2019 during the High-Level Roundtable on Fiscal Relations across Levels of Government, which was jointly organized by the 15th FC, ADB, Organisation for Economic Co-operation and Development (OECD), and the World Bank and was chaired by the 15th FC Chairman, N. K. Singh. The authors would like to thank the 15th FC members and acknowledge their guidance and valuable feedback.

This report—reflective of a One ADB approach—was produced through the collective efforts of ADB experts from several departments with contributions from an external specialist. The authors comprised Abdul D. Abiad (director of the Macroeconomic Research Division, Economic Research and Regional Cooperation Department [ERCD]); Çiğdem Akın (senior public management economist, Central and West Asia Department [CWRD]); Bruno Carrasco (chief of the Governance Thematic Group, Sustainable Development and Climate Change Department [SDCC]); Jurgen Conrad (former principal financial sector specialist, South Asia Department [SARD]); Shikha Jha (former principal economist, ERCD); Navendu Karan (senior public management economist, SARD); Sonalini Khetrapal (social sector specialist, SARD); Abhijit Sen Gupta (former senior economics officer, SARD); Rishav Singh (director, Deloitte Touche Tohmatsu India, LLP and specialist on fiscal transfers in the education sector); and Lei Lei Song (regional economic advisor, SARD).

The authors acknowledge the valuable comments from the internal peer reviewer, Hanif A. Rahemtulla (principal public management specialist, SDCC) and the external peer reviewer, Tapas K. Sen (advisor, PricewaterhouseCoopers Pvt. Ltd., Gurgaon, India and professor, National Institute of Public Finance and Policy, New Delhi, India). The authors also appreciate the knowledge exchanges with M. Govinda Rao (counselor, Takshashila Institute and adviser, Centre for Public Policy, Indian Institute of Management, Bangalore, India) and Sean Dougherty (senior economic advisor, OECD, Paris) on Indian and international experiences on fiscal decentralization.

The report would not have been possible without the support and guidance of ADB management, particularly Bambang Susantono (Vice-President, Knowledge Management and Sustainable Development) and Shixin Chen (Vice-President, Operations 1). The paper also benefited from the valuable suggestions of Hun Kim (former director general, SARD); Kenichi Yokoyama (director general, SARD); Diwesh Sharan (deputy director general, SARD); Takeo Konishi (country director, India Resident Mission, SARD); Sabyasachi Mitra (deputy country director, India Resident Mission, SARD); Rana Hasan (director of the Development Economics and Indicators Division, ERCD); Takuya Hoshino (financial sector specialist, SARD); Kavita S. Iyengar (country economist, Southeast Asia Department); Hiranya Mukhopadhyay (principal public management specialist, CWRD); and Rachana Shrestha (public management specialist, SDCC).

The authors thank Emmanuel Alano (consultant, ERCD); Pilipinas Quising (senior economics officer, ERCD); and Jian Zhuang (senior economics officer, East Asia Department) for providing excellent assistance in background research and data analysis.

The authors appreciate the outstanding support provided by Monica Mei V. Cariño, June A. Gacutan, Kristina Hidalgo, Sheila Marie Foronda-Mariano, and Jackie B. Moreno for editing this report.

Finally, the authors thank Rodel S. Bautista (senior communications assistant) and the staff of ADB's Department of Communications for their excellent technical support in preparing the manuscript for publication.

Abbreviations

ADB	Asian Development Bank
ABF	activity-based funding
ABS	Ayushman Bharat Scheme
CGC	Commonwealth Grants Commission
CGS	central government subsidy
COAG	Council of Australian Government
CPC	Communist Party of China
CPI	consumer price index
CRS	civil registration system
CSS	centrally sponsored scheme
DAK	Dana Alokasi Khusus
DAU	Dana Alokasi Umum
DBH	Dana Bagi Hasil
DDRF	District Disaster Response Fund
DRF	disaster risk financing
EU	European Union
FC	Finance Commission
FII	financial independence index
FRBM	Fiscal Responsibility and Budget Management
FY	fiscal year
GDP	gross domestic product
GOI	Government of India
GPDP	Gram Panchayat Development Plan
GER	gross enrollment ratio
GSDP	gross state domestic product
GST	goods and services tax
HDI	Human Development Index
HFE	horizontal fiscal equalization
HFWD	Health and Family Welfare Department
HWC	health and wellness center
HMIS	health management information system
HLMC	high-level monitoring committee
IMR	infant mortality rate
IT	information technology
IFI	international financial institution
IGA FFR	Intergovernmental Agreement on Federal Financial Relations
JER	Japan Earthquake Reinsurance Co., Ltd
JSY	Janani Suraksha Yojana
LAT	local allocation tax
LGU	local government unit
LPFP	Local Public Finance Program
LST	local shared tax
LTT	local transfer tax
MIC	Ministry of Internal Affairs and Communications
MOEF	Ministry of Economy and Finance
MOF	Ministry of Finance
MOHFW	Ministry of Health and Family Welfare
MOIS	Ministry of Interior and Safety
MTEF	medium-term expenditure framework
MTFF	medium-term fiscal framework
MHRD	Ministry of Human Resource Development
NAS	National Achievement Survey
NDMA	National Disaster Management Authority
NDRF	National Disaster Response Fund
NEP	national efficient price
NHM	National Health Mission
NPP	national partnership payment
NSPP	national specific purpose payment
OECD	Organisation for Economic Co-operation and Development
ONRN	Observatoire National des Risques Naturels
PAI	Public Affairs Index
PRC	People's Republic of China
PM-JAY	Pradhan Mantri Jan Arogya Yojana
PSU	public sector unit
PTR	pupil–teacher ratio
PWD	Public Works Department
RMSA	Rashtriya Madhyamik Shiksha Abhiyan
ROK	Republic of Korea

RTE	Right to Free and Compulsory Education Act	SPP	specific purpose payment
SDMA	State Disaster Management Authority	SSA	Sarva Shiksha Abhiyan
SDRF	State Disaster Response Fund	SSE	social sector expenditure
SED	School Education Department	TOR	terms of reference
SEQI	school education quality index	U-DISE	Unified District Information System for Education
SFC	State Finance Commission	UGC	University Grants Commission
SFD	standard fiscal demand	ULB	urban local body
SFN	standard fiscal need	VAT	value-added tax
SFR	standard fiscal revenue		

Executive Summary

In comparison to central or national governments, subnational governments, in general, have higher expenditure responsibilities—in line with its subsidiarity principle—and lower own revenues. Fiscal transfers address the large vertical imbalance among the various levels of government. Moreover, there could be economic disparities across regions—or horizontal imbalance—which also need to be addressed so that each subnational government is equally placed to provide a standard quality of service to all citizens.

The challenge in the design of intergovernmental transfers is to strike a balance between preserving the autonomy of subnational governments and mitigating against moral hazard issues related with higher level of equalization transfers from central to subnational governments. The intergovernmental fiscal transfers system in India has attempted to address these aspects. The strength of the fiscal transfers system in India arguably lies in its adaptability toward emerging requirements and the flexibility to introduce best practices to improve the system. The Fifteenth Finance Commission (15th FC) in India has taken office almost coinciding with the dissolution of the Planning Commission, thus relegating the responsibility for advice on fiscal transfers almost entirely on the FC except for transfers from central ministries.

This report discusses the country systems in Australia, Indonesia, Japan, the People's Republic of China (PRC), and the Republic of Korea (ROK) to draw learnings for India in the design of intergovernmental transfers. While there are other countries in Asia with prominent features of fiscal decentralization, the selection in this report was based on the interest expressed by the 15th FC to learn about the intergovernmental fiscal transfer systems in these countries and their experience with the use of performance-based transfers in promoting subnational governance and outcomes in social sectors such as education and health.

While most countries in the sample are not federal, there are important learnings to draw from unitary systems such as the PRC, which has strong decentralization features given its geographic size and population. The Indonesian case is relevant for its transition toward a decentralized structure where the transfers to the third tier of government gain prominence over the second tier. Indonesia is also comparable to India in terms of its size, population diversity, heterogeneity in economic development across the country, fiscal imbalances, and capacity constraints in fiscal management and service delivery at the subnational level. Thus, for both countries subnational fiscal needs, cost disability, and equity considerations constitute crucial factors for the design of intergovernmental fiscal transfer system. Japan and the ROK have unitary structures but their experience in incentivizing performance could be of relevance to India. Australia is highlighted as it is a federal state that most closely aligns with the federal structure of India.

The first section of the report provides a comparative institutional review of the Finance Commission in India vis-à-vis equivalent institutions in the selected Asian countries. It emphasizes the importance of a permanent secretariat to the FC and the need to strengthen the subnational State Finance Commissions.

The second section compares the intergovernmental fiscal transfer systems in the selected Asian countries with that in India. Sharing of central government revenues is a major source of transfers in most countries. There could also be other untied grants that allow subnational governments to spend based on their specific priorities. Invariably across countries, untied (or unconditional) transfers constitute the highest proportion of total transfers. Specific purpose grants like the national specific purpose payments in Australia and Special Allocation Fund (Dana Alokasi Khusus) in Indonesia serve to promote desired outcomes in the specific sectors that are decentralized such as health and education. Specific-purpose transfers can aim toward equalization of service standards across regions and can be more efficiently monitored than general purpose transfers in achievement of outcomes. Performance-based grants have been used by Australia and the ROK to reward targeted achievements by subnational governments. An effective fiscal transfers system must employ the right mix of unconditional equalization transfers, specific-purpose transfers, and performance-based transfers to incentivize subnational governments to achieve desired outcomes without sacrificing their fiscal autonomy.

The third section delves into the design of performance-based transfers. This report recommends that about 2% of the divisible pool of the central government in India be reserved for performance-based transfers, similar to the proportion under the 12th and 13th FC recommendations. It considers a possible framework for performance-based programs for better results and how this framework can be supported and leveraged by international financial institutions. Various studies have noted that quality of governance acts as a determinant in the delivery of services. This report constructs a governance index that can be used to incentivize state governments to show improvements in this index during the 15th FC period. Similarly, it suggests a health index and a school education quality index to promote better services in the respective sectors.

The fourth section provides this report's conclusions.

Keywords: fiscal policy, intergovernmental fiscal transfers, vertical and horizontal fiscal devolution, federalism, subnational government, performance-based grants, public sector budgeting, governance, health and education, India.

I. Mechanisms for Fiscal Transfers

A. The Institutional Arrangement for Fiscal Transfers in India

1. The Finance Commission (FC) in India is an autonomous constitutional body with the mandate to recommend to the President the distribution between the union and states of the net proceeds of shareable taxes, the principles that should govern provision of grants-in-aid to the states, and any other matter referred to the FC by the President. Article 280 of the Constitution prescribes that the FC shall be constituted every 5 years or less and consists of a chairman and four other members appointed by the President.

2. While the responsibility of designing intergovernmental transfers is vested with the FC, central government ministries also provide grants to state governments as central share for centrally sponsored schemes (CSS), central sector schemes and specific-purpose grants in their respective sectors. With the dissolution of the Planning Commission on 1 January 2015, which is now replaced by NITI Aayog, the Finance Commission is the main source of transfers to state governments and local governments besides transfers from central ministries (Figure 1).[1]

B. Strengths of the Institutional Arrangement in India

3. Since the 1st FC was appointed in 1951, all FCs have comprised distinguished experts working independently and under a defined context-specific remit to develop an intergovernmental fiscal transfer system based on economic principles. The chairman of the FC has the equivalent rank to a cabinet minister.

4. The FCs operate under a transparent, inclusive, and accountable framework through a process of deliberations with and across key stakeholders. FCs visit states that in turn make representations to the FC. The FC frames recommendations based on the specific remit entrusted to it and with the goal of collating the experiences and lessons across the consultative process and to the extent possible developing a consensus in terms of its recommendations to the President of India. The FC frames recommendations to address both vertical and horizontal imbalances. The recommendations fall into three categories: (i) those to be implemented by an order of the President, (ii) those to be implemented by law of parliament, and (iii) those to be implemented by executive order. As constitutionally mandated, the President shall cause the FC recommendations together with an explanatory note by the Ministry of Finance on actions taken thereon to be laid before both houses of the parliament.

---

[1] Other channels for intergovernmental coordination are the Inter-State Council and the National Development Council. The State Finance Commission (SFC) is expected to be constituted at least once in every 5 years to review the financial position of the local bodies and to make suitable recommendations to the Governor on the distribution of both shared taxes and grants between the state and the urban and rural local bodies. It can also recommend measures to strengthen the financial position of the local bodies and deliberate on any other matter referred to it by the Governor.

Figure 1   Institutional Structure for Intergovernmental Transfers in India

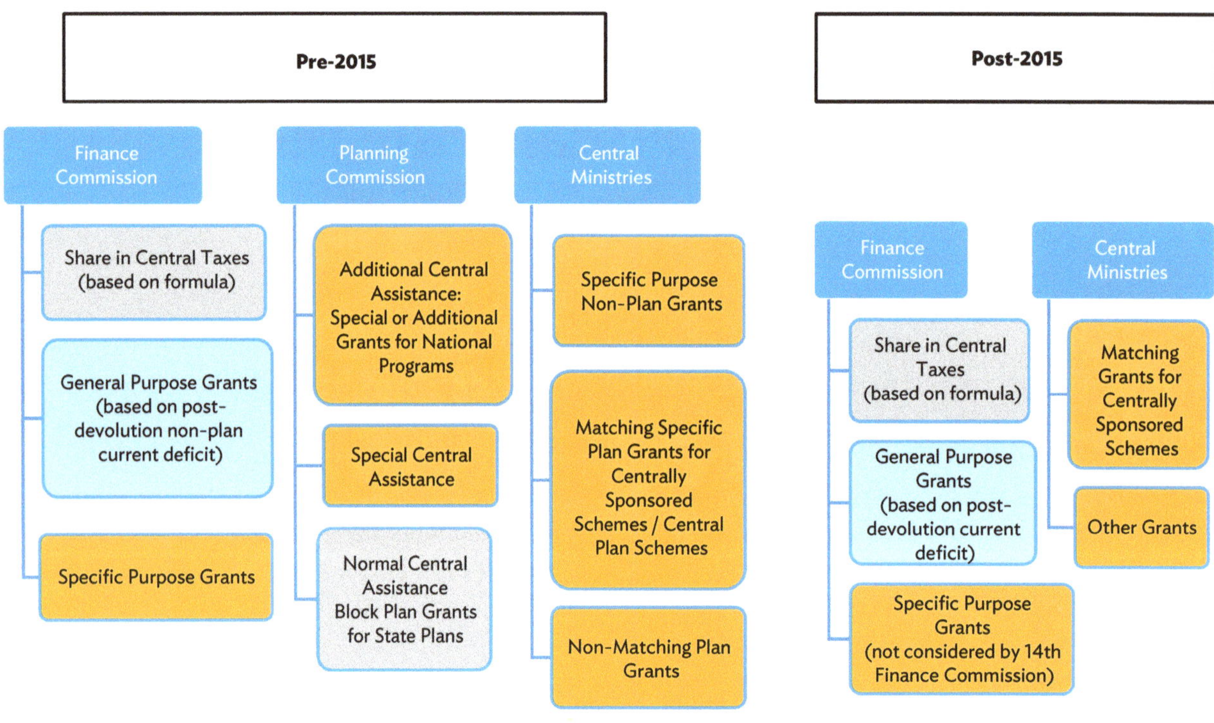

Source: Asian Development Bank.

5. By convention, the Finance Minister accepts FC recommendations and it falls on the Government of India (GOI) to implement them over the following 5 years before the next FC is constituted. The FC proceedings and meetings with stakeholders are shared in the FC reports, available in the public domain.

6. Although the broad contour of the role of the FC is provided in the Constitution, the terms of reference (TOR) of an FC can be specific to emerging requirements, referenced under "other matters." Thus, the 11th FC and 12th FC were asked to examine the issue of fiscal sustainability in their respective TORs. The TOR of the 15th FC lays much stress on examination of performance-based transfers in line with the development agenda of the GOI. While such specific changes are a subject of much debate

in the context of central involvement in the state government's fiscal management, FCs have been found to be fair in their examination of such matters.

C. Limitations of the Institutional Arrangement in India

7. The FCs review the intergovernmental transfers from the center to the second tier of government, namely, the states and with effect from the 10th FC, also recommend grants for the third tier (urban local bodies and panchayats). However, since the mandate is primarily focused on the transfers to state governments, the FC recommendations can be deemed to be partial from a wholistic federal fiscal framework perspective.[2] While states

---

[2]   Central FCs have been providing grants to the third tier of government to augment their resources. However, detailed recommendations are expected to be framed by the SFCs.

in turn, are mandated to establish State Finance Commissions (SFCs) to review the transfers to the local governments, these do not have the full authority of the national FCs and often the states are not actively involved in supporting transfers given limited resources available to transfer to local governments and/or limited absorptive capacity of local governments to implement programs. This is one of the reasons why while there may be differences across coverage and quality of service delivery across states, these are likely to be more pronounced across local bodies within states than across states and thereby accentuating horizontal imbalances.

8. The FCs are constituted with a fixed term of 2 years, extendable on a case-by-case basis, and subsequently disbanded. While this avoids institutional or mission creep, it constrains institutional memory as there is no permanent secretariat that can ensure close bridging from one commission to the next. Furthermore, an incoming commission must sort out all logistical arrangements, including staff recruitments, working arrangements, and office space before it can get set to work. The process can take anywhere between 3 to 6 months and leads to inefficiencies.

9. The FC has a list of sanctioned posts but the process of appointing suitable staff for an incoming commission is another time-consuming process. Staff gets deputed from government departments based on their ability, willingness, and suitability, as also obtained from other sources including direct recruitment. A major drawback with the system of recruitment through deputation is that it requires several levels of clearances. Even after requisite permissions by the Ministry of Finance (MOF) and relevant agencies are obtained, officials may not be immediately released by the lending departments and ministries. The FCs then recruit contractual staff, but this takes away from the productive time.

10. The legacy data and files of the previous FCs get transferred to the Finance Commission Cell in the MOF after the term of the FC is complete. Although these data and information again get transferred to

the new incoming FC on appointment, they are more than 5 years old by the time the new FC begins its work. The system lacks institutional memory, which would otherwise be useful for a new FC. Since there is no permanent secretariat to maintain and update data from time to time, the new commission must undertake the task afresh.

11. Finally, being a temporary body, the FC does not have a system of monitoring sector-specific grants. For the same reason, it is difficult to recommend fiscal transfer models that involve changes and updates during the FC implementation period.

D. Comparison of the Institutional Arrangement with Other Asian Countries

12. A comparative institutional review of FCs and/or their equivalents across selective countries in Asia was undertaken. These include Australia (federal constitutional monarchy), the People's Republic of China (PRC) (unitary republic), Indonesia (unitary republic), Japan (unitary monarchy), and the Republic of Korea (ROK) (unitary republic). Australia is highlighted as its federal structure most closely aligns with that of India (Appendix 1).

13. Australia has an independent permanent body, the Council of Australian Government (COAG) operating in tandem with the Commonwealth Grants Commission (CGC) under the Intergovernmental Agreement on Federal Financial Relations (IGA FFR). The COAG, headed by the Australian Prime Minister as Chair, is the highest intergovernmental decision-making body, responsible for vertical fiscal devolution. The CGC is a small independent body, responsible for horizontal fiscal devolution, that collects data for research and analysis, and measures relative fiscal capacities and needs for fiscal transfers. Section 96 of the Australian Constitution provides for the federal parliament to "grant financial assistance to any State on such terms and conditions as the Parliament thinks fit." The CGC comprises (i) a Commission,

and (ii) a Secretariat. The commission decides policy issues based on the advice received from all stakeholders as well as the secretariat and directs the work of the secretariat. The Commission consists of a chairperson and not less than two other members. On advice from the Federal Executive Council[3] and under the Commonwealth Grants Commission Act 1973, the Governor-General of the Commonwealth of Australia, appoints CGC commissioners on a full-time or part-term basis. Their term is not less than 1 year or more than 5 years, but they are eligible for reappointment.

14. The Secretariat oversees administrative, financial, and human resources management matters. The Secretariat employees are civil servants, headed by a Secretary who, as the Chief Executive Officer and Accountable Authority, is responsible for the Secretariat's activities. The Secretary is assisted by two assistant secretaries and a chief operating officer. In fiscal year (FY) 2018, the Secretariat had 30 staff with an annual budget of A$6.2 million.

15. Australian experience shows that a permanent secretariat is essential to the CGC. The Secretariat conducts high-quality research and analysis for CGC and provides effective support to the Commission's Chair and members to discharge their responsibilities, as well as help ensure sound corporate governance and financial management. With a permanent secretariat, these functions are performed continuously, and institutional knowledge and memory are maintained. The financial costs of running a permanent Secretariat may be higher than a temporary one, but at A$6 million a year, it is less than 0.01% of goods and services tax (GST) revenues that the CGC is mandated to distribute to the states.

16. **Consultative process in Australia.** The Commission in Australia consults with the states before it finalizes its recommendations on GST revenue-sharing relativities before the Commonwealth and states release their budgets. The Federal Treasurer would accept those recommendations and use them in the forthcoming Commonwealth Budget to share the estimated GST for that year among the states. Thus, a permanent secretariat provides the benefit of an institutional memory, which enables implementation of annual updates on even complicated transfer mechanisms.

17. In other countries (in this report), the authority for intergovernmental fiscal arrangement is vested within the MOF with varying degrees of independence. In Indonesia and the ROK, the MOF makes decisions on fiscal transfers, whereas in Japan the MOF works out the arrangement in association with the Ministry of Internal Affairs and Communications (MIC). In the PRC, fiscal policies and central–local fiscal relations are under the MOF, but its autonomy is limited over the government and most importantly, party organizations in fiscal policy making and implementation (Appendix 1).

E. Recommendations for the 15th Finance Commission

18. **Establish a permanent secretariat for the Finance Commission.** As in the Australian case, a permanent secretariat can (i) provide flexibility to introduce transfer mechanisms based on annual fiscal updates; (ii) retain institutional knowledge, data, and information that can quickly bring the incoming commission up to speed after taking charge; (iii) introduce and implement complex transfer systems on a relative shorter notice, if their benefit can be established; and (iv) make advance administrative arrangements, including clearances, for the incoming commission members. Although Australia has an elaborate secretariat, the cost is only a fraction of total transfers. The cost can be further reduced in India by strengthening the existing Finance Commission Cell in MOF, GOI such that the key

---

[3]   The Federal Executive Council, established by the Constitution, is the formal legal body responsible for advising the Governor-General and comprises all current and former Commonwealth Ministers and Assistant Ministers.

positions in this cell transfer to the incoming Finance Commission as soon as it takes charge.

19. **Strengthen State Finance Commissions.** The state governments have appointed their respective SFCs at different intervals, thus making it difficult to synchronize SFC periods with the central FC. In some cases, state governments either rejected the SFC recommendations or did not specify the time frame for implementation in the action taken report presented to the legislature as discussed by the 14th FC report (2015). The FC can incentivize states directly through transfers or indirectly through nonbinding recommendations to strengthen their SFCs to enhance the outreach and quality of services across local governments. In many outer lying local governments, public spending, no matter how small it is, has important multiplier effects in the local community so that it can be an important catalyst for economic activity in these areas. Empowering of SFCs and local governments could be instrumental in closing the horizontal imbalances across India.

II. Design of Intergovernmental Fiscal Transfers

A. The Need for Intergovernmental Fiscal Transfers

20. Intergovernmental fiscal transfers from central government to subnational governments serve three main objectives. First, they address the vertical imbalance (fiscal gap) between the central government and subnational governments as the expenditure requirements of the subnational governments typically exceed their own revenues due to insufficient tax capacity. Thus, they compensate subnational governments for differences between incurred expenditures and own revenues. Second, they address the horizontal imbalances between subnational governments. Third, they ensure national uniformity in the provision of public services to citizens across the country and incentivize good performance in service delivery by the subnational governments (Bessho 2017). This section will primarily focus on addressing vertical and horizontal imbalances using intergovernmental fiscal transfer system and building on the Asian experience. The third objective will be to assess performance considerations of transfer programs focusing on health and education and covered in detail in section III of this report.

21. **Vertical Imbalance.** In general, subnational governments have higher expenditure responsibilities in line with the subsidiarity principle—local governments are better able to respond to the needs of the local citizens and communities—and lower own revenues as compared to the national government. The need for fiscal transfer reflects large vertical imbalance among the various levels of government. Table 1 presents subnational expenditure as a ratio of total general government expenditure and compares it with subnational revenues as proportion of total general government revenues for various countries in Asia. The difference is particularly noteworthy in Indonesia where the central government collects more than 90% of the overall government revenue while being responsible for around 55% of expenditure, and the PRC where the central government collects 46% of general government revenue and spends 15% of general government expenditure. In comparison, the central government in India collects over 60% of general government revenue and spends about 45% of general government expenditure.

Table 1   International Comparison of Subnational Government Expenditure and Revenue as Proportion of Total General Government Expenditure and Revenue

	Australia*	Indonesia**	PRC*	Japan**	India***
SNG Expenditure/Total General Government Expenditure (%)	43.0	45.2	85.3	58.9	55.4
SNG Own Revenue/Total General Government Revenue (%)	25.9	7.4	53.6	41.0	33.2

IMF = International Monetary Fund, OECD = Organisation for Economic Co-operation and Development, SNG = subnational government.
* 2012–2017 period average; ** 2012–2015 period average; *** 2016–2018 period average.
Sources: Authors' calculations based on Government Finance Statistics, Australia, 2016–2017 and Australian Bureau of Statistics, April 2018; OECD Stats and OECD's White Paper on Local Public Finance (various issues, 2014–2017); IMF Article IV reports (2015 and 2017) and Statistik Indonesia, various issues; People's Republic of China, Ministry of Finance data accessed through CEIC database; and Reserve Bank of India (RBI) Study of State Budgets (2016–2017, 2017–2018 and 2018–2019); RBI Handbook of Statistics on Indian Economy 2017; and Annual Financial Statement, Annual Budget 2018–2019, Government of India.

22. Australian states finance about 60% of their spending from "own revenues," with the remainder being covered by federal grants. Including GST, the Commonwealth or federal government raises around 75% of total tax revenue and controls broad-based taxes such as personal and corporate income, and customs and excises. Large vertical imbalances require sizeable transfers from the Commonwealth to state governments. State taxes are about 15% of the national tax revenue, smaller than many other Organisation for Economic Co-operation and Development (OECD) countries. The rest of about 5% is from local governments (property tax). Australian states can set their own-tax bases and rates. Yet, the Commonwealth and the state governments do not have overlapping tax bases, unlike other decentralized federations, such as Canada and Switzerland.

23. **Horizontal Imbalance.** Regional disparities within a country could arise from structural, fiscal, or governance issues. There could be differences in fiscal capacities and needs among subnational governments, resulting in varying fiscal gaps among them. Transfers from the central government are expected to equalize the capacities commensurate with their fiscal needs so that service standards can be equalized across the regions.

24. The difference in income and fiscal capacity among the subnational or second tier of government in Australia, Japan, and the ROK is much smaller than in India. In Australia, for example, Table 2 shows that the household disposable income per capita of the richest state (Australian Capital Territory or ACT) is just a little over twice of the poorest (Tasmania). The own revenue capacity of the highest (ACT) almost doubles the lowest (Tasmania). On the other hand, in some states, such as Northern Territory and Western Australia with a large area and small population, it is costlier to deliver public services.

25. In Indonesia, on the other hand, the provinces greatly differ in their socioeconomic indicators. Vujanovic (2017) argues that variance in per capita income across Indonesian provinces is higher than other emerging economies like the PRC, India, Brazil, and Mexico. For example, in 2017 the average per capita income of the top five provinces, was more than six times that of the average per capita income in the five poorest provinces (Figure 2).

Table 2   Australian States and Territories—Key Statistics

	NSW	VIC	QLD	SA	WA	TAS	NT	ACT
Area (%)	10.40	3.00	22.50	12.70	33.00	0.90	17.50	0.03
Population (%)	32.00	25.20	20.10	7.00	10.80	2.10	1.00	1.60
Gross state product (ratio to national average)								
2010	0.99	0.94	0.94	0.88	1.36	0.80	1.26	1.28
2017	1.03	0.90	0.93	0.84	1.34	0.78	1.47	1.31
Gross household disposable income per capita (ratio to national average)								
2010	1.01	0.92	1.00	0.95	1.07	0.92	1.17	1.71
2017	1.07	0.91	0.92	0.91	1.08	0.86	1.32	1.93
Tax revenue per capita (A$)								
2010	2,707	2,522	2,131	2,249	2,743	1,716	1,806	3,118
2017	3,990	3,412	2,621	2,579	3,312	2,112	2,463	4,114
Own-revenue per capita (A$)								
2010	4,808	4,205	5,419	5,226	5,974	4,058	5,832	6,383
2017	6,196	5,283	6,432	5,311	7,264	5,700	6,933	7,784
Total revenue per capita (A$)								
2010	8,407	8,155	9,022	9,551	9,566	9,044	20,246	10,545
2017	10,363	9,512	11,402	10,729	10,406	12,411	23,799	12,665

ACT = Australian Capital Territory, NSW = New South Wales, NT = Northern Territory, QLD = Queensland, SA = South Australia, TAS = Tasmania, VIC = Victoria, WA = Western Australia.
Note: A$ = Australian dollar.
Source: Authors' compilation from the Australian Bureau of Statistics, Government Finance Statistics.

Figure 2   Subnational Socioeconomic Disparities across Indonesia

2.1   Per Capita Income and Poverty Rate across Provinces (2017)

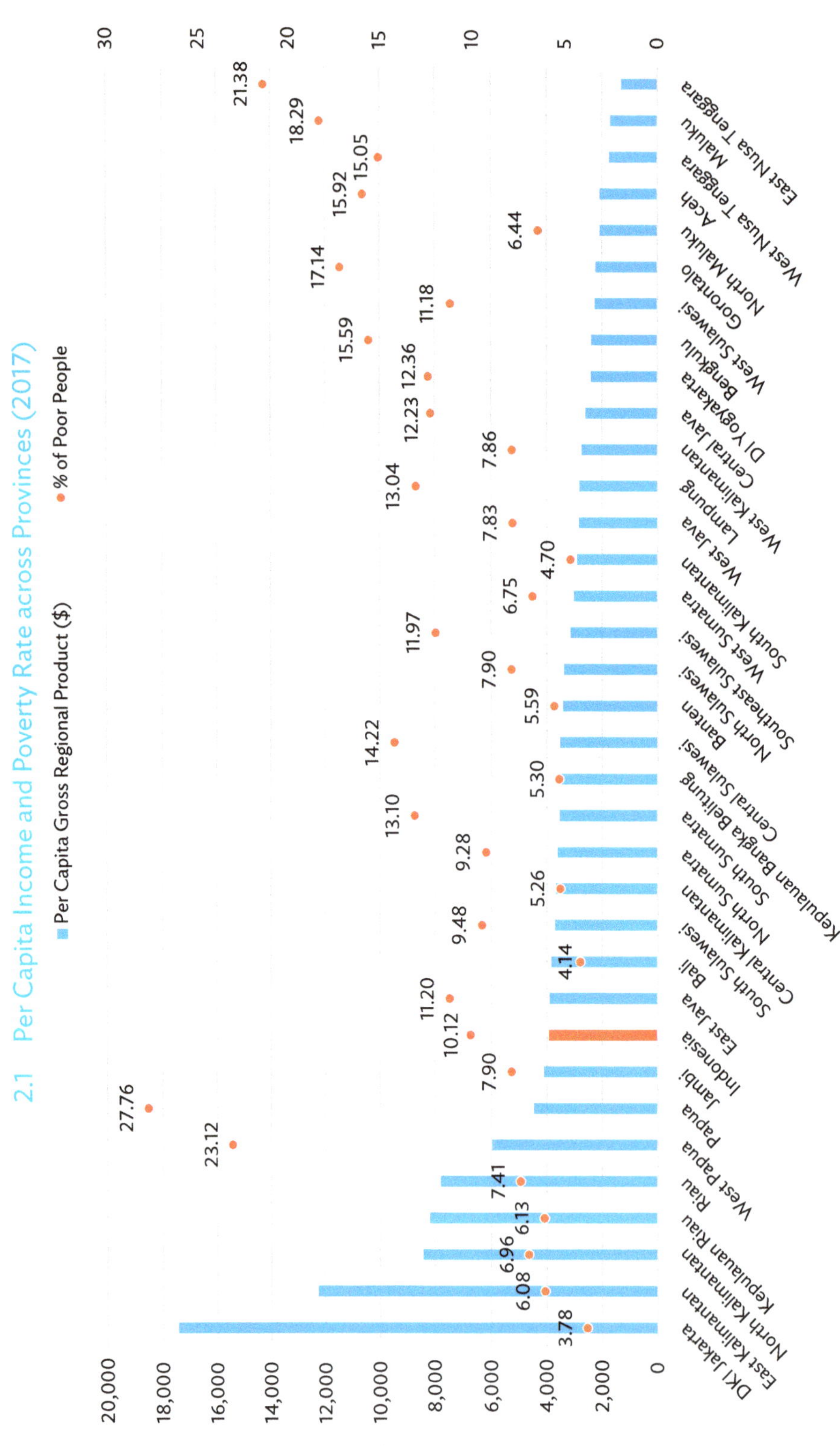

Sources: Data for % of Poor People in 2017 are from Statistical Yearbook of Indonesia 2018. Statistics Indonesia. Table 4.6.2; and data for Nominal per Capita USD 2018 are from Wikipedia. https://en.wikipedia.org/wiki/List_of_Indonesian_provinces._by_GRP_per_capita#PPP.

2.2   Human Development Index across Provinces (2015)

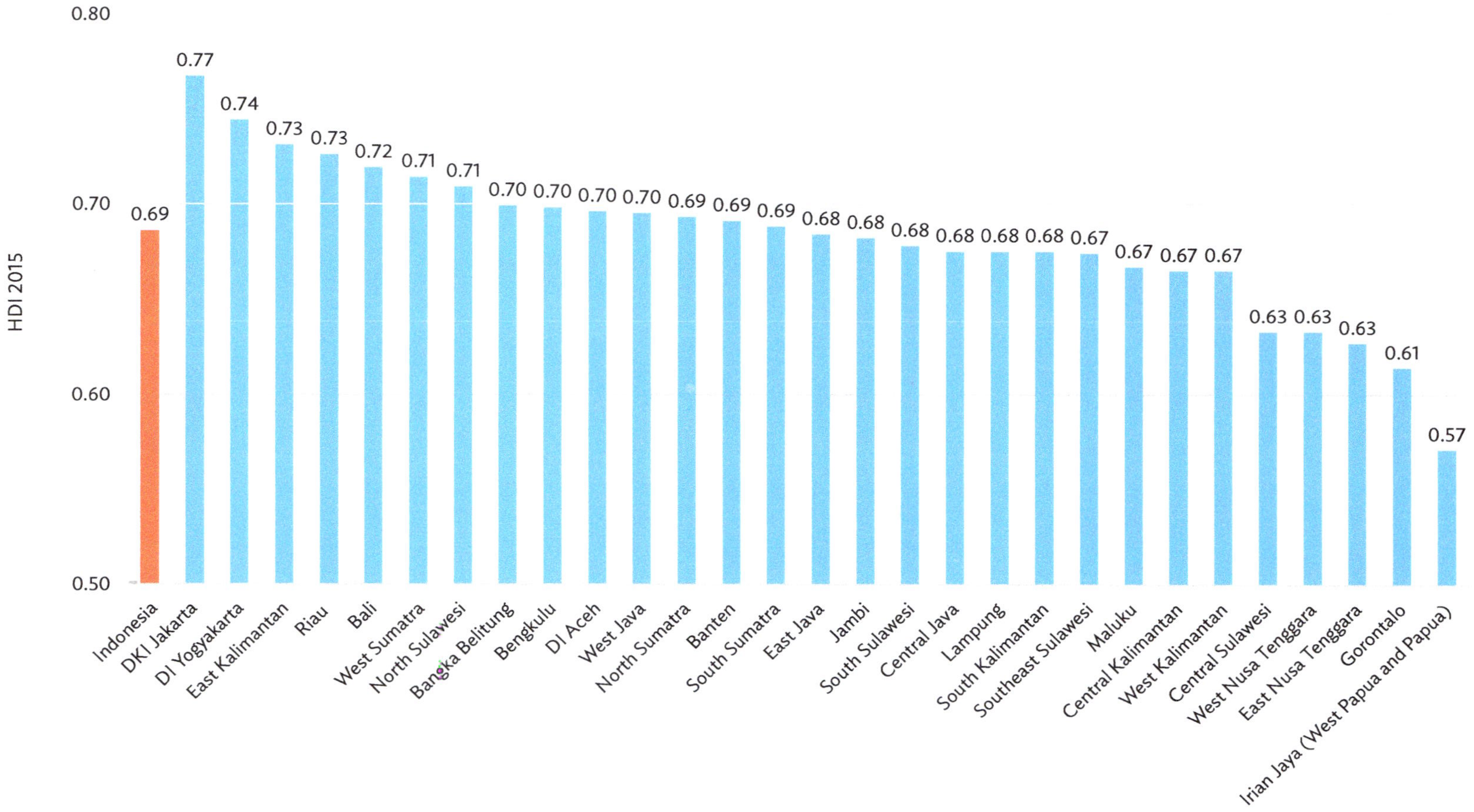

HDI = Human Development Index.

Sources: Per capita income and poverty rate across provinces are from Badan Pusat Statistik Indonesia. 2018. Statistical Yearbook of Indonesia. Jakarta; and Human Development Index is from the Institute for Management Research. Global Data Lab Subnational Human Development Index. https://globaldatalab.org/shdi/shdi/.

26. In some instances, per capita income may not be the best measure of living standards. For example, in resource-rich provinces like Irian Jaya (West Papua and Papua), a large part of the income from extraction of natural resources flows outside the province, resulting in high poverty rates, even though provinces have the sixth and seventh highest per capita income out of 34 provinces.

27. The divergence in living standards across Indonesia is also reflected in living conditions with poverty rates ranging from around 4% in Daerah Khusus Ibukota Jakarta (DKI Jakarta) and Bali to 28% in Papua. The Human Development Index (HDI) in provinces like Papua remains below 60 while in DKI Jakarta it is close to 80. Similarly, while in DKI Jakarta, 91.3% of the population has access to improved sanitation and 92.4% has access to improved drinking water, in Papua only 31.4% and 52.4% of the population, respectively, has access to these services. Vujanovic (2017) documents large disparities across the provinces in terms of health, education, and access to infrastructure.

28. While some variation in economic conditions across regions is unavoidable, the design of intergovernmental fiscal transfers becomes more challenging when disparities are huge. The challenges lie at differentiating among structural deficiencies, governance issues, and capacity constraints to effectively equalize vertical and horizontal imbalances. An international review of fiscal transfer systems by Dougherty (2019) points out that revenue equalization through transfers from the central government may reduce the tax effort of the subnational governments to develop their own fiscal base. In addition, the lack of a system of standardized cost assessments for service provisions could provide perverse incentives to subnational governments for inflating their reported expenditure needs in order to obtain higher central transfers. Insurance against shocks provided by equalization transfers may distort a subnational government's own fiscal decision-making. If the subnational deficits can be easily financed by

additional fiscal transfers on request, then the cost is shared by all subnational governments, leading to moral hazard. Lack of fiscal discipline could also pose challenges for the central government budget stability. In line with "flypaper effect," large lumpsum transfers can carry the risk of fiscal profligacy leading to wasteful use of public resources, and inefficient and low-quality outcomes in public service delivery if the governance and accountability measures are not in place for subnational governments. Martínez-Vázquez (2011a) also provides mixed evidence on poverty reduction outcomes from fiscal transfers, which are dependent on the governance of subnational governments. Thus, the design of the intergovernmental fiscal transfer system should be carefully calibrated to strike the right balance between preserving the autonomy of subnational governments and recognizing capacity constraints while offsetting moral hazard risks and incentivizing performance and accountability.

29. The following section provides an overview of the structure of the intergovernmental fiscal transfer system in India and key issues related to the Indian system before discussing the experience of other selected Asian countries. The learnings from these countries will be gathered to derive recommendations for India.[4]

B. Intergovernmental Fiscal Transfers in India

30. Following the dissolution of the Planning Commission in 2015, there are two operating channels for transfer of resources from the central government to the states in India: (i) statutory transfers through the FC awards, comprising (a) formula-based tax devolutions and (b) grants-in-aid, which are deficit grants based on post-devolution current deficit; and (ii) discretionary transfers by various union ministries for CSS and specific-purposes.

31. **Vertical sharing.** As per Article 270 and Article 280(3)(a) of the Indian Constitution, the FC determines

---

    In addition to the countries covered in this report, Asian Development Bank (ADB) reports by Martínez-Vázquez (2011b) and Smoke (2016) provide a review of the fiscal decentralization experience in other Asian countries such as Bangladesh, Pakistan, and Sri Lanka in the South Asia region; and Cambodia, the Philippines, Thailand, and Viet Nam in the Southeast Asian region.

the percentage of the divisible pool that is to be assigned to the states (vertical distribution) and the percentages that are to be allocated to states inter se (horizontal distribution). Once the formula with different weights to parameters is applied, no conditions can be set on the right of the state to receive such funds. Starting with the 11th FC, the divisible pool has been prescribed as a fixed proportion of all central government taxes to be shared to correct for the vertical imbalance between revenues and expenditure responsibilities of states.[5]

32. Prior to the introduction of GST in 1 July 2017, during FY2011–FY2015, on average, taxes raised by the central government accounted for 60.7% of total taxes. The states' revenue receipts before central government transfers accounted for 38.1% of total government revenue receipts, whereas the states' net revenue receipts after receiving devolution and grants from center accounted for 63.7%.[6] The 14th FC recommended an increase in the share of states in the central divisible pool from 32% to 42%, giving states more spending autonomy while there was a corresponding reduction in transfers through sources such as CSS. Aggregate transfers to states recommended by the 14th FC as proportion of gross state domestic product (GSDP) of all states was around 7.3% while the tax-to-GSDP ratio of the states was estimated at 8.7% during the 14th FC period.

33. **Horizontal sharing.** As shown in Figure 3, considerable income and developmental disparities exist across states in India despite steady but uneven progress over time.

34. The basic approach of the past FCs regarding the horizontal sharing across states has been to specify the key criteria and assign weights for distribution of the shareable tax revenue among the states to correct for these horizontal imbalances. Although selection of factors and the weights assigned to them have largely remained subjective and do not seem to flow from any comprehensive theoretical framework, overall, fiscal devolution formulas in India have evolved over time based on consensus, and flexibly incorporated

various indicators covering three key principles. For the fiscal needs and cost disability, indicators such as population size, area, forest cover, and infrastructure index distance (from average of top three states) were used by earlier FCs. For equalization, indicators such as per capita income distance (from the average of top three highest states), inverse income, poverty ratio, index of backwardness including share of scheduled castes, scheduled tribes, and backward classes were considered. For performance, indicators measuring tax collection, tax effort (tax/GSDP), and fiscal discipline were incorporated in various FC formulas (Appendix 2). Outside of the formula-based transfers, grants for gap filling of current deficit were considered. The indicators used by the recent FCs are shown in Table 3.

35. Recent FCs have attempted to strike a balance between fiscal needs, equalization, and performance objectives while trying to minimize the moral hazard risk. Under the 11th FC, the recommendation to reduce the weight of the population to 10% and to assign a weight of 62.5% to per capita income distance reduced the shares of high-income and middle-income states in tax devolution. Due to the objection by some states that they would be penalized, the subsequent 12th and 13th FCs increased the weight of population from 10% to 25% and reduced the weight assigned to distance of per capita income as an equalization measure from 62.5% for the 11th FC to 50% for the 12th FC and to 47.5% for the 13th FC. The 13th FC introduced a new approach based on the distance between estimated per capita taxable capacity for each state and the highest per capita taxable capacity. However, the 14th FC observed that the relationship between income and tax was nonlinear with different consumption baskets across states and decided to revert to income distance methodology used by the 12th FC and assigned 50% weight. The combined weight of performance parameters like tax effort and fiscal discipline increased over time from 12.5% for the 11th FC to 15% for the 12th FC and 17.5% for the 13th FC to incentivize states for improving their fiscal situation. To capture demographic changes in terms

---

[5]   Most broad-based taxes have been assigned to the center, such as customs duties, income tax, corporation tax, and central GST while state taxes include state GST, motor vehicle tax, value-added tax (VAT) on petroleum, stamp duty and registration fees, state excise duties, and electricity duty.

[6]   Government of India. Ministry of Finance. 2016. *Indian Public Finance Statistics, 2015–2016*. New Delhi.

Figure 3   Subnational Socioeconomic Disparities across India

3.1   Human Development Index 2015 and Per Capita Gross State Domestic Product (PPP $) 2017

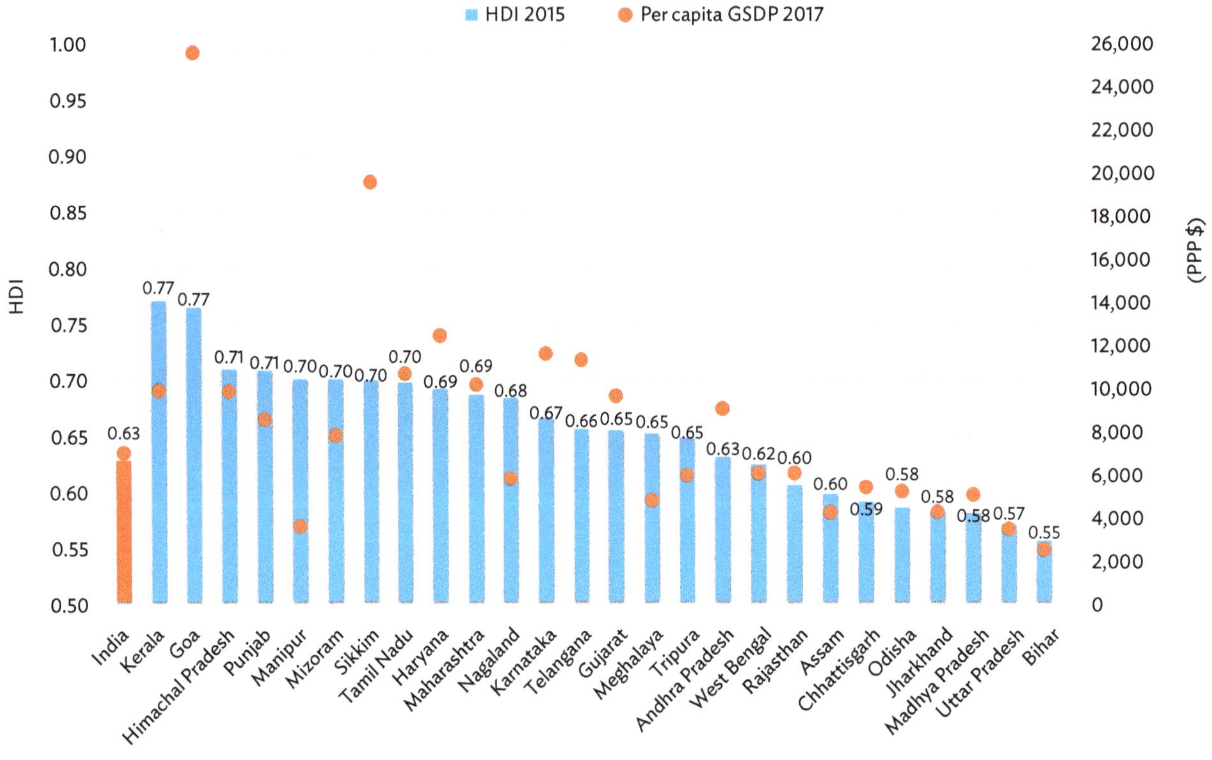

3.2   Change in Human Development Index (1990 vs. 2015)

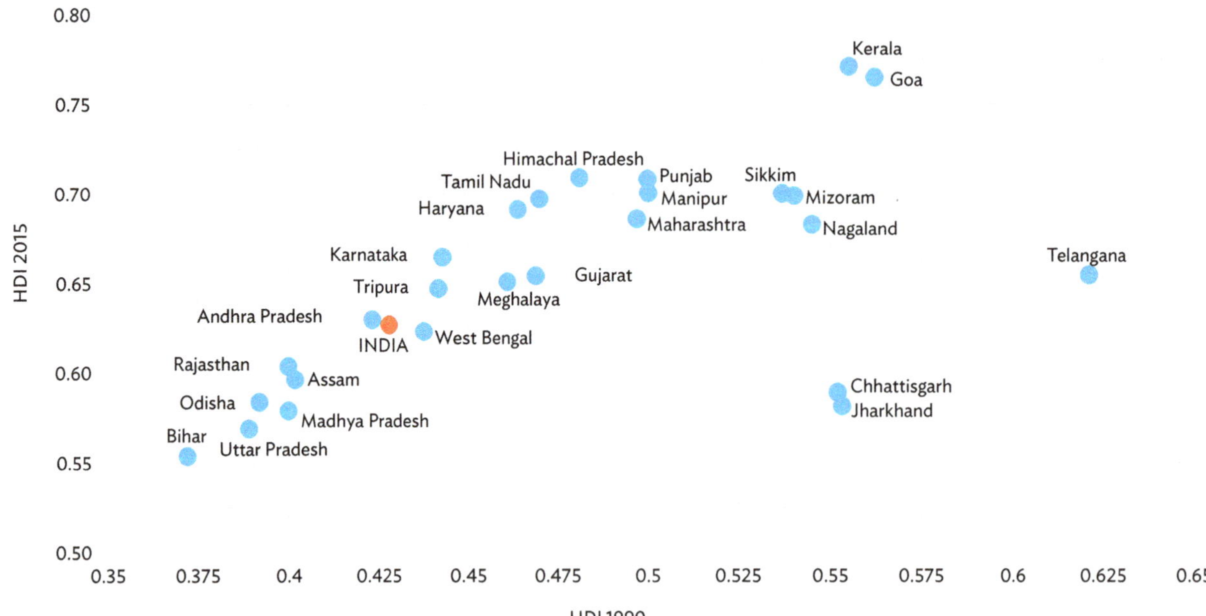

GSDP = gross state domestic product, HDI = Human Development Index, PPP = purchasing power parity.
Sources: State-level GSDP is from Ministry of Statistics and Programme Implementation adjusted by International Monetary Fund PPP conversion rate and Human Development Index is from the Institute for Management Research. Global Data Lab Subnational Human Development Index. https://globaldatalab.org/shdi/shdi/.

Table 3   Recent Fiscal Devolution Formulas in India

Objective	Fiscal Need/Cost Disability					Equalization	Performance	
Indicators (Weight in %)	Population (1971)	Population (2011)	Area	Forest Cover	Infrastructure Index Distance	Income Distance	Tax Effort	Fiscal Discipline
11th FC (2000–2005)	10.0		7.5		7.5	62.5	5.0	7.5
12th FC (2005–2010)	25.0		10.0			50.0	7.5	7.5
13th FC (2010–2015)	25.0		10.0			47.5		17.5
14th FC (2015–2020)	17.5	10.0	15.0	7.5		50.0		

FC = Finance Commission.
Sources: Data compiled from the Finance Commission Reports, and D. K. Srivastava and B. C. Rao. 2009. *Review of Trends in Fiscal Transfers in India*. Madras School of Economics. See Appendix 2 for details.

of fertility, age structure, and migration, the 14th FC decided that allocation based on the outdated population census would be unfair, and thus reduced the weight assigned to the 1971 population to 17.5% and introduced an additional 10% weight to the 2011 population. The latest 14th FC dropped the fiscal performance parameters while increasing the weight of cost disability factors such as area and forest cover. The inclusion of forest cover in the devolution formula reflected the compensation related to the cost of maintaining the forest land for ecological benefits as well as the opportunity cost of having an area that is not available for other economic activities.

36. **Grants-in-aid.** Under Article 275 of the Indian Constitution, FCs recommend conditional or unconditional grants-in-aid to help states provide comparable levels of services, at comparable tax rates, while ensuring a budget balance in the revenue account. Although over the years, there has been a considerable extension in the scope, there are broadly three types of grants-in-aid.

(i)   **Gap-filling grants** are predominantly in the nature of general-purpose grants to meet the current deficit, i.e., the difference between the assessed expenditure on the non-plan revenue account of each state and the projected revenue including the share of a state in central taxes.

(ii)   **Local bodies grants** are recommended by the FCs following the 73rd and 74th Amendments to the Constitution to supplement the resources of local bodies. These grants are input-based for specific type of spending such as roads, drinking water, sanitation, etc., as well as output-based for improvement of performance in local capacity and maintenance of proper accounts.

(iii)   **Specific-purpose grants** are conditional transfers given to states to (i) ensure minimum standards of certain basic services, (ii) provide grants for natural calamities, (iii) cover capital expenditure needs of states in certain sectors, and (iv) incentivize better fiscal management and planning among states. Certain upgradation grants were given to selected states in areas like general administration, law enforcement, primary education, public health, and welfare of backward classes. The 14th FC excluded the sector and state-specific grants, except for grants to local governments and for disaster management, with the rationale that (i) they constitute a small fraction of the proposals submitted by the states; (ii) these grants were not allocated based on any formula or any uniform principle; (iii) the schemes are best identified, prioritized, and financed at the state government level; and (iv) state governments raised the issue of limited flexibility in the use of such grants.

37. Figure 4 shows the general trend in FC transfers to states. They have been on the rise since the 10th FC, reaching from 34.9% of gross central revenue to 47.9% during the first four years of the 14th FC period.[7] The states' share of central taxes reached about 28.6% of gross central revenue, thus constituting about 60% of total transfers during the 14th FC period until FY2019 (budget estimate). Grants-in-aid accounted for 19.2% of gross central revenue and made up about 40% of total transfers during the 14th FC period. This leads to further dependency of states to transfer of central government revenues and creates a risk of moral hazard at the state level.

38. **Grants for natural calamities.** Based on the data provided by the National Disaster Management Authority (NDMA), more than 75% of the Indian coastline faces the risk of cyclones and tsunamis; 68% of the cultivable area is vulnerable to droughts; 58.6% of the Indian landmass is prone to earthquakes of moderate to very high intensity; and 12% is prone to floods and river erosion. Economic shocks from natural disasters not only carry the risk of fiscal unsustainability, they also have high socioeconomic costs unless appropriate and timely measures are undertaken for quick recovery. The poor and marginalized sectors of society are the worst affected when natural disasters occur and have low capacity to recover quickly.

39. In India, the basic responsibility of leading relief measures after a disaster lies on the state government concerned. The Disaster Management Act 2005 provides the mechanisms for disaster management and the system for funding disaster relief. In accordance with the act, central and state governments have constituted the NDMA and the National Disaster Response Fund (NDRF) at the national level, and the State Disaster Management Authorities (SDMAs) and State Disaster Response Funds (SDRFs) at the state level. However, the District Disaster Response Funds (DDRFs) have not been constituted by most state governments to avoid spreading thinly the limited resources available for disaster financing across districts. Relief activities at the district level are carried out by the state government through transfers from SDRF. State Disaster Mitigation Funds envisaged under the act have also not been set up by most states.

40. The importance of disaster relief financing finds resonance in the FC transfers. Successive finance commissions since the 2nd FC have considered disaster relief in the scheme of transfers, and it has been formalized in the FC's terms of reference from the 6th FC onward. The 14th FC recommended that the contribution by central and state governments, respectively, in SDRF should be in the ratio 90:10. Funds are first released from SDRF for disaster relief and the contribution from NDRF comes after adjusting the contribution already made by the central government toward the respective SDRF.

41. **Discretionary transfers by various union ministries.** Under Article 282 of the Constitution, central government ministries give input-based conditional matching grants to states for CSS and central sector schemes to ensure minimum standards in "merit" services or services with significant interstate spillovers. After the rationalization of CSS in 2015, they are classified as "core of the core", "core," and "optional" schemes, and the states are required to contribute a progressively higher proportion of the cost of the schemes under these respective categories. There are 6 "core of the core" schemes, which are mainly for social protection and social inclusion, and 22 "core" schemes at present—mostly on the subjects in the concurrent list or state list under the Constitution. The total amount of funds spent on all central sector schemes and CSS in FY2017 amounted to about 1.5% of gross domestic product (GDP), constituting 24% of total transfers. Of these, five schemes—(i) the National Rural Employment Guarantee, (ii) National Health Mission, (iii) Elementary Education, (iv) Rural Roads, and (v) Housing schemes—constituted 66% of total grants under central schemes (Rao 2017).

---

[7]   The rise can also be attributed in part to the fact that, with effect from FY2013–FY2014, release of funds for CSS from central ministries directly to the state implementing agencies bypassing the state budget was stopped, and it was required to route plan transfers through the state budgets. These direct transfers were approximately 10% of gross central revenues.

Figure 4   Central Government Transfers as a Share of Gross Central Revenues

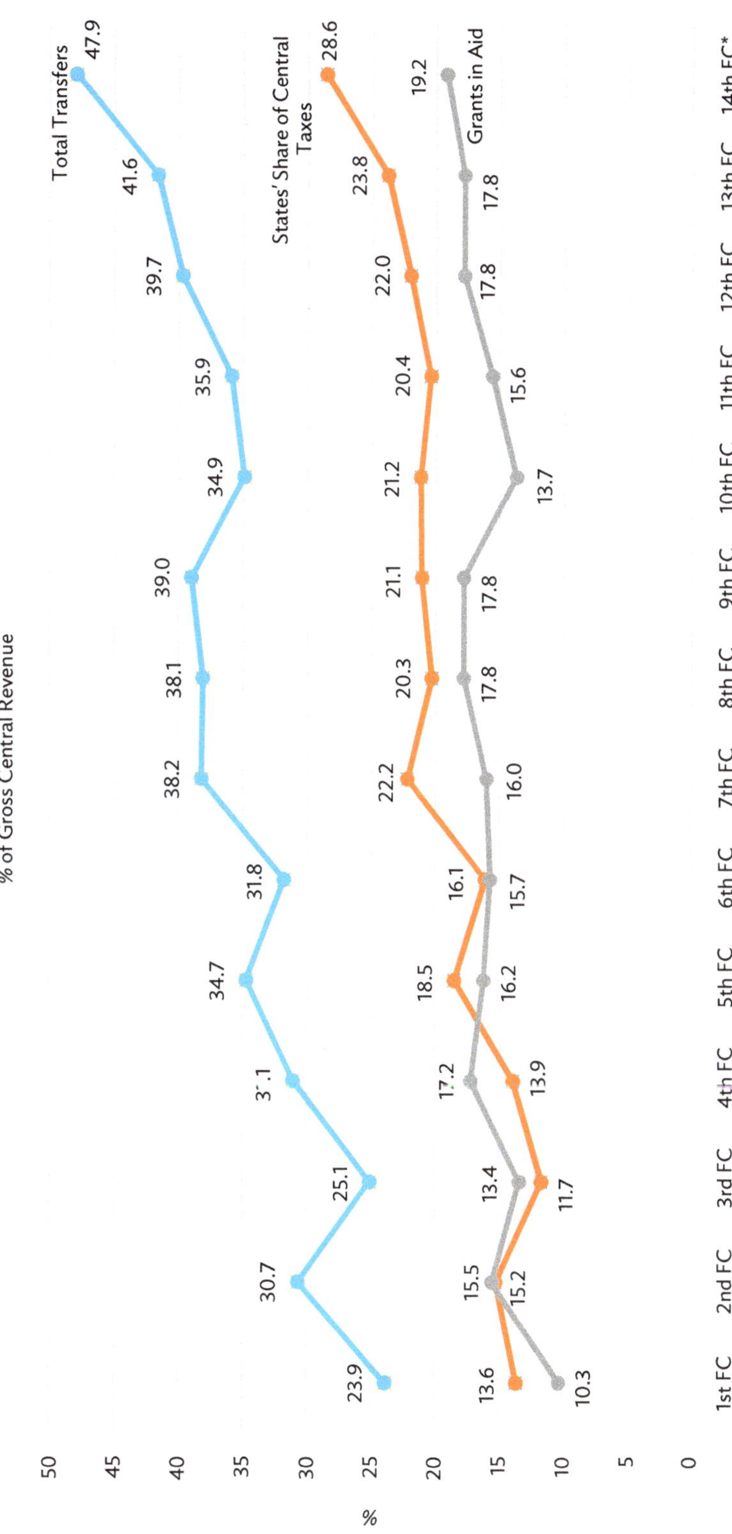

FC = Finance Commission.

Note: * 14th FC period covers fiscal year (FY) 2016, FY2017, FY2018 (revised estimate), and FY2019 (budget estimate).

Sources: Data compiled from Reserve Bank of India. *State Finances—A Study of Budgets*. Mumbai (various issues); and D. K. Srivastava and B. C. Rao. 2009. *Review of Trends in Fiscal Transfers in India*. Madras School of Economics.

Table 4   Trends in General and Specific Transfers in India

Period	General Purpose Transfers % of GDP	Specific Purpose Transfers % of GDP	Total Transfers % of GDP	General Purpose Transfers % of total transfers
FY2012	3.60	1.57	5.17	69.59
FY2013	3.48	1.47	4.94	70.32
FY2014	3.47	1.29	4.76	72.91
FY2015	3.33	2.13	5.46	61.04
FY2016	4.50	1.64	6.14	73.34
FY2017	4.90	1.54	6.44	76.07

Source: Authors' compilation from the Reserve Bank of India. State Finances: A Study of Budgets. Mumbai (various issues).

42. Table 4 shows the trends in general and specific transfers. The importance of general-purpose transfers over specific-purpose transfers has increased over the years.

43. Several issues have been observed in India's intergovernmental fiscal transfer system:

(i)   **Risk of moral hazard.** Given that FC transfers to states have been rising with a growing share of untied general-purpose transfers and gap-filling grants, this has exacerbated the dependency of states to central government transfers and increased the risk of moral hazard. A study by Rajaraman and Vasishtha (2000) points out that unconditional transfers from the center are negatively associated with states' revenue efforts in India. Jaitley (2018) also finds that in comparison with other federal countries, states and local governments rely much more on devolved resources and much less on their own-tax resources, and they collect less direct taxes. Thus, the intergovernmental fiscal transfer system in India has not adequately incentivized own-tax effort on the revenue side and the effectiveness and efficiency of state-level expenditures on the expenditure side given the composition of transfers in India.

(ii) **Backward-looking performance indicators in devolution formula.** Even though earlier fiscal devolution formulas have incorporated indicators related to tax effort and fiscal discipline, the amount of central government transfers was determined based on past fiscal performance, and thereby did not guarantee that the states will make any improvements going forward. An improvement over the 14th FC approach would require including only the fiscal needs/cost disability and equalization considerations in designing a horizontal devolution formula while addressing the performance requirements under the conditional grants using forward-looking indicators.

(iii) **Need for a well-designed system of conditional transfers.** The 14th FC increased the share of states in the central divisible pool from 32% to 42%, while recommending a corresponding reduction in transfers through sources such as CSS and eliminating specific-purpose transfers, most of which went to health and education sectors, with the intention to grant more autonomy to states in their spending decisions. In effect, without improvements in the state's institutional capacity, increased transfers have not been effectively used by state governments for growth-enhancing investments and social spending. Although the social sector expenditures (SSEs) as percentage of GDP has increased during the 14th FC implementation period until FY2019 (budget estimate [BE]), there has been a shift away from education and health expenditures to water and sanitation, housing, and urban development. This is apparently due to the implementation of CSS schemes such as the Swachh Bharat Mission, affordable housing schemes, and the smart cities mission. Since the CSS schemes are specific-purpose in nature, there is a case for reintroduction of specific-purpose and performance-based transfers in FC transfers as well.

(iv) **Need to strengthen enforcement mechanisms.** Institutional capacity enhancements for effective use of funds, collection of reliable data for measurement of performance, and enforcement mechanisms by the central government can further strengthen India's fiscal transfer system. A smart design of fiscal transfers requires greater collaboration between central and state governments in the design of conditional transfers, setting the right performance targets and incentives for compliance, including rewarding of good performance and penalizing of weak performance through discontinuation, reduction or reallocation of funds, and independent assessment and monitoring of achievements.

(v) **Need to strengthen disaster relief financing in federal fiscal relations.** While the National Policy on Disaster Management in India lays emphasis on both pre-disaster and post-disaster measures, the attention toward pre-disaster measures needs strengthening. These include risk awareness, risk assessment, risk reduction (prevention), and risk preparedness. Moreover, disaster risk coverage should extend beyond budgetary measures to include options like disaster insurance, and the provision of financial guarantees. It is advisable to involve the finance sector in managing the contingent liability of a disaster by providing coverage against that risk. Both public and private disaster risk financing (DRF) tools can support pre-disaster and post-disaster measures. Funds like NDRF and SDRF are ex-ante public DRF tools. Other ex-ante public DRF tools would be disaster insurance, contingent credit arrangements, and catastrophe bonds. Budget reallocation, debt financing, taxation, multilateral borrowing, and international aid have also been widely used as ex-post public DRF tools in Asia and the Pacific. Ex-post tools have the advantage that they do not involve holding costs. However, they are useful only for low-level and high frequency disasters. Private sector DRF tools can be effectively employed to strengthen the resilience of businesses and individuals against disasters. The public and private sectors have complementary strengths in disaster management, and they can work together for an effective response to a calamity (Juswanto and Nugroho 2017). Observatoire National des Risques Naturels or

the National Observatory for Natural Hazards in France is a good example of public–private effort in data collection for DRF (Nussbaum 2015). Japan's earthquake insurance scheme covers risk coverage against earthquakes for personal property as an option along with fire insurance (Box 1). Quick disbursing disaster relief financing from international financial institutions (IFIs) can also be quite useful to minimize the holding cost as suggested in section III. For cost optimization, it is recommended to employ a mix of ex-ante and ex-post public and private DRF tools.

Box 1   Examples of Disaster Risk Financing Tools in France and Japan

Observatoire National des Risques Naturels (ONRN) or the National Observatory for Natural Hazards in France is a collaborative public–private partnership effort among the state, local authorities, specialized agencies, academia, and the private insurance and reinsurance sector. The ONRN facilitates sharing of natural hazards data for risk assessment, risk mitigation, emergency preparedness, and financial planning purposes. The ONRN was developed in 2012 following the disaster hit by the windstorm Xynthia in 2010 and the integration of the French national disaster risk reduction platform. The data providers of the ONRN are governed by special contractual agreements to guarantee the consistency and reliability of the shared information, and the end users also have a role in providing inputs to the ONRN.

Introduced by the Act on Earthquake Insurance in 1966, Japan's earthquake insurance scheme is a state-sponsored program, which covers the loss or damage of residential use and personal property buildings due to burial, destruction, fire, or flooding caused by an earthquake. Japan Earthquake Reinsurance Co., Ltd. (JER) acts as an earthquake reinsurance pool, retaining some portion of the liability and transferring the rest back to the private insurers and to the Government of Japan through reinsurance treaties. Private insurers involved in this scheme have to fully insure their risk with JER. The indemnity limit for a single disaster event is approximately ¥11.13 trillion currently.

Source: W. Juswanto and S. Nugroho. 2017. Promoting Disaster Risk Financing in Asia and the Pacific. Asian Development Bank Institute Policy Brief. No. 2017-1.

C. Intergovernmental Fiscal Transfers—Asian Experience

44. Based on this background about India's intergovernmental fiscal transfer system, this section provides an overview of the Asian experience from Australia, Indonesia, the PRC, and the ROK by looking at how these countries are addressing vertical and horizontal imbalances, and how the performance of subnational governments is incentivized and monitored through various types of central transfers. This section provides the learning and recommendations for India. Further details on country-wise fiscal transfer systems, addressing vertical and horizontal imbalances as well as conditional transfers are presented in Appendix 3.[8]

C.1. Australia

45. The CGC in Australia pursues full horizontal fiscal equalization (HFE) so that each state would have the fiscal capacity to provide services and the associated infrastructure at the same standard after allowing for material factors affecting revenues and expenditures, provided that each state made the same effort to raise revenue from its own sources and operated at the same level of efficiency.[9] GST revenues in Australia collected by the Commonwealth are used as a means to achieve HFE. The goal of Australia's HFE system is to compensate the states for their structural disadvantages and give them almost complete degree of equalization of both revenue and expenditure capacity. This is unique among OECD countries. In contrast, many other countries try to achieve a minimum standard of services, rather than full equalization. After distributing GST among the states as grants, the fiscal capacity of all states except the Northern Territory is similar and the differences are smaller than those in own revenues. The Northern Territory, with a large area and small population, has the highest total revenue per capita to deliver average services.

C.1.1. Types of Transfers in Australia

46. Australia's IGA FFR specifies that financial support from the Commonwealth to the states includes (i) untied general revenue assistance (mainly through the distribution of the GST revenue); (ii) tied assistance of national specific purpose payments (NSPPs) in six key service delivery sectors, with each payment based on a National Agreement; and (iii) tied assistance of national partnership payments (NPPs), which fund specific projects of nationally significant reforms or service improvements and reward states once certain benchmarks are fulfilled. Figure 5 shows these Commonwealth payments to the states in FY2019.

47. **General purpose transfers (unconditional equalization grants)**. The GST revenue is distributed to equalize states' fiscal capacities to provide services and infrastructure based on the same standard. The CGC recommends how to distribute the GST pool, given the states' revenue capacity, efficiency, and net financial worth. The CGC's recommendations are considered by the Council on Federal Financial Relations. In determining how much GST a state should receive, the CGC makes three assessments: (i) how much expenditure the state requires to undertake to provide the average level of services and infrastructure; (ii) how much own revenue the state could raise under the average of tax regimes in Australia; and (iii) how much each state receives from the Commonwealth in tied funding besides GST distribution (so that needs are not met twice). The GST distribution covers the gap between assessed revenue and expenditure and provides the state the capacity to deliver the average level of services and infrastructure with average taxes.

48. **National specific purpose payments (NSPPs)** are conditional grants based on agreements between the Commonwealth and state governments. A National Agreement specifies the objectives and clarifies the roles and responsibilities of the Commonwealth and the state governments in delivering the services in key sectors, for which they are jointly responsible.

---

[8]   Although this report primarily focuses on Asian experiences, a few country examples outside the region have also been included for their relevance to the subject. Appendix 3 includes a summary of transfer systems in Canada and South Africa, which are non-Asian federal countries.

[9]   Equal efficiency assumes that the same amount of money will deliver the same standard of service across provinces, implying that full horizontal fiscal equalization would be achieved if fiscal capacities get equalized.

Figure 5   Total Commonwealth Payments to the States in FY2019 (A$ billion)

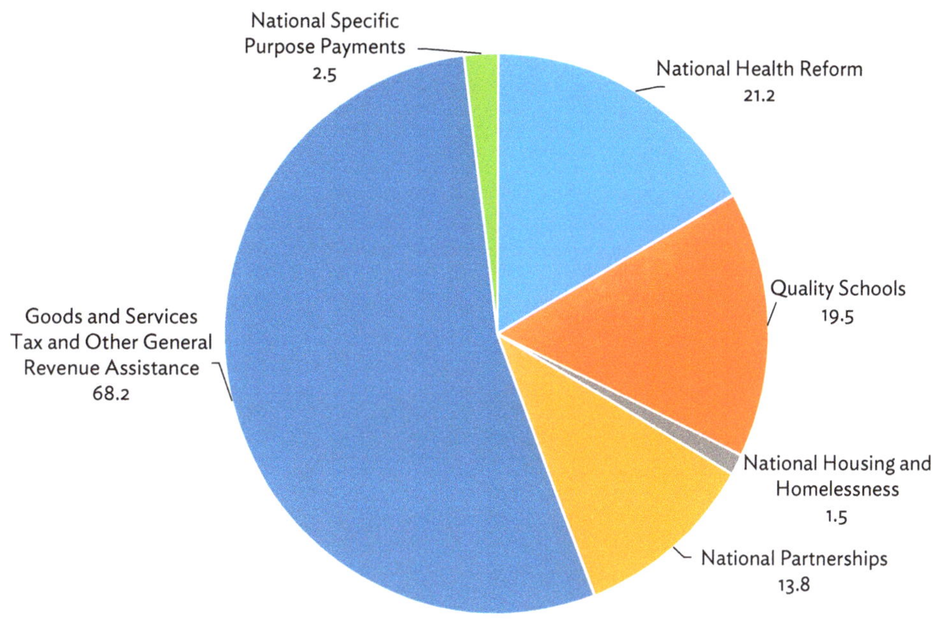

FY = fiscal year.
Source: Commonwealth of Australia. 2018. Budget 2018–19. *Federal Financial Relations Budget Paper No. 3.*

In 2009, six National Agreements were made in the sectors of (i) health (replaced by National Health Reform Agreement in 2011), (ii) education (replaced by National Education Reform Agreement in 2014), (iii) skills and workforce development, (iv) disability services, (v) affordable housing, and (vi) indigenous reform. The independent COAG Reform Council annually monitors and assesses the performance of all governments in achieving outcomes, outputs, and performance indicators, as specified in each National Agreement.

49. **National Partnership Payments (NPPs)** are performance-based conditional grants that are more narrowly focused and carry more conditionalities than NSPPs. Typically, NPPs constitute a small number of grants to the states that are not particularly prescriptive. NPPs are made annually, only after the states achieve performance milestones or benchmarks as specified in National Partnership Agreements. If a performance benchmark or milestone is achieved earlier than the due date, the Commonwealth may make the associated payment earlier than scheduled. National Partnership Agreements specify the terms and conditions of

NPPs in health, education, skills and workforce development, community services, affordable housing, infrastructure, environment, contingent payments, and other sectors.

50. NSPPs and NPPs vary in degree of conditionality. NSPPs are widely used in health and education and accounted for around half of the Commonwealth payments to states (equivalent to around 3% of GDP). NPPs comprise around a third of specific payments (Figure 6).

51. **Performance of the fiscal transfer system in Australia.** The distribution of the GST has been a frequent point of debate among states, as each state requests a larger share of the GST pool. In 2014, the Federal Government agreed to produce a White Paper on Reforming Federation, but gave up the effort in 2016, in fear of the repercussions of reforms in that election year. In 2017, the Commonwealth Government asked its review and advisory body, the Productivity Commission, to undertake an inquiry into Australia's system of horizontal fiscal equalization and assess its performance.

Figure 6   Payments for Specific Purposes in FY2019 by Function (A$ billion)

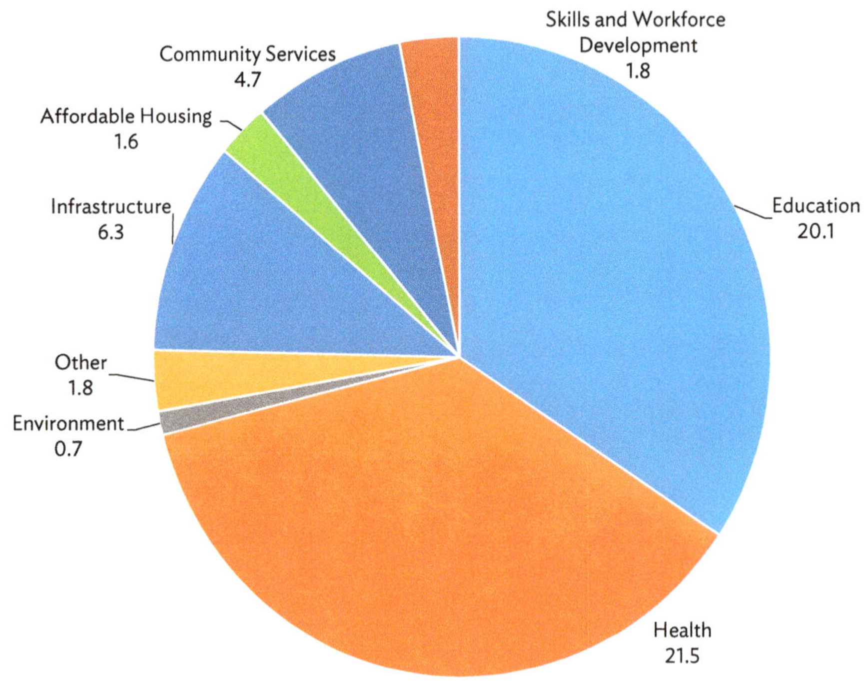

FY = fiscal year.
Source: Commonwealth of Australia. 2018. *Budget 2018–2019. Federal Financial Relations Budget Paper No. 3.*

52. The report submitted to the Commonwealth Government in May 2018 highlights that in the current horizontal fiscal equalization system, equalizing completely and to the fiscally strongest state requires a redistribution task, which is too big for any jurisdiction to bear, and the distributions are too volatile when there are significant cyclical and structural changes. The report concludes that the current system discourages reforms in policies related to mineral and energy resources (royalties and development) and major tax reform by the states (a costly first-mover disadvantage). The current equalization system is complicated and poorly understood by public officials within the governments, which leads to confusion and erodes accountability and confidence in the system.

53. Despite the shortcomings, particularly on sharing GST revenues among the states, this fiscal devolution mechanism has served Australia well, equipping all states with a similar capacity to deliver services to Australians. The National Agreements on conditional payments (NSPPs and NPPs) negotiated between the Commonwealth and states provide a transparent and centralized funding arrangement given that the roles and responsibilities of different levels of government as well as objectives for each sector are clearly specified. This framework also provides incentives for delivering outcomes and reform. Australia is unique that GST, as a federal tax, is shared only among the states as general revenue support to equalize fiscal capacity of the states.

C.1.2. Learnings from Australia and Relevance for India

54. **Transparent and performance-based transfers.** Australia uses both unconditional and conditional transfers with specific and performance-based transfers to balance the autonomy of each state with the measures to offset the risks of moral hazard. In a similar vein, a combination of fiscal reform legislations adopted by states in India, normative and formula-based transfers for equalization, specific-purpose transfers, and performance-based transfers could offer the right mix to address the economic and fiscal disparities across states.

55. **Rationalization of transfers and programs**. Consolidation of conditional grants under NSPPs and NPPs based on agreements between the Commonwealth and state governments is a good model for setting clear objectives, outcomes, outputs, and performance indicators for a few selected priority sectors, followed by a rigorous performance monitoring by an independent agency such as the COAG Reform Council. Australia's experience also underscores the importance of clarifying roles and responsibilities of different layers of government in concurrent subjects to avoid accountability issues and inefficient outcomes in service delivery. There have been some instances that the Commonwealth government has intervened in the states' decisions in their expenditure (particularly on education, health, housing, and infrastructure).

56. In India, the rationalization of CSS to 6 "core of the core" schemes and 22 "core" schemes at present has to some extent addressed the overlap in roles and responsibilities of different layers of government. Further reforms would include reduction of multiple indicators to focused targets, and rationalization of state government schemes while strengthening integrated data collection and independent monitoring mechanisms for the achievement of targets.

C.2. Indonesia

57. Indonesia poses an interesting case of decentralization, having transitioned from a very centralized economy at the time of the Asian financial crisis in 1997–1998 to a very decentralized system by early 2000. The decentralization largely took place through the legal process with the passage of a series of laws in 1999. The legal basis of decentralization is articulated under two laws, namely, Law No. 22/1999 and Law No. 25/1999 (Wibowo 2015). These laws have been subsequently modified to Law No. 32/2004 and Law No. 33/2004 to provide authority to the district governments in a wide range of areas including health, education, public works, agriculture, industry, trade, investment, and labor while limiting the authority of the central government to only areas related to defense, religion, justice, foreign policy, debt, and financial management. Similarly, Law No. 25/1999 (Law No. 33/2004) regulates the fiscal relationship between the levels of the government in Indonesia following the principle of "money follows function."

58. However, the decentralization process has been lopsided. The subnational governments in the provinces, regencies or cities, and villages were given expenditure responsibility across several key areas, and thus the share of subnational expenditure increased from less than 10% to nearly 50% of total government spending. However, revenue powers of subnational governments remained limited, accounting for about 10% while 89% of total government revenue was collected by the central government in 2015 (Vujanovic 2017). The central government has also been reluctant to relinquish some of its revenue-raising powers. The vertical imbalances have resulted in a system of fiscal transfers with subnational governments becoming heavily dependent on transfers from the central government that finance around 85% of their expenditure. Transfers to subnational governments constituted about 40% of general government spending in 2016. Furthermore, until 2017, the subnational governments have not issued any local currency bonds to attract financing for long-term infrastructure investment (Nasution 2016).

59. Another key feature of the fiscal transfers in Indonesia is the relatively small role played by the second tier of the government, i.e., the provincial governments, and allocation of greater responsibilities and resources to the municipalities/districts. While provision of greater resources to lower tiers of government could help improve service delivery by providing funds to governments that are close to the public and make the best expenditure decisions, a plausible reason for the limited role of the provinces is to stem apprehensions of secession (Sen et al. 2014). The bypassing of the provinces has helped maintain the authority of the central government as the sub-provincial local governments are too disaggregated to pose a challenge.

60. Furthermore, despite the move toward decentralization, the process continues to be mostly top–down with the central government wielding most of the power in determining the volume and composition of the transfers. The reluctance of the central bureaucracy to devolve greater powers and jurisdictions has resulted in the mechanism of intragovernmental transfers being a combination of objectivity and arbitrariness (Sen et al. 2014).

The overwhelming role played by the central government line ministries in many of the decentralized areas like health and education also points to continuing dominance of the central government.

C.2.1. Types of Transfers in Indonesia

61. There are three broad categories of transfers, i.e., Fiscal Equalization Funds (or Balancing Funds), Autonomy Funds and Village funds from central government to subnational governments.

62. **Fiscal Equalization Funds (or Balancing Funds)** account for 90% of the central government transfers and are made available to subnational governments to supplement their own revenues. They are aimed to address the fiscal gaps arising from disparity in revenue and expenditure needs of the subnational governments (vertical imbalance) and ensure uniform service delivery. The key Balancing Funds, i.e., DAU, DBH, and DAK, are allocated through a top–down approach although the subnational governments do provide some inputs.

63. **General Allocation Fund or Dana Alokasi Umum (DAU).** The DAU is a general-purpose grant to reduce the differences between the financial capacity among the regions (horizontal imbalance). The DAU is calculated according to a formula, which is revised every year. The DAU is the most important revenue transfer mechanism from the central government. It accounts for over 50% of the total central transfers.

64. DAU is a needs-based general-purpose transfer made up of two parts: basic allocation to cover wage costs and the fiscal gap grant that is an equalizing tool. The basic allocation covers personnel costs for the subnational government employees and is around 50% of the DAU fund. The remainder of the fund is based on the fiscal gap, divided among the provinces and districts, with the distribution decided by an agreement between the parliament and government.

65. The fiscal gap is the formula-based portion of the DAU which is defined as the difference between fiscal needs and fiscal capacity with both in turn being determined by other variables. 10% of the divisible pool under the fiscal gap is allocated to provinces and 90% to district governments (Hofman et al. 2006; Murniasih 2005).

66. The fiscal capacity comprises own income revenue, tax revenue share under Dana Bagi Hasil (DBH), and natural resource revenue share under DBH, while fiscal needs calculation is based on total expenditure of the provinces and districts. The fiscal need is measured as average expenditure adjusted by various factors including population, area, construction, cost, HDI and per capita domestic product (Table 5). The weights on these adjustment factors are decided between the Ministry of Finance and Parliament under the annual budget process. The subnational governments can request the detailed breakdown of their DAU collection.

67. **Revenue Sharing Fund or Dana Bagi Hasil (DBH)** covers the distribution of tax and nontax revenue that the central government collects from sources like personal income tax, property tax, and revenue from natural resources like oil, gas, mining, fishery, and forestry. The transfer under DBH is not directly related to the provision of services by regional governments (Fadliya and McLeod 2010). In 2015, DBH accounted for 16.6% of central government transfers to subnational

Table 5   Weights of Variables in Fiscal Needs Computation in Indonesia (%)

	Province				Districts			
	2014	2015	2016	2017	2014	2015	2016	2017
Population Index	30	30	30	30	30	30	30	30
Area Index	14	14	15	15	13	13	13	13
Construction Price Index	27	27	27	27	28	28	28	28
Human Development Index	15	17	17	17	15	17	17	17
Per capita Regional Domestic Product	14	12	11	11	14	12	12	12

Source: D. Simandjuntak. 2018. A Special Law for Archipelagic Provinces: Is It Necessary for Kepri? *ISEAS—Yusof Ishak Institute Perspective Working Paper.* No. 10.

governments, which accounted for 13% of the revenue of the provinces and 11% of the revenue of the cities/regencies (Vujanovic 2017).

68. The DBH tax revenue allocation is distributed using a clear formula. In the case of revenue from taxes, 80% of the revenue collected under personal income tax goes to the central government, while 8.4% of the revenue is shared with districts where the taxpayer resides, 3.6% is equally distributed to other districts of the province and 8% is shared with the provincial government. For land and building tax, the originating district gets nearly two-thirds of the revenue while the remaining part is distributed between the central and the provincial government.

69. In the case of revenue from natural resources, the sharing is governed by Law No. 33/2004 and Regulation No. 55/2005. Various technical ministries like the Ministry of Energy and Mineral Resources, Ministry of Home Affairs, and Ministry of Forest are involved in the sharing of revenue. While the central government retains the bulk of the revenue from oil and natural gas, the subnational governments gets a major share of the revenue from mining, forestry, and fisheries. Table 6 shows the basis for distribution of natural resource revenues in 2011.

70. Since 2015, the central government has also started transferring funds directly to the villages, which are the lowest level of the local government. These transfers are guided by Law No. 6/2014 and MOF decree. Under the allocation formula, 90% of the funds are distributed evenly across all the villages while 10% depends on the relative position of the village in terms of population, poverty, and construction cost.

71. **Special Allocation Fund or Dana Alokasi Khusus (DAK).** The funds under DAK became a specific-purpose grant in 2016 budget. They mainly target projects in line with national priorities but come under the responsibilities assigned to the subnational governments. These include health, education, agriculture, rural electrification, and housing, among others. DAK allocations are based on MOF Decree No. 48/2016 (World Bank 2018). The DAK comprises a matching grant system, with the recipient subnational government required to provide at least 10% matching funds. This ensures that the recipient subnational government has ownership of the project and works to ensure improved service delivery.

72. The DAK accounted for 5.6% of central government transfers to the lower tiers and funds 5% of subnational government expenditures in 2014. The structure of DAK was overhauled in 2015 and 2016 and the share of DAK in central government transfers increased to 8.9% in 2015 and 27.1% in 2016. In its original format, DAK was designed to fund activities considered to be a national priority by the central government. DAK was primarily used to fund capital expenditure, although sometimes recurrent expenditures were also financed. In 2015, the non-physical DAK (*DAK Non Fisik*) was introduced to finance recurrent expenditures such

Table 6   Natural Resources Revenue Sharing Arrangement in Indonesia

Revenue Sector (Weight in %)	Central	Province of Origin	District of Origin	Other Districts in Province of Origin	Other Districts
Oil and Natural Gas					
Oil Revenue	84.5	3.1	6.2	6.2	–
Natural Gas Revenue	69.5	6.1	12.2	12.2	–
Mining and Forestry					
Land Rent	20.0	16.0	32.0	32.0	–
Royalty	20.0	16.0	32.0	32.0	–
Forest Concession License Fees	20.0	16.0	64.0	–	–
Reforestation Fund	60.0	–	40.0	–	–
Fisheries					
Fisheries' Revenue	20.0	–	–	–	80.0

– = not applicable.
Source: C. D. Agustina et al. 2012. Political Economy of Natural Resource Revenue Sharing in Indonesia. *Asia Research Centre Working Papers.* No. 55. London, United Kingdom: The London School of Economics & Political Science.

as operation and maintenance costs in areas like health and education for efficient service delivery. The original DAK was renamed DAK Fisik (Physical DAK) and comprised three parts: (i) regular DAK to finance priority sectors and eligible districts; (ii) affirmation DAK for remote and less developed regions; and (iii) special assignment DAK for funding priority projects in priority areas.

73. For DAK Fisik allocation, the Ministry of National Development (Bappenas) is responsible for identifying priority sectors that are in alignment with the national development plan while the technical ministries use sectoral criteria to decide on the allocation. In the case of DAK Non Fisik, the DG Fiscal Balance determines the allocation for individual districts.

74. The central government sets the DAK criteria covering (i) general fiscal criteria, (ii) specific criteria, and (iii) technical criteria (Sen et al. 2014). The fiscal criteria are driven by the fiscal positions of subnational governments excluding the cost of personnel. Only those governments found to be below average are eligible under these criteria. Specific criteria are aimed to accord preference to some of the vulnerable regions like coastal regions and islands, regions bordering neighboring countries, disaster-prone regions, and less-developed regions. Special criteria are determined by the concerned ministry in consultation with Ministry of Home Affairs, Ministry of Finance, and Ministry of Planning. Finally, technical criteria are determined by the technical ministry or the program or activity implementer based on several factors including macro, service-related, administrative, and needs indicators. The allocation and eligibility of the subnational government for DAK transfers are based on formulas, which tend to be information intensive. However, the formula-based approach is believed to have been insulated from political interference.

75. **Autonomy transfers.** There are two other kinds of fiscal equalization funds, namely, autonomy transfers and village transfers. Under the autonomy transfers (Dana Otonomi Khusus Dan Penyeimbang) the central government allocates a larger share of resource revenues to provinces like Aceh, Papua, and West Papua through the tax-sharing mechanism.

76. **Direct transfers to villages (Dana Desa).** In 2014, a new system of direct transfers to villages from both central government and regency/city governments was introduced, which was phased in over the next 3 years. The regencies/cities were required to contribute 10% of own-source revenue, revenue-sharing funds (DBH), and general allocation fund (DAU).

77. Table 7 summarizes the breakdown of central government transfers in Indonesia by type, and Box 2 presents the limitations of Indonesia's intergovernmental fiscal transfer system.

C.2.2. Learnings from Indonesia and Relevance for India

78. Given that India also maintains a three-tiered structure of governance comprising the union or central government, the state governments, and the urban and rural local bodies, some lessons for India can be drawn from the Indonesian experience.

79. **Incorporate HDI in devolution formula.** Despite the commonalities between the horizontal devolution formulas, the HDI used by Indonesia could also be considered as an additional indicator in India's devolution formula to help compensate for social development disparities across states.

Table 7   Central Government Transfers to Subnational Governments in Indonesia

Breakdown by Type	2014	2015	2016
% of total transfers to regions and rural funds			
General Allocation Fund (DAU)	59.5	53.1	50.0
Revenue Sharing Fund (DBH)	18.1	16.6	13.8
Special Allocation Fund (DAK)	5.6	8.9	27.1
Autonomy and other funds	16.8	21.5	9.1
% of general government spending excluding interest			
Transfers to regions	34.9	36.3	40.3
TP/Dekon	1.1	0.9	1.6

Notes: TP/Dekon = a deconcentration fund for regional development. DAK transfers in 2016 include school operational assistance (BOS) and additional teachers' allowance fund. Sources: Organisation for Economic Co-operation and Development. 2016. *OECD Economic Surveys: Indonesia 2016.* Paris; and authors' compilation from the Government of Indonesia, Ministry of Finance.

Box 2 Limitations of the Fiscal Transfers System in Indonesia

One of the major drawbacks of the intergovernmental transfer mechanism in Indonesia is that transfers under DAU and DBH are at conflict with each other. The funds received under DAU are inversely related to the fiscal capacity, a part of which is the revenue generated from DBH. Thus, despite the entitlement of subnational governments under DBH, when total intergovernmental transfer is considered as a whole, the amount under DBH is deducted from the entitlement under DAU. Similarly, the inclusion of own income revenue for entitlement under DAU reduces the incentive of the subnational governments to increase their own revenues in a typical moral hazard fashion.

Furthermore, the assured coverage of wage expenditures of subnational governments under DAU have resulted in prioritizing such expenditures over development needs. The DAU gives no incentive to subnational governments to reduce or avoid growth of their employees because a reduction in the employee wage bill will also reduce the DAU entitlement. Besides overemployment, management practices that can enhance efficiency and improve cost-saving such as using contract workers or public–private partnerships are discouraged.

Under the current mechanism, the various subnational governments are treated in the same manner under the DAU transfers. Given that the weights on different indices are the same across all provinces or across all districts, this results in erroneous measurement of subnational fiscal needs. Per capita regional GDP is disproportionately used in the calculation of DAU transfers. Per capita GDP is not a good proxy for the expenditure needs. Provinces with high per capita regional GDP due to natural resources such as Papua and Papua Barat also have high poverty rates. In such cases overwhelming emphasis on per capita regional GDP in designing transfers can be inequitable.

Since the subnational budget realizations are not published regularly, monitoring of expenditures requires strengthening. Compared with DAU, DAK is better managed because it is validated by both local and central governments. The outcomes are verifiable with project funding contingent on delivery of agreed outputs. However, the DAK fund distribution varies from year to year with no consistency in procedure. There is subjectivity in the choice of the weights, technical criteria, and manner of combining special criteria for each sector. Furthermore, medium-term planning and expenditure framework for utilization of DAK funds is generally missing.

Sources: F. McLeod and R. McLeod. 2010. Fiscal Transfers to Regional Governments in Indonesia. *Working Papers in Trade and Development.* No. 2010/14. Canberra: Australian National University; and M. Harjowiryono. 2012. *Development of Indonesia's Intergovernmental Financing System: Fiscal Decentralization in Indonesia a Decade after the Big Bang.* Jakarta: Ministry of Finance.

80. **Strengthen subnational service delivery.** Indonesia has one of the largest intergovernmental transfer mechanisms among the emerging countries, but still the quality of public service delivery at the subnational level remains weak, raising questions about the capacity and leakages at the local level. From a holistic perspective and to avoid distortions from an unequally developed fiscal decentralization architecture and roll-out, it is critical for India and Indonesia to improve the capacity of local governments in making expenditure decisions and executing key projects, while providing them with greater expenditure responsibilities to improve local service delivery. The 2018 decision to incentivize urban local bodies (ULBs) in India covered under the Atal Mission for Rejuvenation and Urban Transportation to issue municipal bonds is a welcome step in this direction. Use of outcome-based medium-term planning and budgeting frameworks and regular monitoring will improve the effectiveness of subnational expenditures in local service delivery.

81. **Incentivize tax effort by subnational governments.** The use of the same formula with similar weights for transfers to provinces and districts in Indonesia does not incentivize local governments to improve fiscal health. The current mechanism discourages improvements in own-tax revenue effort by considering it as a negative factor for the allocation of DAU. In India, states with experience in increasing tax effort in the first couple of years of fiscal award period, can be provided a time-bound incentive for the remaining period.

82. The Indonesian case presents guidance on the distribution of revenues from natural resources. As pointed out by previous FCs, augmentation in nontax revenues can be useful to supplement resources of local bodies. In this regard, it is suggested to (i) address the ambiguity in reporting of mining auction proceeds in state budgets, and (ii) allocate some proceeds from the mining royalty and auction proceeds to the mining district in accordance with the Mines and Minerals Development and Regulation Amendment Bill, 2015.

83. **Transfers to rural areas.** While some of the better placed ULBs in India can strive to issue bonds to raise revenue, the villages do not have such an option. In such a case a dedicated transfer to the villages like the recently introduced Village Funds in Indonesia can help provide resources to villages to improve local delivery.

C.3. Japan

84. In Japan, MOF coordinates resource allocation between the central and local governments. The MIC engages in fiscal supervision of local governments and represents their interests within the central government during the national budget allocation to ensure adequate vertical fiscal transfers and the equitability through the horizontal fiscal transfers (Aoki 2008; Mochida 2001). The Local Public Finance Bureau and the Local Tax Bureau under MIC are responsible for the planning, implementation, and supervision of the local finance system and the local tax system. During the national budget preparation, the Local Public Finance Program (LPFP) estimates for revenue, expenditure, and intergovernmental transfers for all local governments are combined with estimates for national policies and programs. To establish a consistent national budget policy, the LPFP guarantees sufficiency of financial resources for the local governments, facilitates the coordination of central and local governments, and sets guidelines for the financial management of local governments (Ichimura and Bahl 2009). As shown in Table 1, the ratio of central to local government expenditure in Japan is 40:60 while the ratio of central to local tax collection is the opposite (60:40).

C.3.1. Types of Transfers in Japan

85. Three types of funds are transferred to local governments: (i) the local allocation tax (LAT) grants and (ii) local transfer tax (LTT) grants, both of which are general-purpose transfers, and (iii) the central government subsidies (CGS) or national treasury disbursements, which are specific-purpose transfers.

86. **Local allocation tax (LAT) grants.** LAT grants are legally linked to the amount of five national taxes (corporate tax, consumption tax, income tax, liquor tax, and tobacco tax) and constitute the largest transfer from the central government to the local governments. The LAT Law [Article 6(1)] allocates 32% of revenues from corporate tax, income tax, and

liquor tax; 29.5% of revenues from consumption tax; and 25% of revenues from tobacco excise to the LAT grants. These percentages are periodically amended to ensure the adequacy of LAT at the macro level. If the LAT turns out to be insufficient, the central government sometimes tops up supplementary grants from the general budget to the LAT before allocation to the local bodies.

87. The LAT is paid each year to the local governments as a general-purpose transfer. It has two components: an "ordinary" LAT, accounting for 94% of the total, and a "special" LAT, comprising the remaining 6%. The former covers local services and has also an equalization function. The special LAT covers extraordinary and emergency expenses for natural

Box 3   Computation of Ordinary Local Allocation Tax

Ordinary LAT = SFD – SFR

If SFR > SFD, the local government cannot receive LAT grants, and need not pay back funds to the central government.

SFR = Standard local tax revenues x 75% + Local transfer tax

SFD = Unit expense x Measurement units x Adjustment coefficient *where*

(i) standard local tax revenue is computed using standard rates in Local Tax Law, and not the actual tax rates;

(ii) unit expense = expense per unit of each item (e.g., roads, elementary schools);

(iii) measurement unit = the number or size of the beneficiaries of a particular expenditure (e.g., length of roads, number of teachers); and

(iv) adjustment coefficient = adjustment for differences in administrative expenses among local governments due to natural and social condition of each local government (e.g., additional maintenance cost of roads in cold conditions, heating expenses in schools in winters).

LAT = local allocation tax, SFD = standard fiscal demand, SFR = standard fiscal revenue.
Sources: S. Bessho. 2017. A Study of Central and Local Government Finance in Japan. In N. Yoshino and P. Morgan, eds. *Central and Local Government Relations in Asia*. US: Edward Elgar Publishing, Inc.; and United Nations Habitat. 2012. Fiscal Decentralization in Japan. *The Global Urban Economic Dialogue Series*. Nairobi.

disasters. These two funds are calculated separately for each local body. The amount of ordinary LAT grants that each prefecture and municipality receive is set as the difference between estimated expenditures and the sum of local tax revenues, the CGS, and local borrowing (Box 3). Given all these components are estimated by the central government, this system is regarded as top–down, but the universal allocation formula ensures transparency in allocation of LAT among different municipalities. Therefore, political intervention for the allocation is avoided.

88. In Japan's equalization system, both fiscal capacity and cost differences are equalized. Because public service provision costs are influenced by many factors including geography and socioeconomic and institutional characteristics in each area, the equation has modification coefficients applied to it to adjust for these factors. The suitability of these factors and the associated adjustments are periodically reviewed and published to ensure transparency.

89. Since Japan's LAT system uses a uniform formula based on basic fiscal needs and basic fiscal capacity relatively independent of its tax effort, it not only corrects the horizontal fiscal imbalance in Japan but also provides an incentive for local governments to perform well.

90. **Local transfer tax (LTT).** The LTT consists of taxes collected at a national level and then transferred directly to local governments. The national government collects these taxes such as local gasoline transfer tax on behalf of the local governments as a matter of taxation convenience as the amount is relatively small; hence, these are regarded as local government revenue resources. Each local government receives an amount based on its population and the number of employed people in its jurisdiction.

91. **Central government subsidies (CGS).** The CGS is composed of categorical grants directly disbursed from the budgets of central ministries. Other than LAT grants, CGS encourages local governments to undertake projects that contribute to national objectives. Since these subsidies are purpose-specific, use of these grants are decided by the national government. The CGS allows local governments to maintain uniform services required by national laws

as well adopt projects that contribute to national objectives (Bessho 2017).

92. Recent reforms for intergovernmental fiscal transfers in Japan are presented in Box 4.

Box 4   Recent Intergovernmental Fiscal Reforms in Japan

The Trinity Reforms, implemented in Japan from 2004 to 2006, consisted of reducing national grants by ¥4 trillion and local allocation tax (LAT) by ¥5 trillion, and the transfer of ¥3 trillion income tax base to local government units (LGUs) (UN Habitat 2012). Although the initial objectives were met, regional disparity eventually widened as richer LGUs benefited more from transfer of tax sources while poor LGUs suffered from grant cuts and generated lower additional tax revenue from a small base.

The Fiscal Reconstruction Law in 2009 introduced an "early warning system" based on fiscal indicators, which requires a local government to create a fiscal reconstruction plan if a warning is triggered.

Reforms to enhance local autonomy were passed in FY2010. In June 2010, the government launched a "regional sovereignty" strategy which replaced earmarked grants with lumpsum block grants and gave LGUs full autonomy to spend the grants. The bill creating a forum of dialogue between the central government and local associations was adopted in 2011. Revisions to the Local Autonomy Law, adopted in 2011 and 2012, expanded the scope of local government assemblies.

The Comprehensive Decentralization Law established a system for local governments to utilize an "advance consultation system." With effect from 2005, the local governments could issue bonds. However, local governments cannot include repayment costs in the standard fiscal demand in the LAT formula nor can they borrow central government funds if they issue bonds without the approval of the Ministry of Internal Affairs and Communications or the prefectural governor. Local governments that cannot satisfy specific financial criteria are required to obtain permission to issue bonds while those with severe financial situations are restricted to issue bonds.

Sources: I. Aoki. 2008. Decentralization and Intergovernmental Finance in Japan. *Policy Research Institute Discussion Paper Series.* No. 08A–04. June. Ministry of Finance; Organisation for Economic Co-operation and Development (OECD). 2017. *Multi-level Governance Reforms: Overview of OECD Country Experiences.* OECD Multi-level Governance Studies. Paris: OECD Publishing; and United Nations Habitat. 2012. Fiscal Decentralization in Japan. *The Global Urban Economic Dialogue Series.* Nairobi.

C.3.2. Learnings from Japan and Relevance for India

93. **Objective measurement of fiscal gap.** Since standard fiscal revenue (SFR) is computed based on the standard rates of local taxes instead of actual rates, LAT is determined independently from the tax effort in Japan. If a locality increases its tax effort by raising its tax rates above the standard rates, the amount of LAT that the locality will receive will not decrease. Local governments therefore have the incentive of improving their local tax effort. It also allows local governments to implement their own policies, which are not included in the standard fiscal revenue, and address fiscal needs not fully captured by the standard fiscal demand (Bessho 2017; Uda 2015). In India, the major portion of the transfer is untied and supplemented with gap-filling grants. India should strengthen objective standards for computation of fiscal gap and incentivize state governments to improve their tax efforts.

94. **Standard service delivery benchmarks.** Since LAT allocation is based on the standardized unit expense for each public service (Box 3), local governments have an incentive to lower the actual unit expense to create fiscal space while ensuring the service quality. Most recently, incentive mechanisms have been introduced for local governments to be more results oriented. For example, unit expenditure for LAT allocation for certain types of public services is periodically adjusted to reflect best practice in operational efficiency (top-runner method), and the allocation of budget for local revitalization projects are made based on quantitative performance measures (such as increase of the number of companies). In comparison, the transfer system in India focuses on a mix of normative equalization and conditional transfers. While performance incentives have been included in the scheme of transfers earlier, it has not been attempted to link transfers directly with service standards and penalize states for not maintaining service levels.

95. **Holistic performance evaluation.** Since Japan has a top–down budgeting system, the central government's effectiveness in achieving budgetary targets is monitored through multiple agencies such as MOF, MIC, Government Revitalization Unit, Public Sector Activity Screening, Public Sector Activity Review, and Board of Audit. Under the Central Government Reform Program, guidelines for ministries and agencies were introduced in 2001 for assessing policies and activities and incorporating results into future planning and budgeting. Accordingly, line ministries develop medium-term budget plans and submit their annual evaluation reports based on key performance indicators. The local governments also conduct their own self-evaluation (Matsuura et al. 2010). In India, linkages between central government and state-level medium-term fiscal planning and performance-based budgeting need strengthening (see section III).

C.4. People's Republic of China

96. The present framework of intergovernmental fiscal relations was created in 1994 following a far-reaching restructuring of the relations between the central and subnational governments since 1949. Although the PRC is a unitary state, the governance structure appears rather decentralized with governments at the provincial, prefecture, county, and township levels accounting for 80% to 85% of expenditure.[10] The share of central government is small to effectively accommodate expenditures involving redistributive goals, social protection including pension and health care, and significant externalities. Hence, on the spending side, the PRC is more fiscally decentralized than most developing countries (Shen et al. 2012). However, there are large vertical imbalances on the revenue side with the subnational governments controlling minor taxes with narrow bases.

97. Until 2015, subnational governments were not allowed to borrow to finance budget deficits. In practice, they have extensively borrowed and spent off-budget, particularly since the global financial

---

[10]   The PRC has five levels of government: the central government, 31 provincial level governments, 334 governments at prefecture level, 2,850 governments at county level, and governments of more than 40,000 townships. Provincial level governments include 22 provinces; 5 autonomous regions; and the cities of Beijing, Chongqing, Shanghai, and Tianjin. These four cities have populations comparable to that of other provinces. Regarding administration and financial arrangements, they are just like other provinces.

crisis, mostly through urban development investment companies and/or special purpose finance vehicles. While this allowed local governments to meet infrastructure development needs, it has led to serious concerns in fiscal transparency, accountability, efficiency, and sustainability, and potentially accentuated horizontal imbalances.

98. In recognition of these risks, in 2014, the PRC's legislature adopted a revision to the budget law, issuing directives to implement budget and public financial management reforms. Key issues in subnational public finances have included lack of consolidated budget accounts, ad hoc local fiscal policies through subsidies, tax exemptions and preferential credit, and using public enterprises as off-budget vehicles. The State Council regulations have set directives for streamlining the subnational government budgets. The revised budget law permitted subnational borrowing through the provincial governments, subject to the limits set by the central government (as codified in the 2015 budget law). The revised budget law also tried to build a warning system to help avoid insolvency. However, these measures have not fully eliminated the incentives for the subnational governments to find ways around restrictive laws and borrowing quotas and thus the extent of off-budget borrowing is not fully known in the PRC (Bahl 2019).

99. With the recent administrative reforms initiated by the central government, work is ongoing to improve the reallocation of fiscal responsibilities, expenditure and revenue assignments, and the fiscal transfer mechanism in line with the emerging needs of the country in response to rapid economic growth and urbanization (ADBI 2018). Since 2016, the central government has been reassigning various expenditure items step-by-step to different levels of government. This process has reached big-ticket items like transport, environment, education, and health. In 2018, the government has approved plans to increase expenditures particularly for social services and the flow of transfers to subnational governments.

100. The plans also included adjustments in revenue assignments, expansion in the tax base, and reductions in fees related to cost of doing business on the revenue side. The central government decided to merge local and central tax bureaus, as an essential step to increase the efficiency of tax collection. Under the economic and social program presented by the State Council in 2018, the central government has committed to reviewing the revenue powers of the subnational governments. The degree of tax autonomy has not yet been increased, but the introduction of a municipal property tax is envisioned (Box 5).

C.4.1. Types of Transfer in the People's Republic of China

101. The present system of intergovernmental transfers in the PRC has the following components:

102. **Equalization transfers** use needs-based criteria. These transfers (and through them indirectly fiscal needs) are determined based on (i) the standard revenue (standard tax rate and estimate of tax base); (ii) standard expenditure of a province; and (iii) the share of the provincial standard fiscal gap of the total fiscal gap. Standard expenditures cover categories such as spending on administration, education, heating, safety, social services, and urban maintenance, among others. Costs are calculated based on factors such as altitude, number of civil servants and students, population density, wage differentials, temperature, transport distance, and the size of minority groups. In 2012, MOF revised and improved the formula for equalization transfers.

103. The central government annually determines the size of the pool for equalization transfers on an ad hoc basis, largely based on macroeconomic considerations such as the need to provide fiscal support for the economy. The government is now working to define a minimum public service delivery level countrywide as a "more scientific" yardstick to assess fiscal needs.

104. Three categories of needs-based intergovernmental transfers between the central and local governments are as follows (Sen et al. 2014):

(i)   **General transfers.** Revenue sharing from value-added tax (VAT), profit tax, and personal income tax are used to lower disparities in expenditures across local governments. These account for about 46% of the total transfers. The main form of these transfers is equalization transfers, which

Box 5   Property Tax in the People's Republic of China—Strong Potential but Difficult Implementation

The People's Republic of China (PRC) already has a range of property taxes, but most are one-off taxes on transactions rather than recurrent taxes. Property taxation was introduced in 1951 through the Provisional Regulations on Urban Real Estate Tax. After 1985, with additional regulations, real estate tax, urban land use tax, land value-added tax, cultivated land occupation tax, and deed tax were introduced. These property taxes generate only modest revenue, accounting for 24.7% of subnational government tax revenues in 2016, which is low compared with 73% in the United States, and almost 100% in Australia and the United Kingdom. Local governments in the PRC thus rely on other financing sources, such as land sales or off-budget borrowing.

Introducing a recurrent tax on residential property—preferably following a broad-based and low-rate approach—has been hotly debated for years, given its potential to substantially increase fiscal revenues and autonomy at the local level. A recurrent tax would also facilitate a move toward the densification of cities and away from extensive urban development, which allows cities to sell more and more land, but also requires more infrastructure spending. It would also reduce speculative housing investment, which becomes less profitable with a regular tax on real estate.

Property tax pilots were launched in Chongqing and Shanghai in 2011. However, their impact has been limited as both cities opted for low rates with high exemptions, focusing on luxury units in Chongqing and new purchases in Shanghai. The recurrent property tax in Chongqing was levied on merely 11,000 units or less than 1% of all properties. Hence, the tax

yielded less than 1.0% of local government tax revenues. The results have been similar in Shanghai.

Other constraints have prevented the introduction of a recurrent tax on residential property: (i) inadequate property and land registration data; (ii) separate authorities for land and building registration; (iii) difficulty assessing the market value of land, rural housing, and subsidized government housing for the employees of state-owned enterprises; (iv) weak capacity and lack of independence of property appraisal firms, dominated by local government-owned companies; and (v) resistance of vested interests.

Despite these issues, the government still aims to introduce residential property tax. A nationwide property registration system is being built to ensure accurate assessment and collection of property taxes when eventually introduced. A new registration system for transactions was launched in 2015 but it will take up to 5 years before information on the existing stock of properties is added. The 19th National Congress of the Communist Party of China in October 2017 reconfirmed that a comprehensive reform of property taxes is needed, with legislative reforms and the improvement of information systems being the next steps. More specifically, the Congress urged the government to proceed in line with the principle "legislation first, full authority, step by step" to ultimately levy real estate tax on commercial real estate and personal housing based on the assessed value. In line with this party guidance, the government decided to advance property tax legislation in 2018. A law was drafted to be presented at the National People's Congress, i.e., the Parliament, to prepare the ground for public consultations.

Sources: Asian Development Bank. 2014. *Money Matters—Local Government Finance in the People's Republic of China.* Manila; and Asian Development Bank Institute. 2018. *Tax and Development—Challenge in Asia and the Pacific.* Edited by S. Araki and S. Nakabayashi. Tokyo.

accounted for about 19% of total transfers in 2011 but their share has been incrementally increased since 2014.

(ii)   **Earmarked transfers** subsidize projects subject to matching expenditures by subnational governments. These accounted for about 42% of total transfers in 2011 but their share is now incrementally reduced, mainly to lessen the need for local governments to finance matching expenditures, as they find them difficult to mobilize due to lack of own-tax revenues and borrowing constraints.

(iii)   **Compensation transfers** include VAT rebates equal to the previous year's rebates plus 30% of the growth in VAT and consumption tax revenues in the respective jurisdiction. Their objective is to reduce the revenue loss from the 1994 tax reforms that affected some subnational governments. They accounted for about 12% of the total transfers in 2011.

105. **Special-purpose transfers** are earmarked grants for subsidizing specific expenditure programs. They include grants for wage payments, rural tax benefits, rural subsidies grandfathered by the reforms in 1994,

rural education and health programs, support of minorities, and other grants financed by central government line ministries. Special-purpose transfers involve over 200 different grant programs and have complex conditions. Under a countrywide fiscal reform initiative launched in 2013, the share of targeted transfers, which typically require matching expenditure by subnational governments, has been incrementally reduced (and the State Council called for further reductions in 2018) while increasing the share of equalization transfers.

C.4.2. Learnings from the People's Republic of China and Relevance for India

106. While the unitary system and single party rule in the PRC allows a tighter control over subnational governments than in India, there are a few learnings from the PRC that India can adopt.

(i)   **Recognition of performance.** The biggest incentive for bureaucrats is the possibility of career advancement and recognition. In the PRC, political and bureaucratic interests are closely aligned with meeting regional GDP targets, which in turn require execution of infrastructure projects. Blanchard and Shleifer (2000) find that in the PRC, local governments have actively contributed to the growth of new regional businesses, and decentralization has been more effective in reducing the risk of local elite capture because of the central government's ability to reward and/ or punish local governments. In India, besides performance-based transfers, a recognition program for the best performing subnational governments and officials could be considered.

(ii)   **Infrastructure development with fiscal sustainability.** An excessive focus on infrastructure has created excess capacities in the PRC and increased debt and contingent liabilities to an unsustainable level in many municipalities. The incentives in the present system lean toward development spending at the expense of investment in social services. A solution could be to target a mix of physical and social infrastructure, service standards benchmarking, and including fiscal sustainability as an explicit long-term target.

The Indian state governments can issue bonds and access other means of borrowings subject to a ceiling determined by their fiscal targets, similar to the central government set quotas in the PRC. State governments in India are uniquely characterized—in comparison to other second-tier levels of government across Asia—in having their own state-level fiscal responsibility legislation. This is a powerful instrument to address the soft-budget constraint observed in other jurisdictions. State governments in India also report in their annual budgets their guarantees to state entities for better transparency, which is not yet done regularly in the PRC. While these steps have kept direct state government liabilities within limits in India, a similar attention needs to be paid toward off-budget borrowings (implicit contingent liabilities) by state public sector entities. A standard methodology for risk assessment from contingent liabilities also needs to be devised.

(iii)   **Mobilizing revenues through property tax.** Subnational governments need reliable (on-budget) revenue sources to meet their social and infrastructure funding needs. In regionally diverse countries, such as the PRC and India, part of the solution is to increase the amount of central government transfers as a percentage of GDP (which the PRC has not yet succeeded in doing) and an increase in the share of equalization grants within overall transfers at the expense of earmarked transfers (which the PRC has been doing incrementally since 2014). However, empirical evidence by Liu and Zhao (2011) shows negative incentive effects of central fiscal transfers and equalization grants on provincial tax efforts, while the effects of tax rebates are unclear. Another solution could be a recurrent tax on property levied at the local level (possibly within central government set parameters). However, preparing the ground for such a tax takes a long time. Difficulties that the PRC experienced in implementation of recurrent property tax are not specific to the PRC alone. Other countries, including India, face similar technical and political issues.[11] To minimize taxpayer resistance, it may be prudent to keep tax rates low, introduce objective property valuation methodologies, upgrade taxpayer services, including online payments while providing tax relief to the vulnerable taxpayers. The PRC's approach to introduce a nationwide property registration system offers a solution that can broaden the tax base, improve compliance, and result in high revenues even with low tax rates. However, property taxes can be introduced earlier on a pilot basis when certain localities are ready. The FC in India could incentivize states and municipalities for digitizing property records, introducing scientific property valuation methods, and improving taxpayer services. The IFIs could support local bodies in this endeavor (see section III on how IFI support can be leveraged).

C.5. Republic of Korea

107. Local governments in the ROK are financed mainly by locally generated revenues and transfers and subsidies from the central government. The Local Finance Equalization Scheme was established to (i) determine functional assignments among central and local governments in an efficient manner, (ii) help supply public goods in adequate quantities by addressing externalities among regions, and (iii) redress disparities in fiscal strength among local governments with weak revenue base through central government or higher-level local government transfers. The current transfer scheme consists of the transfer of resources between the central and local governments and transfers between metropolitan units and basic units of local governments and conditional grants. Central government transfers fund about 42% of local expenditures.

108. To improve local fiscal autonomy, local budgeting directives, which had been viewed as a form of central government control, were ended. A new system of overall ceilings on outstanding local borrowing was introduced, accompanied by the removal of the need for individual approvals for local bond issuance. With amendment to the Local Finance Act in 2015, new systems to enhance fiscal accountability such as annual local government fiscal analysis, accrual and double-entry accounting system, citizen participation in the budget compilation process, and a program budget system were introduced (Young 2015). Participatory budgeting is one of the key projects in the 2018 Government Innovation Master Plan. The Local Finance Act gives a certain degree of fiscal autonomy by allowing local governments to adjust tax rates by as much as 50%, however, in practice this has been rarely used due to their reluctance. Information technology (IT) systems were also introduced in public finance and local governance. Implemented in 2002, the Electronic National Tax System or Hometax, enabled taxpayers to process tax duties online without visiting tax offices. The Digital Budget and Accounting System (dBrain), in use since 2007, facilitated the real time management of all national financial activities. The counterpart local system is the Local Government Financial Management System (*e-Hojo*).

C.5.1. Types of Transfers in the Republic of Korea

109. There are two types of transfers in the ROK: (i) general purpose transfers (unconditional equalization payments), consisting of local subsidy; and (ii) specific-purpose grants (conditional transfers), consisting of national subsidy and local education subsidy.

110. **General purpose transfers.** These comprise **local subsidy** or **local shared tax (LST)**, which is an unconditional equalization grant set at a fixed share of 19.24% of the national tax revenue (MOSF 2014). Based on Article 10 of the Subsidy Management Act, different subsidy rates are applied based on degree of financial independence of a local government. Local subsidy for each area is determined by its fiscal

---

shortage, or the difference between its standard fiscal need (SFN) and its standard fiscal revenue (SFR), similar to the Ordinary LAT in Japan.

SFN = Basic fiscal demand + Supplementary demand + Demand incentive
SFR = Basic revenue + Supplementary revenue + Incentive revenue

111. The SFN is calculated based on demographic, geographic, social, and economic characteristics in 12 categories and 31 subcategories, and then summed to arrive at total expenditure need per area. The sum of fiscal shortages across jurisdictions is usually more than the amount of funds available for the LST. Consequently, an adjustment factor (i.e., population and area) is applied to the shortage of each local government to determine their allocation.

112. Currently, local subsidies consist of (i) general subsidies, (ii) special subsidies, and (iii) grants-in-aid for adjustment.[12]

(i)   **General subsidies** ensure adequate fiscal resources to maintain the administrative activities of local governments. These account for 17.75% of internal taxes and are offered to local governments whose standard fiscal income falls below the standard fiscal demand. The local consumption tax, part of the general subsidies, are distributed to 17 provinces (upper-level governments) based on an index of final consumption expenditure in each province. Higher shares are given to poorer provinces. The decentralization subsidy, which accounts for 0.94% of internal taxes, aims to progressively hand over the social welfare projects to local governments. It was included as a part of the general subsidy since 2015 (MOSF 2014).

(ii)   **Special subsidies**, which account for 0.55% of internal taxes, are granted for unexpected fiscal demands such as post-disaster restoration, establishment of public welfare facilities, and special projects promoted by the state. There is also a real-estate subsidy drawn from the Comprehensive Real Estate Tax, which is distributed based on the fiscal conditions of each local government. Based on Article 9 of the Local Subsidy Act, special subsidies are granted to exemplary local governments with achievements in local administration or financial management. These are incentive mechanisms to encourage better performance (ADBI 2017). For example, in 2010, the Ministry of Interior and Safety (MOIS) awarded an additional W10 billion in LST to the best-performing local government.

(iii)   **Grants-in-aid for adjustment**. An upper-level city (*si*) or province (*do*) may provide grants-in-aid or subsidies to *sis*, districts (*gus*) or autonomous *gus* within its jurisdiction and within budgetary limits to meet general and special fiscal demands.[13] General grants-in-aid, used to meet general fiscal demands such as supplementary funding, is equal to 90% of the total amount. Special grants-in-aid for specific community projects is equal to 10% of the total amount. Based on Article 36, enforcement decree of the Local Finance Act, general grants are allocated based on population size (50%), tax collections (20%), and financial situation using the financial independence index (FII) (30%).

113. Based on Article 12 of the Local Subsidy Act, there are provisions to penalize poor performance by a local government. Local subsidies may be returned or reduced when a local government makes excessive expenditures or neglects in collecting revenues. If MOIS deems that a distressed local government underperforms in implementing its financial soundness or rehabilitation plan, it may decrease local subsidies or give other financial disadvantages.

114. **Specific-purpose grants.** The ROK dedicates specific-purpose grants (conditional transfers) to stimulate certain kinds of spending and incentivize

---

[12]   Firefighting safety subsidy was included under general subsidies in 2014.

[13]   City or *do* includes 6 metropolitan cities, 1 special city, 1 special autonomous city, and 9 provinces.

own-source revenues. They consist of (i) national subsidy, (ii) local education subsidy, and (iii) shares in the lottery fund.

115. **National Subsidy (or Subsidy from the National Treasury).** Subsidies for local governments from the national treasury are earmarked as conditional matching grants, aimed to partially or fully subsidize costs related to projects commissioned by the national government. In contrast to other local subsidies, which local governments can use as general financial resources, these are directed toward a specific-purpose. The amount of national subsidies, the charges to be borne by a local government, and borrowings from the government funds are determined by the Ministry of Economy and Finance (MOEF) for the relevant fiscal year.

(i)   **Special Account for Regional Development.** This was introduced under the national subsidy in 2004 to increase resource transfer to regions and target specific national programs at noncapital regions. It includes the Mega Region Account, distributed to different ministries for implementing regional targeted programs in 13 provinces, excluding the capital region; the Regional Development Account, transferred directly to all provinces; and the Jeju Account, only for the Jeju Island province (Yusifov 2018). This account uses an allocation formula using five variables (fiscal capacity index, population, income-proportional resident tax, area, and aging population rate). Ongoing is the Regional Tourism Resources Development Program. This grant is more local demand-based, with three main components: formula-based projects allocated autonomously based on population, size, and fiscal capacity index of local governments, projects for poor regions, and regional innovation projects, allocated based on requests from local governments.

116. **Local education subsidy.** Under the Local Education Subsidy Act, special subsidies support local governments with an excellent track record of operating local educational administration and finance. Public spending for primary and secondary education are managed by local education offices

that are independent elected entities separate from local governments. Education expenditures are financed by central government general grants for education (about 76%), transfers from local governments (about 18%), and tuition and fees (about 6%). Local education subsidies, composed of 20.27% of internal taxes and 100% of education taxes, are granted to 17 city and provincial education offices. This grant is divided into general subsidies (total amount of education tax and 96% of the 20.27% of internal taxes) provided to education units whose standard fiscal income falls below the standard fiscal demand; and special subsidies (4% of the 20.27% of internal taxes) for special fiscal demands of local education offices.

117. **Shares in the Lottery Fund.** Administered by the MOEF, this is allocated to local governments and used for social welfare programs. In 2013, the local government share of total allocation was 6% (W930 million) (NABO 2013).

C.5.2. Learnings from the Republic of Korea and Relevance for India
118. Even in a nonfederal system like the ROK, issues of vertical and horizontal imbalances, revenue-sharing, and incentivizing local public service delivery are present, and lessons can be drawn for India.

119. **Rewarding performance.** The central government of the ROK has effectively used the system of fiscal transfers to reward local governments for their achievements while penalizing poor performers with decreased funds. Besides, the 2006 Framework Act on Government Performance Evaluation established an integrated performance management and evaluation system, which covers central government agencies as well as local governments, public enterprises, and quasi-government organizations. The Government Performance Evaluation Committee, a multisectoral agency chaired by the Prime Minister, primarily oversees these top–down evaluations on key policy goals and programs, which are then used for budget cuts or increases as part of the incentive system. A minimum 10% budget cut is imposed the next fiscal year on government programs graded C or D (Hur 2013). From 2008 to 2012, there were 573 programs deemed ineffective and budget was cut

to as high as 19% (Park 2017). India could consider developing a standard governance index across states for tracking performance and rewarding the states with additional funds if performance benchmarks are met (see section III).

120. **Leveraging technology.** The ROK's success in using integrated IT systems to improve local government financial management and service delivery could be an example for India.

D. Summary of Recommendations for the 15th Finance Commission

121. **Address moral hazard issues.** Equalization transfers could lead to moral hazard as they carry the fiscal profligacy risk, leading to wasteful public expenditures, low tax effort by the subnational governments, and inefficient and low-quality public service delivery. In India, while the major portion of the transfer is untied based on objective measures, it is supplemented with gap-filling grants based on normative assessment of fiscal capacity and fiscal needs. Objective standards for computation of fiscal gap needs to be strengthened like in Japan, and state governments should be incentivized to improve their tax efforts. The FII or share of own-source revenues of local governments is used in the ROK to measure the tax effort of local governments, and transfers are linked with improvement in such an indicator. Section III suggests indicators for measuring and incentivizing improvements in governance, including tax effort and fiscal performance, and health and education service delivery to minimize the moral hazard issues.

122. **Separate equalization considerations and performance requirement in the scheme of transfers.** It is recommended that the FC includes only the fiscal needs/cost disability and equalization considerations in designing the devolution formula, and deal with performance requirements separately under the conditional grants using a forward-looking approach. Inequality-adjusted HDI could be included in India's devolution formula. As discussed in the 14th FC report (2015), compared with the HDI, which averages three dimensions of health, education, and income, this measure is more sensitive to developmental disparities and income distribution across states. As pointed out by the 12th FC report (2003), while inequality adjusted HDI reflects access to social services, the infrastructure index distance reflects the state's relative position in terms of access to physical infrastructure. Thus, both indicators may be considered in the devolution formula.

123. **Employ the right mix of unconditional and conditional transfers.** A combination of unconditional transfers, specific-purpose grants, and performance-based transfers would offer the right mix to address the economic and fiscal disparities across states in India; and reintroducing conditional grants by FC would be recommended.

124. For India, greater collaboration between central and state governments in the design of conditional transfers would be beneficial to ensure greater transparency in the objectives of the transfers, and greater compatibility between central and subnational policy preferences. This can be achieved through agreements between central government and individual state governments to set up processes for management of funds and to jointly develop objectives, conditions, outcomes, and performance metrics, similar to the National Health Reform Agreement, 2011 and National Education Reform Agreement, 2014 in Australia where the states, territories, and the Commonwealth government are jointly responsible for funding and delivering a nationally unified and locally managed public health and education systems.

125. **Establish clear demarcation of responsibilities across programs to avoid overlaps and inefficiencies.** Consolidation of conditional grants under NSPPs and NPPs based on agreements between the Commonwealth and state governments in Australia is a good model for setting clear objectives for a few selected priority sectors, followed by a rigorous monitoring of performance indicators by an independent agency such as COAG Reform Council. Australia's experience also underscores the importance of clarifying the roles and responsibilities of different layers of government in concurrent

subjects to avoid accountability issues and inefficient outcomes in service delivery. In India, the rationalization of CSS has addressed the overlap issue to some extent. Additional reforms would include reducing the indicators further to focused targets and streamlining state government schemes. The schemes should be prioritized based on growth-enhancing capital spending. It is also important that states do not substitute their own expenditures with CSS. Independent monitoring and audit mechanisms of CSS and state schemes need strengthening to improve output and input efficiencies.

126. **Strengthen performance monitoring and enforcement mechanisms.** As underscored in Japan and the ROK, a successful intergovernmental fiscal transfer system involves strong coordination with the central government for effective fiscal planning and performance-based budgeting. In addition, independent monitoring and evaluation mechanisms with the right mixture of incentives are critical to strengthen performance and enforcement at all tiers of the government. India could consider developing a standard governance index across states, incorporating key fiscal and service delivery indicators, for tracking performance and encourage competition across states by rewarding them with additional funds if satisfactory performance benchmarks are met.

127. For conditional transfers, Australia's experience with agreements between central government and state governments on achievement of goals and specific milestones could provide a strong basis for compliance. For India, SFCs and an independent body such as NITI Aayog could oversee implementation and assess compliance in close coordination with central government, state governments, and other national stakeholders. Development of standard benchmarks and collection of data for measurement of performance are critical. In case of noncompliance with conditions, various methods of penalties may be adopted, including reduction, withholding, repayment, return or refund, reallocation of funds, or instituting financial corrections.

128. Besides institutional performance monitoring, incentivizing performance of government officials could also strengthen enforcement mechanisms under the fiscal transfer system. The PRC's experience shows that development reforms can be very effective if the possibility of career growth and recognition is aligned with progressive reforms. In India, besides performance-based transfers for the states and/or local governments, a recognition program for the best performing state and/or local government and the concerned department officials can be initiated.

129. **Encourage resource generation by the second and third tiers to reduce dependence on central transfers.** Although outside the direct purview of the FC, reform of state taxes needs to be encouraged for the third tier of government. Local bodies should be encouraged to be self-dependent in fiscal management and reduce their burden on state governments in financing deficits.[14] The FC can consider incentives for local bodies that take steps toward adoption of participatory planning and state-specific Gram Panchayat Development Plan (GPDP) guidelines based on model GOI guidelines, resource mobilization, effective management of public assets, improvements in budgeting, accounting, and audit systems, and adoption of service level benchmarks. Local governments should be encouraged to synergize funding under state and central schemes, SFC transfers, district development fund with FC grants for the most effective utilization of funds, and accessing capital markets for project financing.

130. Urban and rural local bodies need to be encouraged to broaden their tax base for self-reliance. For example, to minimize resistance from property taxpayers, it may be prudent to keep tax rates low and provide improved taxpayer services, including online payments. The PRC's approach to introduce a nationwide property registration system points toward a solution that can broaden tax-base, improve compliance, and result in high revenues even with low tax rates. The FC in India could consider incentivizing states and municipalities for digitizing property

---

[14]   Rural as well as urban local governments derive powers of taxation only out of subjects specified by the state. Each state government can authorize the local government specific revenues under articles 243H and 243X of the Constitution. As the assigned revenues may differ from state to state, this leads to interstate heterogeneity in the standards and quality of services provided by the local governments.

records, introducing scientific property valuation methods, and improving taxpayer services. IFIs can support state and local governments in these efforts (see section III on leveraging IFI support).

131. **Develop capacity of subnational governments.** It is critical to improve the capacity of state governments and local governments in making expenditure decisions and executing key projects, while providing them with greater expenditure responsibilities to improve service delivery. Use of medium-term budgeting and expenditure frameworks need to be incentivized (see section III). Community participation models in budgeting processes such as those followed in Japan and the ROK can be effective for strengthening public accountability at the local governments and should be encouraged. While some of the better placed local bodies in India can strive to issue bonds to raise resources, the panchayats do not have such an option. Besides capacity building,

a dedicated transfer to the panchayats like the recently introduced Village Funds in Indonesia can help provide the villages with resources to improve local delivery.

132. **Strengthen fiscal transparency, risk assessment, and market discipline.** Indian state governments issue bonds and access other means of borrowings subject to a ceiling determined by their fiscal targets, like the central government set quotas in the PRC. In addition, state governments in India also report their guarantees issued to state entities for better transparency. While these steps—together with the advent of state fiscal responsibility legislation—have kept the direct state government liabilities in India within limits, a similar attention needs to be paid toward off-budget borrowings (implicit contingent liabilities) by state public sector entities. A standard methodology for risk assessment from contingent liabilities also needs to be devised.

III. Incentivizing Subnational Government Performance through Transfers

> "No simple, uniform pattern of transfers will be suitable for all circumstances or objectives in any jurisdiction. Transfers as such are neither good nor bad. What matters are their effects on such policy outcomes as allocative efficiency, distributional equity, and macroeconomic stability" (Bird 1993).

A. Performance-Based Transfers for Improved Governance

A.1. Rationale for Promoting Good Governance

133. The basic guiding principle for the design of intergovernmental fiscal transfer system is that the purpose of transfers should not be only financing of the governmental entities but they should also contribute to an effective provision of services. These transfers can be structured to generate three types of outcomes: (i) correcting for vertical imbalance due to mismatch of revenue and expenditures between the center and subnational governments; (ii) correcting for horizontal imbalance or variations across subnational governments; and (iii) incentivizing performance (World Bank 2016). The previous section has covered the first two points. This section will focus on the third point—how to incentivize better performance and service delivery.

134. In theory, the principle of subsidiarity suggests that decentralization helps bring service delivery closer to citizens because decentralized governments that are democratically elected are more accountable and respond directly to the preferences and needs of citizens, which in turn strengthens spending efficiency at the subnational level (Ryan and Woods 2015). However, in reality, intergovernmental fiscal transfers based solely on funding the needs of the subnational governments, cannot ensure the efficient use of these funds unless the compliance of subnational governments with performance measures is monitored (Bird 1993).[15] An analysis of 23 OECD countries by Abbott and Jones (2012) suggests that intergovernmental fiscal transfers may increase subnational public spending because of pervasive voracity effects. Bessho (2017) suggests that a top-down system of transfers in Japan incentivizes higher local government expenditures. For Indonesia, Tirtosuharto (2017) shows that expansion of fiscal spending have caused inefficiency due to waste, corruption, and rent seeking, while Vujanovic (2017) points out that despite more than 15 years of decentralization, there continues to be great divergence across Indonesian provinces in terms of per capita real GDP, health outcomes, and regional infrastructure, including access to safe drinking water and electricity. Lewis (2017) finds that increase in local spending does not

---

[15] Efficiency entails technical efficiency (use of public funds for maximum feasible outputs), allocative efficiency (productive use of budgetary resources), and attainment of results and outcomes (World Bank 2016).

consistently lead to rising access to quality services. This could be driven by (i) the need to make a minimum threshold level of spending for noticeable results, and/or (ii) inefficient utilization of funds by subnational governments that are dependent on transfers.

135. Heywood and Choi (2010) focusing on the health system across 10 Indonesian districts document the absence of relationship between the government's health care spending and health outputs, driven by low planning capacity, fractured health system, and lack of innovation. A subsequent paper, Maharani (2015) finds that devolving responsibility from the central government to subnational governments does not automatically improve performance of health providers and health outcomes. The study shows that both local governments and hospital managers need time to develop capacity to utilize their authority following decentralization and strengthen accountability mechanisms to improve performance of health providers. Muttaqin et al. (2016) and Sari (2018) find evidence for improvement in educational attainment measured as school enrollment rate and learning outcomes in areas with better infrastructure and urbanization post decentralization in Indonesia. However, there are considerable differences in education outcome across districts. Decentralization may increase accountability and empower subnational governments to improve education provided that the subnational governments have the capacity.

136. Martínez-Vázquez et al. (2017) show mixed evidence about the effectiveness of decentralization on service delivery. The benefits are realized only when all three components of decentralization—fiscal, administrative, and political—are strong. For South Asian economies, a recent survey by World Bank (2019) find misalignments between the actual (de facto) and legal (de jure) decentralization, which contribute to the weaknesses in service delivery. It is therefore critical that the intergovernmental fiscal transfer systems are designed to empower the subnational governments with adequate resources to carry out their mandates, give flexibility in utilization of funds, strengthen institutional capacity, and ensure accountability.

137. The empirical evidence from the literature also stress the importance of good governance for effective and efficient public service delivery. A study by Sow and Razafimahefa (2018) covering 64 countries including Bhutan, India, Maldives, and Pakistan shows that fiscal decentralization improves the efficiency of public services under specific conditions, which include strong local government autonomy, strong accountability, good governance, and strong capacity at the local level. Rajkumar and Swaroop (2008) finds that across 91 countries, public spending does not yield expected improvements in outcomes in the presence of poor governance proxied by level of corruption and quality of bureaucracy. They find that with more effective use of public spending on health and primary education, child mortality rates decline faster, and primary education attainment increases more in countries with good governance. Brixi et al. (2013) point out the importance of defining outcome and output targets to strengthen accountability and using independent monitoring and evaluation mechanisms to improve the provincial government's performance in delivery of primary health care services in the PRC. Similarly, Hauner (2007) find that efficiency differences between regions in the Russian Federation in public expenditures in social sectors (health and education) are positively related to per capita income, quality of governance, and democratic control and accountability, while they are negatively related to the share of federal transfers and level of spending relative to regional GDP. Thus, they suggest that implementing performance-based budgeting, overcoming financial management shortcomings, and extending more autonomy in policymaking and accountability to subnational governments are key for improving efficiency in service delivery.

138. The subsequent sections deal with the core elements of governance and its strong interlinkage with two main sectors—health and education. Service delivery systems in health and education sectors are

not only among the indicators of governance quality, but they are directly affected by it.

A.2. Quality of Governance and Efficiency of Social Sector Expenditures in India

139. A study by Mohanty and Bhanumurthy (2018) reviewed the public expenditure efficiency in attainment of social sector outputs (Millennium Development Goals composite performance index), health sector (infant mortality and life expectancy at birth), and education sector (gross enrollment for school education and higher education) among 27 states in India during FY2003–FY2016. The study shows that output efficiency score for all states is 0.69 for social sector spending, indicating that with the same level of inputs, all states are on average producing 31% fewer outputs than they should if they were efficient. The output efficiency score is 0.78 for the education sector and 0.92 for the health sector. Input efficiency score for all states in social sector spending is 0.71, indicating that on average, all states can attain the same level of output by using 29% less of current inputs. Input efficiency score is 0.75 for education and 0.71 for health sectors.

140. The study finds large variations in efficiency of public spending among Indian states. The regression analysis shows that quality of governance has a significant effect on efficiency of public spending in the social sector, including education and health. The study measured the quality of governance using the Public Affairs Index (PAI), estimated by the Public Affairs Center based in Bengaluru, Karnataka in India. The PAI is a composite indicator of 10 broad themes, comprising economic freedom; essential infrastructure; fiscal management; support to human development; transparency and accountability; social protection; environment; women and children; delivery of justice; and crime, law, and order. The PAI in 2016 includes 68 individual indicators; PAI in 2017 includes 81 indicators and PAI in 2018 includes 100 indicators under these themes. The PAI score enables ranking of 30 states in India on an annual basis.[16] Figure 7 shows a strong positive relationship between PAI and output and input efficiency scores in the social sector.

A.3. Measuring Quality of Governance in India—The Governance Index

141. The latest version of PAI in 2018 is quite comprehensive and contains 100 indicators across 10 themes. Most of these indicators capture quality of physical infrastructure, rule of law, human development, and social protection that are already targeted under sectoral state and central level programs and schemes. While these indicators are effective for measurement of governance quality, it may be difficult to use the substantial number of indicators for performance targeting. State governments may find it unpractical to target multiple objectives. To improve the ease of measurement and monitoring, a streamlined governance index with eight indicators (seven PAI indicators and one additional indicator) that have equal weightage across three themes is proposed to determine allocation of performance-based grants (Table 8).

A.3.1. Transparency and Accountability

142. Transparent and accountable government institutions will increase citizens' awareness about their rights and responsibilities, which will further improve the quality in public service delivery due to greater oversight. An accountable government also achieves better outcomes in use of public resources. Under the governance index, two indicators are proposed:

(i)   For transparency, services provided on a digital platform by states under the e-governance plan can be measured. IT systems have improved accessibility of services, standardization of service quality, and prevention of leakages and corruption.

(ii)   For accountability, the Panchayat Devolution Index can be measured, which looks at the depth of devolution of funds, functions, and functionaries by the states to the Panchayat Raj Institutions in compliance with the 73rd Constitutional amendment. The 14th FC recommended strengthening of the panchayats and duly constituted municipalities and greater devolution of formula-based grants from states

---

[16]   Public Affairs Index, Governance in the States of India. Public Affairs Index. Bengaluru: Public Affairs (Years: 2016, 2017, and 2018).

Figure 7   Public Affairs Index and Efficiency of Expenditures in Social Sector

Relationship between PAI and Efficiency of Social Sector Expenditure in Selected Indian States

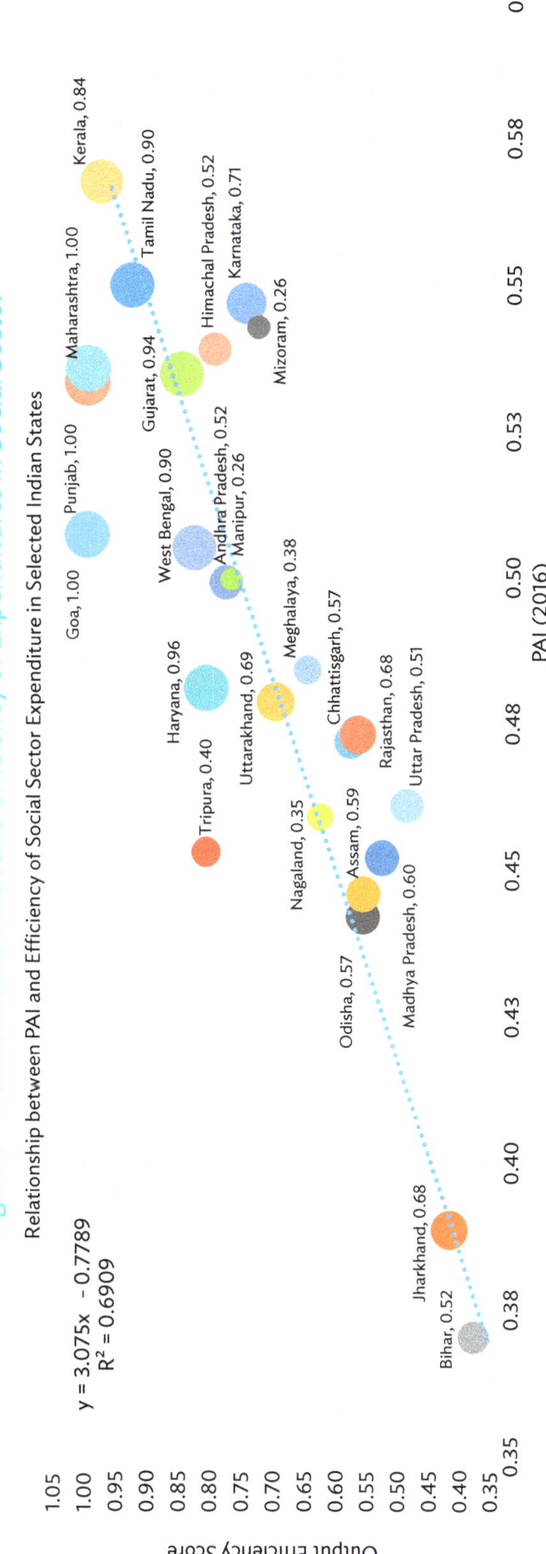

PAI = Public Affairs Index.

Source: Output and Input Efficiency Scores are from R. K. Mohanty and N. R. Bhanumurthy. 2018. Assessing Public Expenditure Efficiency in Indian States. *National Institute of Public Finance and Policy Working Paper.* No. 225; and Public Affairs Index is from Public Affairs Center Governance in the States of India 2016 report. http://pai.pacindia. org/#/2016/public-affairs-index.

Table 8   Components of Governance Index for Performance-Based Grants

Themes	Subthemes	Indicators	Overall Weight in %
1. **Transparency and Accountability**	Transparency	1) Number of services provided under e-governance plan	12.5
	Public accountability	2) Panchayat devolution index score	12.5
2. **Fiscal Management**	Own-revenue generation	3) States own-tax revenue growth	12.5
	Development expenditure	4) Per capita development expenditure	12.5
	Outcome-based budgeting	5) Adoption of MTFF and MTEF under state-level FRBM rules	12.5
3. **Economic Freedom**	Business promotion	6) Number of industrial entrepreneur memorandum filed	12.5
		7) Ease of doing business	12.5
		8) Value of micro, small and medium-sized enterprises' assets (% of GSDP)	12.5
		Total	100.0

FRBM = Fiscal Responsibility and Budget Management, GSDP = gross state domestic product, MTEF = medium-term expenditure framework, MTFF = medium-term fiscal framework, PAI = Public Affairs Index.
Notes: The indicators for each state are normalized by PAI methodology with respect to the deviation from the sample group minimum and variance to avoid a priori correlation with state income. Outcome-based budgeting is a binary indicator reflecting the adoption of MTFF and MTEF by the state as part of their FRBM rules and whether they are actively implemented as part of the state budgeting process.
Source: Seven indicators are from Public Affairs Index, Governance in the States of India, 2017, Public Affairs Center, pp. 145–147.
http://pai.pacindia.org/#/2017/public-affairs-index.

to local bodies to strengthen their service delivery subject to conditions such as auditing of their accounts, further own-tax revenue mobilization, and adherence to performance benchmarks in service delivery.

A.3.2. Fiscal Management

143. Effective and efficient fiscal management is essential for development. States with weaker fiscal performance will find it difficult to allocate resources for physical and social infrastructure. The GOI enacted the Fiscal Responsibility and Budget Management (FRBM) Act in 2003 to institutionalize fiscal discipline both at the central and state level and prescribed a trajectory for eliminating current deficits, reducing fiscal deficits to 3% of GSDP, and reducing debt burden over time. The 12th FC introduced an incentive mechanism by making the enactment of FRBM legislations, which provided for, among other things, elimination of current deficit by a given deadline, and reducing fiscal deficit to or below a target level, a condition for state governments to receive debt relief from the central government loans. As pointed out by the FRBM Review Committee in 2017, while improvements in debt ratios and deficits were observed under the debt relief scheme during 2005–2010, once these incentives ceased to exist, several states were unable to meet their own debt, revenue, and fiscal deficit targets.[17]

144. Considering the variability in attainment of fiscal targets across states, there is a need to establish stronger incentive mechanisms to improve the fiscal management through performance-based grants from the FC. The following three indicators are proposed under the governance index:

---

[17] Several factors contributed to the partial success in implementation of rule-based fiscal policy at the state level. As pointed out by the 14th FC, states have resorted to borrowings from public accounts—particularly the National Small Savings Fund for financing fiscal deficits. The FRBM Review Committee expressed concerns about the opacity of states' budgetary data related to off-budget borrowings by the parastatals and/or state public sector undertakings, accumulated losses of public enterprises, and contingent liabilities arising from guarantees. In return, the 14th FC recommended that both union and state governments should report the total extended public debt as a supplement to the budget document and develop a standardized methodology for risk-weighted ceiling on guarantees to incorporate into the FRBM legislations. The cash accounting system adopted by states also made it easier to postpone the payments, collect taxes in advance, and show lower deficits and debt in a year. Thus, the 14th FC reiterated the need to introduce accrual-based accounting system for both union and state governments.

(i)   **Own-revenue generation** is measured by state's own-tax revenue growth achieved by expanding tax base and/or efficiency of tax administration.

(ii) **Development expenditure** is measured by per capita development expenditure.

(iii) **Outcome-based budgeting** indicates whether the medium-term fiscal framework (MTFF) and medium-term expenditure framework (MTEF) have been adopted under the state-level FRBM rules and whether they are actively used for budgeting process.

145. Recent central government initiatives will contribute to the successful implementation of the proposed incentive mechanism under the governance index. The nationwide rollout of GST in India with effect from 1 July 2017 subsumed a range of local and state-level taxes under the GST regime, which is now harmonized and uniformly applied across India. The GST regime will foster states' own-revenue generation by (i) boosting the tax base through increasing the number of indirect tax filers; (ii) unifying fragmented tax jurisdictions, which could reduce compliance costs for businesses and prevent potential double taxation issues; and (iii) increasing the efficiency of collection with IT-based tax administration. The GST regime will also help lower internal trade barriers for creating a common domestic within the country for more effective flow of goods and services. For the implementation of outcome-based budgeting, monitoring compliance with the FRBM rules is equally critical. For that purpose, the 14th FC and the FRBM Review Committee recommended the establishment of an independent agency such as a fiscal council at the central level by amending the FRBM Act.[18] This will also strengthen the implementation of FRBM rules at the state level. Furthermore, incentivizing outcome-based budgeting will likely reinforce effective planning of development expenditures. As shown in Figure 8, the quality of essential infrastructure is strongly correlated with the efficiency of SSEs.

146. Infrastructure development can also help reduce regional disparities in India. The PRC presents a good example of how focused public investments can reduce regional disparities (Box 6) as reflected in reduced migration from the poorer southwestern regions toward the more prosperous east, although other factors such as declining demand for unskilled workers, lower population growth, and population aging have also contributed (Crane et al. 2018). Further, infrastructure investment might be a necessary condition for raising income levels but not a sufficient one, as demonstrated by the example of northeastern and western provinces of the PRC (Box 6). Careful project selection and fiscal sustainability should not be neglected when using infrastructure to boost economic growth and employment.

A.3.3. Economic Freedom

147. This theme deals with the efforts made by the states to enhance economic growth through business promotion and other private sector led investment initiatives. A state can remove stringent regulations, provide tax incentives to entrepreneurs, and create a business environment to attract investors. Apart from private investment's direct contribution to capital asset formation including infrastructure, stronger economic growth led by private sector growth will also have positive effects on the own-revenue mobilization by states and potentially free up more resources for development expenditures, which in turn will improve the delivery of public services. Performance-based grants can incentivize improvements in the following three indicators:

(i)   number of industrial entrepreneur memorandum filed in the state to capture the new business creation;

(ii) ease of doing business index, based on annual World Bank study, to measure quality of business climate; and

(iii) micro, small and medium-sized enterprises' assets as percentage of GSDP to measure size of the private sector and job creation.

---

[18]   Independent fiscal councils have been established in several countries to improve the policy makers' incentives to pursue prudent fiscal policies and strengthen the oversight and enforcement of fiscal rules (Akın et al. 2017).

Figure 8   Essential Infrastructure and Efficiency of Expenditures in Social Sector

Relationship between Quality of Infrastructure and Efficiency of Social Sector Expenditure in Selected Indian States

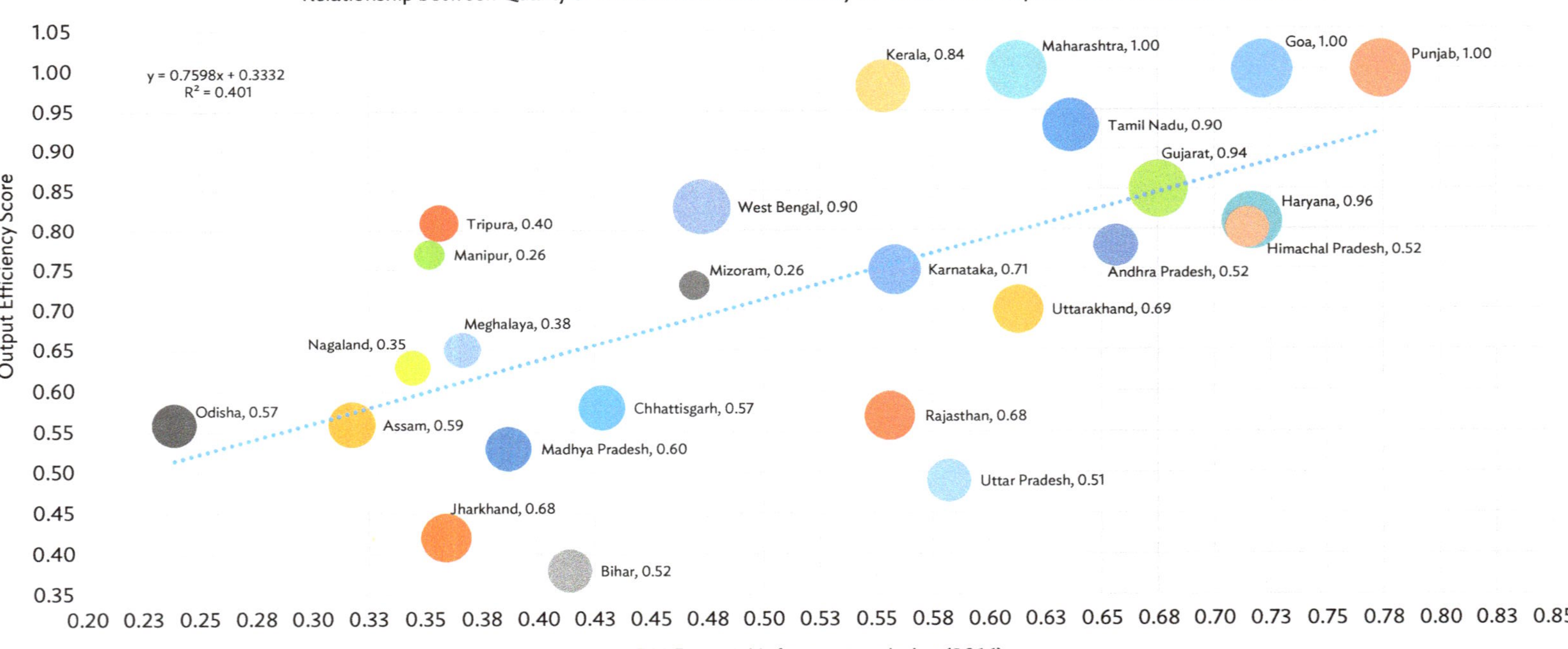

Bubble sizes reflect input efficiency score as reported next to the names of the states

PAI = Public Affairs Index.
Sources: Output and input efficiency scores are from R. K. Mohanty and N. R. Bhanumurthy. 2018. Assessing Public Expenditure Efficiency in Indian States. *National Institute of Public Finance and Policy Working Paper*. No. 225; and Public Affairs Index (Essential Infrastructure) is from Public Affairs Center Governance in the States of India 2016 report. http://pai.pacindia.org/#/2016/public-affairs-index.

Box 6   Investment Programs in the People's Republic of China for Underdeveloped Provinces

For almost 2 decades, the People's Republic of China (PRC) invested in inland provinces to help them catch up with the prosperous coastal provinces. This spending spree has added to the PRC's debt load, but many provinces, particularly in the northeast and far west, nevertheless remain far behind. Some southwestern provinces have fared better. Major cities have been modernized, and incomes have risen to such a degree that people stay instead of leaving to seek their fortune elsewhere. Better infrastructure and industrial relocation have created self-sustaining growth.

Ringed by mountains and far from the developed east coast, the southwest had long been a byword for backwardness. Southwestern provinces saw central government directed investment in the late 1960s and early 1970s as part of the "Third Front" strategy of relocating the military–industrial complex away from the coast, but still lagged behind in the export-driven boom since 1980s. The central government's next attempt to boost the west began in 2000, when the Great Western Development strategy led to an increase in infrastructure spending. However, for another decade, workers migrated to the coast, and western provinces such as Sichuan, Guizhou, and Guangxi saw their share of population decline.

Still, by around 2010 the cumulative effect of infrastructure spending was becoming apparent, and an effective transport network took shape. In the next 5 years, the eastward shift of population began to slow. Over 2011–2016, prosperous Jiangsu, Shanghai, and Zhejiang did not see their population share rising, while Anhui, Guangxi, and Sichuan switched from falling to rising shares. The turnaround in Sichuan was particularly dramatic since the province had traditionally been a big exporter of labor. It mainly had its capital Chengdu to thank for the boom: the city's population surged by 20% from 2011 to 2016, reaching 14 million, as residents of other parts of Sichuan migrated to the southwest's biggest city. In Guangxi and Guizhou, though, every single prefecture-level city recorded a rising number of residents. What caused population flows to change to such an extent? A key factor

clearly was that public sector infrastructure investment and preferential land and tax policies attracted industries.

Chengdu benefited from large investment from technology firms that took advantage of lower labor cost and helped to shift manufacturing jobs west. This has formed a vibrant industrial cluster, attracting many upstream materials manufacturers and creating hundreds of thousands of jobs. Another major employer is tourism. Served by the PRC's fourth busiest airport, Chengdu pulls in well over 100 million visitors every year. Much of Chengdu's investments in tourist infrastructure, transport systems, and real estate have been paid for by debt, but nonetheless incomes have risen. With a per-capita GDP of around $12,000, the city is on course to clear the World Bank's threshold for "high-income economies." This compares to $1,500, little more than 15 years ago.

Nanning, the capital of Guangxi that borders Viet Nam, had population growth of 5.7% in 2011–2016, well above the national rate of 2.6%. With an urban population of 2.9 million, Nanning is a little larger than England's Manchester and just a mid-sized city by the PRC's standards. Its huge investment in urban infrastructure—housing, roads, expressways, bridges, a metro system—is staggering in its ambition and well planned. A new high-speed rail line whooshes passengers to Guangzhou, 575 km away, in barely 3 hours. Incomes are still much lower in Nanning than in bigger cities—but so are costs.

The latest plan to boost development in Guangxi focuses on its slice of coastline—45 minutes south of Nanning on a high-speed train that opened in 2016—and deepening ties with the countries of Southeast Asia. Three small ports have been consolidated into the larger Beibu Bay Port, creating one of the PRC's top 20 ports. Beibu handled 140 million tons of cargo in 2015, up from 80 million in 2010. Positioning itself as Guangxi's gateway to the Association of Southeast Asian Nations, Beibu has begun providing joint customs clearance with Viet Nam and Malaysia. Its Free Trade Port Area has a bonded zone for cars and tax-free outlets for goods.

Source: Asian Development Bank.

Figure 9   Proposed Governance Index and Efficiency of Expenditures in Social Sector

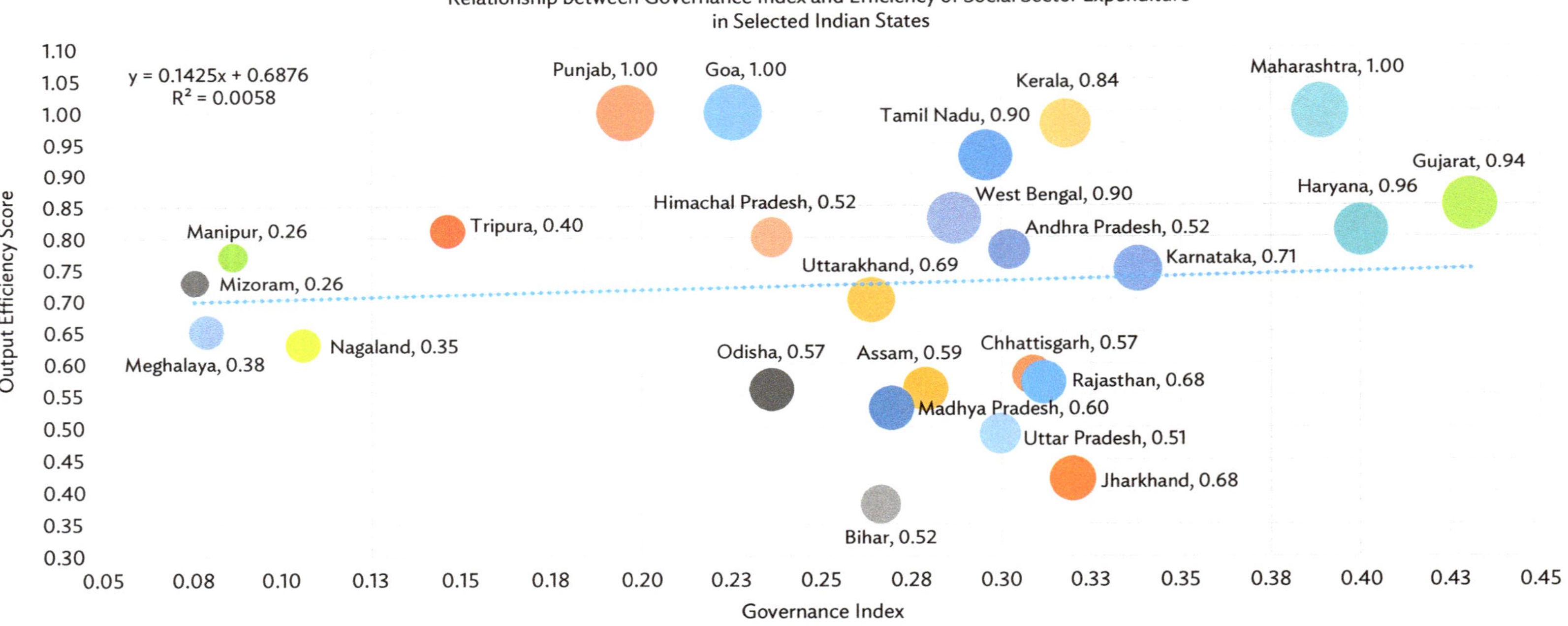

FRBM = Fiscal Responsibility and Budget Management, MTEF = medium-term expenditure framework, MTFF = medium-term fiscal framework.
Note: Outcome-based budgeting is a binary indicator reflecting the adoption of MTFF and MTEF by the state as part of their FRBM rules and whether they are actively implemented during the state budgeting process. This is assumed to be zero for the calculation of the index values given that comprehensive data are not yet available to measure the extent of adoption of this budgeting tool across states.
Sources: Output and input efficiency scores are from R. K. Mohanty and N. R. Bhanumurthy. 2018. Assessing Public Expenditure Efficiency in Indian States. *National Institute of Public Finance and Policy Working Paper*. No. 225; and seven indicators are from Public Affairs Center. 2018. Public Affairs Index, Governance in the States of India. http://pai.pacindia.org/#/2018.

148. Figure 9 shows the positive relationship between the proposed governance index (using seven PAI indicators, excluding the MTFF- and MTEF-related indicator) and the efficiency in SSEs. The association between the proposed governance index and efficiency of SSEs is expected to get stronger for states, effectively implementing outcome-based budgeting using MTFF and MTEFs.

A.4. Strengthening Allocative Efficiency of Budget with Medium-Term Expenditure Framework

149. An analysis of the overall quality of expenditures by state governments in India in Figure 8 shows that while the ratio of capital to current expenditures improved significantly between FY2001 and FY2005 with capital expenditure being almost a third of the current expenditure, there has been a steady decline since then with the capital expenditure accounting for only one-fifth of current expenditures in FY2018 (RBI 2018).

150. However, focusing solely on ratio of capital expenditure to current expenditure to assess the expenditure quality could be misleading as certain types of current expenditures play a significant role in improving service delivery. In social sectors such as health and education, expenditure on salaries of medical professionals and teachers are vital for the provision of these services. Another indicator is related to SSEs, which include expenditures on education, health, water supply, and sanitation and welfare of vulnerable sections. The SSEs by the state governments has Increased from 28.4% of overall expenditure in FY2004 to around 44.0% in FY2018 (Figure 10). However, there has been a distinct change in the composition of SSEs. Education and health, which accounted for 56.4% of SSEs in FY2004, have witnessed their share declining to 45.2% in FY2018, driven by a drop in the share of current expenditure in education in overall expenditure.[19] In contrast, there has been an increased focus on other components including water supply and sanitation, housing, and urban development.

151. In assessing the quality of expenditures, it is also important to look at the share of committed expenditures relative to capital outlay. The average capital outlay to GSDP ratios for 18 non-special category states in India remained at 2.6% in FY2017 and FY2018 (RE) compared with an increase in current expenditures to GSDP ratio from 13.6% in FY2017 to 14.6% in FY2018 (RE) (RBI 2018). In Punjab for example, committed expenditures comprising salaries, pensions, and interest payments make up over 75% of current expenditures. Even though SSEs such as education and health (i.e., salaries for teachers and doctors) are likely to contribute to human capital development, their shares in the states' overall budget allocation are not very high. The current expenditures in nonsocial sectors are mainly driven by the size of the state governments, presenting a large opportunity for rationalizing such inefficient expenditures.

152. Based on this overview, strengthening the allocative efficiency and effectiveness of the states' budgetary expenditures critically hinge upon improving the quality of recording and publishing of subnational fiscal data, and the fiscal management. For India, while the state-level spending data are published regularly, the full picture, comprising all on-budget expenditures at a granular district and/or municipality level, may not be available given the quality issues with public spending data at the local government level. This is also a general pattern observed across other South Asian economies by the OECD's 2019 World Observatory of Subnational Finance and Investment Database. Key identified weaknesses in India's fiscal management are the inadequate linkages established between overall fiscal policy, budgeting process, and implementation. An analysis of state budget cycles in India points out that budgets (i) lack a multiyear perspective; (ii) have weak prioritization of resources with unrealistic targets and lack performance measures; and (iii) have large variability in outturns, which undermine their credibility. During the implementation stage, service standards are

---

[19]   Here, expenditure on education also includes expenditure on sports, arts, and culture.

Figure 10   State Expenditures in India
10.1 Ratio of Capital Expenditure to Current Expenditure (3-Year Moving Average)
10.2 Components of Social Sector Expenditure
% of Aggregate Expenditure
45%
41%
38%
34%
30%
26%
23%
25%
23%
20%
18%
15%
13%
10%
% of Aggregate Expenditure
FY2001
FY2004
FY2007
FY2010
FY2013
FY2016
FY2019
Education (Revenue)
Health (Capital)
Education (Capital)
Health (Revenue)
Social Sector Expenditure (Right Axis)
Source: RBI, State Finances: A Study of Budgets 2017–18 and 2018–19 and CMIE.
36%
30%
24%
18%
35.6%
34.6%
32.5%
30.4%
30.0%
29.4%
28.5%
27.6%
26.2%
25.3%
25.0%
22.5%
21.8%
22.6%
22.0%
22.0%
21.8%
20.5%
21.4%
19.7%
FY2001
FY2002
FY2003
FY2004
FY2005
FY2006
FY2007
FY2008
FY2009
FY2010
FY2011
FY2012
FY2013
FY2014
FY2015
FY2016
FY2017
FY2018
FY2019
FY = fiscal year.
Source: Reserve Bank of India (RBI) State Finances 2017–18 and 2018–19 and Centre for Monitoring Indian Economy (CMIE).

not effectively followed. Multiple schemes with multiple targets and fragmentation of resources also result in higher implementation costs and lower efficiency. Monitoring and evaluation of the state budget cycles are weak in the absence of evidence-based assessment of spending outcomes, structured performance indicators for departments, and results-based evaluation mechanisms.

153. A critical step to improve allocative efficiency of state budgets in any intergovernmental fiscal transfer system is to ensure that budget formulations are based on an MTFF that is guided by fiscal responsibility rules and fiscal policy strategy. This should then be reconciled with aggregate revenue and spending estimates to arrive at a common medium-term budget framework. For the next step, the budgetary framework should be used to formulate MTEFs at the sectoral and departmental level with specific sectoral and departmental performance targets. To supplement this work, efforts should also focus on improving the timely and comprehensive reporting of fiscal operations and adopting a reliable accounting framework. Collection of public finance data at all levels of subnational government is fundamental to linking subnational spending with subnational outcomes effectively and improving the quality of local service delivery.

154. An MTEF is an important public expenditure planning tool, designed to link policy and planning, which has a medium- to long-term outlook (3 to 5 years) with the annual budgetary expenditures. This framework enables the government to allocate budgetary resources to programs, activities, and projects that promote the strategic socioeconomic priorities of the national and/or subnational governments. MTEF was pioneered as a concept by Australia in the early 1980s, followed by Denmark, New Zealand, the Netherlands, and Norway in the early 1990s.

155. MTEF bridges the crucial gap between the long-term Five-Year Plan (along with operational annual plans) of states and annual departmental budgeting exercise by focusing more on strategic result-oriented public expenditures planning and supporting multidimensions from sector to programs as compared with earlier versions that served more as rather a static accounting or bookkeeping exercise. For the case of India, in the annual budget preparation exercise, the concerned departments

can prepare their annual budget requests premised on the estimates of the first year of their rolling MTEFs as the baseline. MTEFs could therefore serve as a bridge between the long-term objectives for the sector and departmental annual budgeting exercise to ensure that resources are programmed to realize defined objectives in a targeted manner.

156. Budget preparation using MTEF involves the following steps: (i) preparation of a top–down budget for linking the fiscal consolidation road map and the fiscal policy resource envelope for total expenditures under the MTFF; (ii) estimating a 3-year sector plan resource envelope consistent with the explicit long-term sector priorities; (iii) preparing a bottom–up budget with estimates of expenditure requirements to sustain the current level of performance in service delivery under the trend scenario, and then estimating additional cost required to achieve the desired targets under suggested interventions; (iv) preparing the framework for sector outputs and outcomes of various schemes and programs; (v) developing performance monitor indicators; and (vi) reconciling and reprioritizing the bottom–up budgeting estimates (i.e., expenditure requirements) with top-down estimates of resource availability to identify potential savings and efficiency gains. Details are provided in Appendix 4.

157. Adoption of MTEF improves fiscal governance and enhanced allocative efficiency of public financial resources due to the following reasons (Boex et al. 2000; Schiavo-Campo and Tommasi 1999; World Bank 1998):

(i)   Budgetary allocations are aligned to the macro-fiscal objectives of the state and targets committed under FRBM Act through estimation of a resource envelope so that aggregate fiscal discipline is maintained subject to resource availability and cost-efficiency in delivery of goods and services;

(ii)   Allocations are clearly linked with the long-term sectoral priorities (both inter and intra sectoral resource allocation) of the state envisaged under its five-year plan and annual plans which improve the allocative efficiency of the budget allocations;

(iii) Allocation estimates are updated annually on a rolling basis based on actual performance on physical indicators through preparation of logical framework and performance tracking so that greater transparency and accountability of public finances are explicitly targeted; and

(iv) Allocations are made by making explicit recognition of the medium-term perspective in implementation of schemes and/or programs giving predictability to the budgetary commitments, and they enable better linkages between national and state-level planning, budgeting, implementation, and monitoring and evaluation.

158. The MTEF has been implemented successfully in several states in India. West Bengal and Punjab's experience with MTEFs under the public resource management programs of the Asian Development Bank (ADB) is presented in Appendix 5.

A.5. Recommendations for the 15th Finance Commission

159. In summary, to improve the effectiveness of intergovernmental fiscal transfers in India, it is recommended that the 15th FC incentivizes (i) improvements in quality of governance across states in India through performance-based grants by tracking the progress using the proposed governance index, (ii) strengthening of public financial management through adoption of MTEFs as part of the states' budget preparation process to improve allocative efficiency of public resources, and (iii) comprehensive monitoring of attainment of performance-driven outcomes and service delivery results at the subnational government level. Details on the design of performance-based transfers for incentivizing governance are provided in the section D.

160. Building on the above analysis, the following two subsections take a more in-depth look at how performance-based transfers can be designed to improve quality of service delivery in health and education sectors. These two sectors were included given their relative importance in subnational public expenditures. These two sectors are arguably the most important from the perspective of sustainable development given their relevance to human capital formation, improvements of

people's livelihood opportunities, and long-term spillover effects on the economy.

B. Performance-Based Transfers for Improved Service Delivery in Health Sector

B.1. Overview of Health Sector in India

161. Investment in social sectors like health and education is necessary for human capital development, which is a prerequisite for sustainable economic growth. Although the National Development Agenda in 2015 identified health, education, nutrition, women, and children as priority sectors under the shared responsibility of the central and state governments, Indian policymakers have faced resource constraints in increasing expenditure on health and education. India's estimated public health expenditure to GDP ratio for FY2018 is 1.3% (CBHI 2018)—among the lowest in the world while the total current health expenditure to GDP ratio is close to 3.9% (WHO 2018) with the private sector making up for the difference. Correspondingly, despite significant economic growth over the past decades in India, achievements in health have not been commensurate.

162. The GOI has renewed its commitment to accelerate the achievement of the Sustainable Development Goals, including Goal 3 related to ensuring healthy lives and promoting well-being for all at all ages (NITI Aayog 2018b). The GOI's budget for FY2019 had an increase of nearly 11.5% over the budget of FY2018 with an allocation of ₹548 billion ($8.4 billion) for the Ministry of Health and Family Welfare (MOHFW). Although the budgetary allocation to the health sector has increased three times in the last decade in nominal terms, as proportion of GDP, it has increased only marginally from 1.1% to 1.3% (Lahariya 2018). This would go up to 2.5% by 2025, according to the National Health Policy 2017.

163. Health being a state subject in India, health-related interventions are largely done by the states (NITI Aayog 2018a). The central government intervenes through CSS to support state governments

Table 9   Public Spending on Health across the World

	Total Health Spending per Capita (PPP $)	Share of Health Expenditures by Government (%)	Share of Public Health Spending at Subnational Level (%)	Year
Argentina	1,287	55	57	2004
Brazil	1,028	47	54	2009
Ethiopia	51	54	67	2005
India	132	29	68	2007
Indonesia	112	58	69	2005
South Africa	935	44	81	2005

Sources: A. Glassman and Y. Sakuma. 2014. *Intergovernmental Fiscal Transfers for Health: Overview Framework and Lessons Learned.* Centre for Global Development; and World Health Organization data. https://www.who.int/healthinfo/statistics/en/.

in achieving national-level objectives. The GOI has recently launched the Ayushman Bharat Scheme (ABS) in 2018 to fulfill the vision of universal health coverage as envisaged in the National Health Policy 2017 (Appendix 6).[20]

164. India is not an exception where provision of health care services falls within the responsibility of the state governments. In several decentralized countries, subnational governments finance more than half of the public health care expenditures (Table 9).

165. A close examination of Table 9 shows that public share of health spending in India is very low. While there is a commitment to increase the government's health spending, this has not been adequate to achieve the desired goals given the divergent absorptive capacity across states to plan and implement health-related interventions and to utilize the earmarked National Health Mission (NHM) budget effectively at state level.

166. The utilization of funds allocated for the NHM was quite low in FY2016 and FY2017, when only about half (55%) of the funds allocated to the state governments were utilized (Choudhury and Mohanty 2018). The constraints in effective utilization of funds are primarily related to the states' capacities to scale up implementation such as (i) cumbersome procedures on fund disbursements; (ii) lack of

availability of human resources; (iii) weak capacities to plan and execute programs (Berman et al. 2010). Effective and timely utilization of funds calls for addressing existing inefficiencies, utilizing alternative approaches to service delivery, and a greater focus on outputs and outcomes (Berman et al. 2010).

167. Additionally, a rapid increase in funding from the center's budget has resulted in unintended consequences. Central support has created incentives for states to reduce their own health expenditures, especially on lower-level services. The NHM has addressed this issue by putting conditions, i.e., requiring states to increase their own spending at a specified rate parallel to the increased central funding. However, given the complexities of India's government finances, central government's ability to monitor results may be delayed. States also have some discretion on whether to use center or state funds for specific expenditures in case of flexible grants.

168. Nonetheless, the National Health Policy 2017 envisages that the resource allocation to states will be linked with (i) state development indicators; (ii) absorptive capacity; and (iii) financial indicators (MOHFW 2017). Currently, India spends only 1.3% of its GDP on health care but under the new health policy the government has proposed to increase the public health care spending to 2.5% of the GDP by 2025 with a special focus on the underprivileged

---

[20]   The universal health care coverage service index for India stood at 56 out of 100 in 2015, compared with 49 in Indonesia, 76 in the PRC, and 80 in Australia, Japan, and the ROK (World Bank).

(MOHFW 2017). The ABS will employ mechanisms like contracting out primary health care services and increased health-seeking behavior through improved access via insurance.

B.2. Transfers in Health Sector in India

169. In India, the recommendations for health-specific transfers have varied across FCs. The approach of the 12th FC was based on expenditure needs while the 13th FC's approach was based on health outcomes (Yamini et al. 2015). The 12th FC recommended equalization grants for health to the seven Indian states with the lowest health indicators to reduce inequality in per capita expenditure and to encourage these states to prioritize health-related spending (Clements et al. 2012). However, nearly 20% of the funds remained unused because of the conditions attached to the transfers (Choudhury and Nath 2012).

170. Under the 13th FC, allocations to states were conditional on reducing states' infant mortality rate (IMR) as the outcome indicator (Yamini et al. 2015).[21] The allocation formula considered the relative improvements from the median to calculate the share of the funds going to each state (Choudhury and Nath 2012).

171. Since the 13th FC formula was designed without considering the population or state health expenditure while calculating the weights, this led to a situation where 65% of allocations went to states that accounted for less than 10% of India's total population (Choudhury and Nath 2012). The top three states to gain from this performance incentive were small states from the northeast, which already had better IMRs. In contrast, the formula did not adequately compensate states with large populations for achieving substantial declines in infant mortality. For example, Uttar Pradesh reduced its infant mortality rate from 67 in 2009 to 57 in 2012 and has 16.8% of the national population,

but still received only 0.3% of national allocations (Choudhury and Nath 2012). Formula aside, the IMR had its own limitations as a performance indicator as it was not strictly comparable across states and exhibited variation in the upper and lower bounds. These inherent measurement issues skewed the grant distribution (Bloom and Fan 2015).

172. The transfers from MOHFW under NHM have also ignored the measurement of outcomes. For example, the Janani Suraksha Yojana (JSY) program accounts for nearly 30% of the flexible pool funds for Bihar and Uttar Pradesh and over 10% of total National Rural Health Mission expenditure (Yamini et al. 2015). For evaluation of the program, the central government focused on the increase in institutional deliveries while NHM focused on decrease in IMR and the maternal mortality ratio. The performance results showed that institutional deliveries may have increased, but the impact on IMR and the maternal mortality ratio is questionable (Fan et al. 2018).

B.3. Transfers in Health Sector—Asian Experience

173. Similar to India, experiences of other countries regarding the effect of decentralization on health outcomes is mixed and depends on the details of their design, implementation, and accountability arrangements.[22] Improving health outcomes depends on the efficiency and effectiveness of health expenditures at the local level. In many countries, even though health services may be provided by subnational governments, performance-based incentives have been incorporated by the central governments into the national public health systems and social insurance schemes to ensure equitable, efficient, high quality, and cost-effective delivery of health care services (Beazley et al. 2019). The Asian experience along with other international examples are

---

[21]   Consistent data for IMR were available every year from the Sample Registration System, which is a relatively independent source of data from the Registrar General of India.

[22]   Cantarero and Pascual 2008; Habibi et al. 2003; Jimenez-Rubio 2011b; Jin and Sun 2011; Mahal et al. 2000; Robalino et al. 2001; Samadi et al. 2013; Soto et al. 2012; Uchimura and Jütting 2009; and Yee 2001.

provided below on specific-purpose transfers and performance-based transfers in the health sector.[23] Appendix 3 provides the country-wise summary of fiscal transfers, including health.

B.3.1. Australia

174. The Australian health system is decentralized with responsibilities shared by the federal, state, and territory governments (Government of Australia 2011). As of 2012, health system financing is a combination of formula-based need-based transfer from the federal government to the state government through the National Health Reform Funding (previously specific-purpose payments) and complemented by the fiscal resources of the states and territories. While an extensive list of over 30 performance indicators exist under the National Health Agreement 2011, funds are generally not withheld if a subnational fails a benchmark (Mackay 2011). The National Health Reform Agreement, 2011 is the principal federal-level legislation that sets out the partnership and joint responsibility of the Commonwealth, and state and territory governments in improving health outcomes and sustainability of the Australian health system.

175. Under National Health Reform Funding, the bulk of health spending is on hospital services. The federal government increased its funding contribution to 45% in FY2015 and to 50% in FY2018 to support public hospital services by state. The funding comprises two elements: base funding and efficient growth funding, under which the Independent Hospital Pricing Authority annually determines the efficient price.

176. The efficient growth funding comprises (Government of Australia 2011):

(i)   services funded based on activity, i.e., the increase in the efficient price of delivering public hospital services, and the increase in service provision; and

(ii)   services funded based on block grants, i.e., increase in the efficient price of delivering those services.

177. For FY2013 and FY2014, the National Health Reform Funding was equivalent to the National Health Care Specific Purpose Payment (SPP) indexed by each state's growth factor (Government of Australia 2011). The intergovernmental agreement defined the growth factor for the National Health Care Specific Purpose Payment as the product of

(i)   a health-specific cost index (a 5-year average of the Australian Institute of Health and Welfare health price index);

(ii)   the growth in population estimates weighed for hospital utilization; and

(iii)   a technology factor (the Productivity Commission derived index of technology growth).

178. In 2014, there were discussions for the National Health Reform Funding to be replaced. The federal government's contribution will no longer guarantee a 50% funding but will be linked to the movements in the consumer price index (CPI) and population growth. If the CPI moves below the growth in the cost of funding, the states and territories will face a shortfall (Biggs 2018).

179. For FY2017, the federal government of Australia committed to meet 45% of efficient growth in the cost of hospital services for the period 2017–2020 (capped at 6.5% growth in the federal funding annually) and retained the activity-based funding (ABF) and the National Efficient Price (NEP) as the basis for hospital funding (Biggs 2016). The ABF is calculated based on the level of hospital activity, complexity of cases, and their cost based on NEP (Biggs 2016).

180. **Learnings from Australia and Relevance for India.** Similar to the National Health Reform Funding in Australia, activity-based funding for public hospitals exists in India in the case of the national health insurance scheme. The GOI could also consider the efficient growth funding for public hospitals.

---

[23]   A few country examples outside the Asia region have also been included for their relevance to the subject.

B.3.2. Indonesia

181. Health financing is decentralized in Indonesia. The responsibilities are shared between the central, provincial, and district governments. Based on the National Health Accounts, in 2013, the government covered 40% of health expenditures with more than 60% of spending done at the subnational level through complex intergovernmental fiscal transfers (Tandon et al. 2016). The following intergovernmental fiscal transfer programs exist in Indonesia for the health sector:

182. **Dana Alokasi Umum (DAU).** Fiscal transfer for health is a subsection of the general needs-based intergovernmental transfers, most done through the DAU to the district governments (Sen et al. 2014). The health portion of the plan includes number and mix of health workers, drugs, equipment and/or supplies, and infrastructure availability (Tandon et al. 2016).

183. **PNPM Generasi.** A performance-based community-based block grant, focusing on 12 indicators for health and education, was introduced in 2007. There are eight health-related indicators (World Bank 2012):

(i)   Four prenatal care visits for pregnant women

(ii)   Consumption of iron tablets during pregnancy

(iii)   Delivery assisted by a trained professional

(iv)   Two postnatal care visits

(v)   Number of children who receive complete childhood immunizations

(vi)   Adequate monthly weight increases for infants

(vii)   Monthly weighing for children under 3 and biannually for children under 5

(viii) Vitamin A twice a year for children under 5

184. Generasi villages receive allocated funds based on the number of targeted beneficiaries (e.g., children and expected number of pregnant women). In the second year, 20% of funds are transferred based on the performance of the 12 indicators (of previous year) (Olken et al. 2017).

185. **Program Keluarga Harapan.** This conditional cash transfer program to households with children and pregnant women was introduced in 2007. The program is run by the central government through the Ministry of Social Welfare. There are six maternal and child health-related indicators (Hickling Corporation 2008; Sen et al. 2014):

(i)   Infant age 0–11 months with complete immunization protocol (Bacillus Calmette-Guerin [BCG], diphtheria, tetanus, and pertussis [DPT], polio, measles, Hepatitis B, and weighted every month)

(ii)   Infant age 6–11 months given Vitamin A minimum twice a year (February, August)

(iii)   Infant age 12–59 months: complementary immunization and weighed every 3 months

(iv)   Children age 5–6 years: measured for weight; and participation in early childhood education program when there is an early childhood facility at the closest location

(v)   Pregnant mother: undergoes pregnancy examinations at any public health facility up to four times and obtains iron tablet supplements; deliveries by trained professionals

(vi)   Health conditions of post-delivery mothers checked at least twice prior to the baby reaching 28 days old.

186. **Learnings from Indonesia and Relevance for India.** Indonesia uses both (i) community-based block grants, and (ii) household-level conditional cash transfers based on a combination of input and output indicators. Performance-based transfers in India incentivize state governments for achievement of targets. Community-based block grants and direct cash transfers would be useful in encouraging community partnership in achievement of health targets.

B.3.3. People's Republic of China

187. Health outcomes deteriorated quite drastically during the 1980s and the 1990s when the PRC undertook market reforms, restructuring subnational revenue and expenditure assignments. The central government held significant tax power with expenditure functions distributed among the lower tiers of government. In the health sector, subnational governments even account for 90% of expenditure.

The PRC's fiscal reform resulted in unfunded mandates for health services. Decentralization of expenditure and service delivery to lower levels of subnational governments such as districts, municipalities, and rural local bodies along with ad hoc transfers to states without clear guidelines on the nature and type of services have created financing inefficiencies and capacity bottlenecks (Mukherjee 2016). Lack of direct performance measurement and incentives also adversely affected the quality of health care service delivery (Feltenstein and Iwata 2005).

188. **Learnings from the PRC and Relevance for India.** There is a need for a stable intergovernmental fiscal transfer system to achieve equitable financing for the subnational level expenditures. The PRC's experience underscores the critical role of a combination of equalizing transfers, incentives, and performance-based payments to ensure equity and efficiency in health services, especially for the poorer and more disadvantaged regions.

B.3.4. Other Countries

189. **Argentina.** Argentina's Plan Nacer was launched in 2004 after the economic crisis that increased poverty and worsened health outcomes (World Bank 2013). Results-based fiscal transfers from central to provincial governments under Plan Nacer provided incentives to the provinces and health care centers to promote better access and quality of health services with the aim of achieving universal health care (World Bank 2013). Plan Nacer used an innovative pay-for-performance model to enable provincial governments to contract out service delivery, and patients to choose freely among certified providers (Gertler et al. 2014). Plan Nacer provided about 80 services free of charge to uninsured pregnant women and mothers (up to 45 days after delivery), and children under the age of 6 (Vergeer et al. 2011).

(i)   **60% needs-based with monthly capitated payment, based on enrollment of the target population into the program.** Every month, to avoid duplication, the provincial insurance unit has verified enrollment eligibility against other social insurance databases, and this process is also repeated at national level. Payments are transferred from the Ministry of Health's National Health Services Purchasing Team to the provincial health insurance unit (Gertler et al. 2014).

(ii) **40% performance-based capitated payment made once every 4 months based on health service utilization indicators for maternal and child health.** Plan Nacer began with 10 tracers of health. The providers are reimbursed by the provincial health services purchasing team based on a fee-for-service basis (i.e., for the agreed 80 services) (Gertler et al. 2014). As of 2014, an index of 14 indicators covering service delivery and outcomes (ranging from early pregnancy care to immunization coverage) was used for making payments to districts (Gertler et al. 2014).

190. **Learnings from Argentina and Relevance for India.** Unlike Plan Nacer, performance-based fiscal transfers are not included in the design of ABS. For ABS, an effective monitoring and supervision framework, based on improvements in health indicators would be required, which could be used for performance-based transfers. The GOI could make the 60% central contribution subject to the achievement of certain indicators for state-level population or could award improved indicators by providing increased funding to cover additional population.

191. The United Kingdom, Brazil, and South Africa link health transfers using composite indices, comprising a mix of health-related input and output indicators and factors determining health conditions (Shah 2006):

(i)   **The United Kingdom.** Factors include age, gender, mortality, unemployment, and the elderly living alone.

(ii) **Brazil.** Infant mortality; ages 1–64 mortality; ages 65 and older mortality; mortality rate by infectious and parasitic diseases; mortality rate for neoplasia; mortality rate for cardiovascular conditions; adolescent mother percentage; illiteracy percentage; percentage of homes without sanitation; percentage of homes without running water; and percentage of homes without garbage collection.

(iii)   **South Africa**. Percentage female; percentage of children under 5; percentage living in rural area; percentage older than 25 without schooling; percentage unemployed; percentage living in traditional dwelling, shack, or tent; percentage without piped water in house or on-site; percentage without refuse disposal access; percentage without phone access; percentage without electricity access; and percentage living in household headed by a woman.

B.4. Health Sector Recommendations for the 15th Finance Commission

192. **Improve measurement of health sector performance.** The international experience presented above underscores the importance of measurement of outcomes in health care programs as well as designing appropriate incentives for service delivery. The following section discusses approaches in selecting an appropriate health-related indicator in India, which can be used by the 15th FC for designing the performance-based transfers to the health sector.

193. **Maintain close monitoring of infant mortality rate.** In the past, IMR has been regarded as a good proxy for the whole population's health (Blaxter 1981). IMR is more sensitive to policy changes in health service delivery and easier to measure than maternal mortality as its occurrence is more frequent (Yamini et al. 2015). There is also high correlation between disability adjusted life expectancy and IMR (Reidpath and Allotey 2003). In comparison, mortality due to tuberculosis or cardiovascular disease or any other specific disease is not age-standardized, and hence states have different distributions in cause of deaths. Similarly, life expectancy at birth summarizes probabilities of death at every age but it is less sensitive to immediate changes and improvements in health and has higher data requirements than IMR (Yamini et al. 2015).

194. The downside of using IMR is that it often runs the risk of becoming the principal focus of health policy (Reidpath and Allotey 2003). The formulation of health strategies and priorities based on infant health and the skewed allocation of resources may lead to overlooking the population's health as a whole (Murray 1996).

195. In India, IMR remains a valuable indicator for several reasons (Yamini et al. 2015):

(i)   IMR is an indicator chosen by national consensus;

(ii)   IMR is affected both by the functioning of the health care system and by the improvements in health behavior and socioeconomic status;

(iii)   the economic benefits of child health are large in the longer run;[24] and

(iv)   countries of all income levels have delivered continued percentage reductions in IMR.

196. Adopting the single indicator of IMR (similar to the 13th FC) can be considered—however, with a modified formula for transfers to ensure that the observed distortions under the 13th FC are avoided.

197. **Supplement infant mortality rate with composite health index to better monitor outcomes.** To measure health outcomes in a multifaceted way, as discussed, several countries are moving toward adopting composite indices and designing performance-based transfer systems based on such indices. Previous FCs in India when looking for a reliable indicator had to consider IMR only as no other measure was available then. However, the recently released health index by NITI Aayog in collaboration with MOHFW and the World Bank, now offers a comprehensive heath indicator for consideration by the 15th FC (NITI Aayog 2018a).

---

[24]   Children who are well nourished in utero also have lower rates of chronic diseases (Yamini et al. 2015). Child vaccination has economic benefits ranging from $151 billion–$231 billion over 10 years for 72 countries and amounts to a return on investment of 12%–21% (Bloom and Fan 2015).

Box 7   Limitations of the Health Index in India

Data for Health Index may not be exhaustive to capture interstate variation in health status. The state-specific disability-adjusted life years rates for many individual diseases vary 5 to 10 times between the states. Even major differences can be observed between neighboring states at similar levels of development.

Missing data. About 61% of deaths in India is due to noncommunicable diseases (NCDs), which includes heart disorders, cancer and diabetes, and mental health. NCDs and financial risk protection are not captured in the health index.

Lack of private sector data. The health management information system (HMIS) monthly reporting of information on health services delivered by the private sector remains very poor although approximately 70% of health care needs are met by the private sector.

Quality of HMIS data. Data entry errors are rampant in HMIS data. Field verification of HMIS data should be carried out.

Periodic review of the index is not undertaken. Periodic review is imperative given the rapidly changing data availability and to also reestablish the inclusion and exclusion criteria based on available data (proxy measures, field validations, improved availability, etc.)

The proxy indicator "average out-of-pocket expenditure per delivery in public health facility" may not be reflective of actual out-of-pocket expenditure patterns. Research shows that vulnerable population groups tend to spend the largest portion of their out-of-pocket budget on drugs (about 72%), and the least on inpatient treatment (30%–35%). In the poorest states, the proportion of drug sales is even higher. Additionally, this indicator does not capture private sector institutional deliveries. As per the recent National Sample Survey Office (2015), up to 30% of institutional deliveries in rural areas and up to 52.5% of institutional deliveries in urban areas are carried out the private sector.

Sources: Indian Council of Medical Research (ICMR), Public Health Foundation of India, Institute for Health Metrics and Evaluation, and Ministry of Health and Family Welfare. 2017. *India: Health of the Nation's States. The India State-Level Disease Burden Initiative.* New Delhi; S. Kumar. 2015. Private Sector in Health Care Delivery Market in India: Structure, Growth and Implications. *Working Paper 185.* New Delhi: Institute for Studies in Industrial Development. Z. Husain et al. 2012. Opportunities and Challenges of Health Management Information System in India: A Case Study of Uttarakhand. *Munich Personal RePEc Archive (MPRA) Paper.* No. 40014. New Delhi: Institute of Economic Growth; and C. Garg and A. Karan. 2009. Reducing Out-of-Pocket Expenditures to Reduce Poverty: A Disaggregated Analysis at Rural-Urban and State Level in India. *Health Policy and Planning.* 24 (2). pp. 116–128.

198. The composite health index comprises 26 indicators across 3 domains and 5 sub-domains to record the overall performance of the states along with annual improvements in health outcomes, governance, and processes (Appendix 7). The data sources for this index include the sample registration system, health management information system (HMIS), central MOHFW data, national family and health survey (NFHS), civil registration system (CRS), and revised national tuberculosis control program. States can be ranked within three categories: (i) larger states, (ii) smaller states, and (iii) union territories.[25]

199. The use of the health index as a proxy of the population's health in India has several advantages because of the (i) high diversity of health status among Indian states, (ii) existence of large number of datasets that could support estimation of health index, and (iii) IMR's prioritization and bias for maternal and child health. The health index could also help shift from the input-based focus to achievement of health outcomes (NITI Aayog 2018a). Some limitations to the health index exist (Box 7) but improvements will strengthen the effectiveness over time.

200. To improve effectiveness of the public health spending, MOHFW has recently announced that incentives under the National Health Mission will be linked to performance based on the health index. The states have also started using the health index for monitoring their health status. Efforts are ongoing for 10% of the government's health funding under the NHM to be linked to the health index to reward the better performing states. This incentive might

---

[25]   A union territory is a type of administrative division in India. Unlike the states, which have their own governments, union territories are federal territories ruled directly by the union (central) government.

be raised to 20% and could factor the health index while deciding on health project funding to states.

201. The 15th FC could incentivize states to use the health index as a performance measure to strengthen the quality and efficiency of the health care system. It can be extended for performance-based fiscal transfer in the health sector (see section D for details), including the ABS as explained below. Performance evaluation can consider a combination of improvement in the state's ranking among its peers and marginal improvements in health outcomes. This is to ensure that high ranking states with strong baseline levels like Kerala do not lose out on marginal improvement measure. High-ranking states can be incentivized to maintain their ranks.

202. **Ayushman Bharat Scheme (ABS).** India is committed to universal health coverage and has launched ABS, a major step toward this goal. Currently, performance-based fiscal transfers are not included in the design of ABS, as was done in NHM. The health index has indicators related to universal health coverage for monitoring achievement of health outcomes under ABS. GOI could make the central contribution conditional on the achievement of certain health index indicators, and/or coverage of public health facilities under ABS to boost wider health care coverage in India. To ensure state government contribution for Pradhan Mantri Jan Arogya Yojana (PM-JAY), the second component of ABS (Appendix 6), it may be worth considering ring-fencing of the central government's 60% contribution subject to 40% contribution from the state government.

203. To fund the ABS in FY2019, GOI has already allocated ₹20 billion for implementation of PM-JAY.[26] The National Health Policy 2017 proposes raising of public health expenditure to 2.5% of the GDP by 2025. However, in view of the sustainability of ABS, the target of allocating 2.5% of GDP to health would need to be brought forward to 2022.

204. To augment the resources for the health sector, additional budget could be mobilized from the "sin tax," which is a public health tax placed on goods that adversely affect health, most notably tobacco and alcohol. Some countries are already using it to raise resources. A notable example is a funding mechanism under the Thai Health Promotion Foundation (ThaiHealth), which collects about $50 million–$60 million a year from a 2% surcharge levied on alcohol and tobacco excise tax. The Philippines is a recent example where new taxes on tobacco and alcohol have contributed to an increase in the Department of Health's budget from $1.25 billion to nearly $2 billion within 2 years. India already has a cess tax on tobacco products. A cess on alcohol could augment the budget further. The revenue could go to a dedicated account for implementation of ABS.

205. The regulatory environment for the health insurance sector could also be strengthened to (i) raise public awareness on pursuing a healthy lifestyle, (ii) improve collection of insurance co-payments, (iii) minimize incentives for insurance providers to select patients for higher profits (cream skimming), (iv) reduce excessive utilization of medical services paid for by insurance (moral hazard), and (v) prevent overexpansion of insurance coverage by states beyond the eligible groups. These measures can strengthen the sustainability of finances for ABS.

C. Designing Performance-Based Transfers for Improved Service Delivery in Education Sector

C.1. Overview of Education Sector in India

206. The economic growth of a country is dependent on physical and human capital, and education plays a major part in the formation of human capital. Given the high socioeconomic benefits of a developed education sector, following

---

26   Government of India, Ministry of Health and Family Welfare. 2018. Raising Funds to Implement NHPs. Press Information Bureau release. 7 August. http://pib.nic.in/newsite/PrintRelease.aspx?relid=181616.

the Eighty-Sixth Amendment Act, 2002, article 21-A in the Constitution of India and the consequent legislation, Right to Free and Compulsory Education Act, 2009 (RTE) have conferred the right to elementary education to all children, in the age group of 6–14 years as a fundamental right, based on equality of opportunity in a formal school, which satisfies essential norms and standards. The RTE became effective on 1 April 2010.

207. The Constitution of India clearly specifies the legislative, executive, and judicial functions in terms of the union, state, and concurrent lists. Education was a state subject until the 42nd Constitutional Amendment, 1976, which brought about a fundamental change by transferring education from the state list to the concurrent list.[27] The amendment recognizes the federal structure of the country and gives equal responsibility to both the central and state governments to promote education. The institutional arrangements are discussed in Appendix 8. The objective of incorporating education in the concurrent list was to facilitate evolution of all-India policies in the field of education (Box 8).

208. **Public expenditure on education.** The National Policy on Education 1986 set the norm of 6% for public education expenditure to GDP ratio based on the Kothari Commission's recommendation. NITI Aayog (2018b) in a strategy paper has also recommended a targeted education spending of 6% of GDP by 2022. Jain and Dholakia (2009) note that even an allocation of 6% of GDP to the education budget would not be sufficient to fund universal school education until the very distant future if the government school system is used as the only instrument. In comparison, the actual public expenditure in India is significantly below this norm. In fact, as per Economic Survey 2017–18 of MOF, the expenditure declined from 3.1% of GDP

in FY2013 to 2.4% in FY216 and 2.7% in 2018 (BE) (Figure 11). This could be attributed to higher fiscal stress on state governments in the recent years and state governments according lesser priority to the education sector.[28] Further, the plan grants were significantly reduced post the increase in devolution to states (42% from 32% of the divisible pool) as per 14th FC recommendations, a substantive portion of which hitherto went to the health and education sectors.

Box 8   Concurrency in the Education Sector

The concept of concurrency was given an operational meaning by the National Policy on Education, 1986. This policy envisaged concurrency as *"a sharing of responsibility between the union government and the states in the vital area of education"* and further stated, *"While the role and responsibility of the states in regard to education will remain essentially unchanged, the union government would accept a larger responsibility to reinforce the national and integrative character of education; to maintain quality and standards (including those of the teaching profession at all levels); to study and monitor the educational requirements of the country as a whole in regard to manpower for development; to cater to the needs of research and advanced study; to look after the international aspects of education, culture and human resource development and, in general, to promote excellence at all levels of the educational pyramid throughout the country."*

This created an avenue for the center government's intervention in the field of elementary education. The states have powers limited to the extent that these do not impede or prejudice the exercise of the executive powers of the Union.

Source: Government of India, Ministry of Human Resource Development (MHRD). 1998. *National Policy on Education (as modified in 1992)*. New Delhi. https://mhrd.gov.in/sites/upload_files/mhrd/files/document-reports/NPE86-mod92.pdf.

---

[27] The amendment was suggested by a committee headed by S. Swaran Singh. The committee observed that agriculture and education being subjects of primary importance to the country's rapid progress toward achieving desired socioeconomic changes, there was a need to evolve all-India polices in relation to these two subjects.

[28] High fiscal stress on state governments over the recent years is partly attributable to implementation of the Ujwal DISCOM Assurance Yojana (UDAY) program, a debt restructuring scheme for state-owned power distribution companies. Issuance of UDAY bonds in 15 states across India during FY2016 and FY2017 accounted for 0.7% of GDP (Chakraborty et al. 2018).

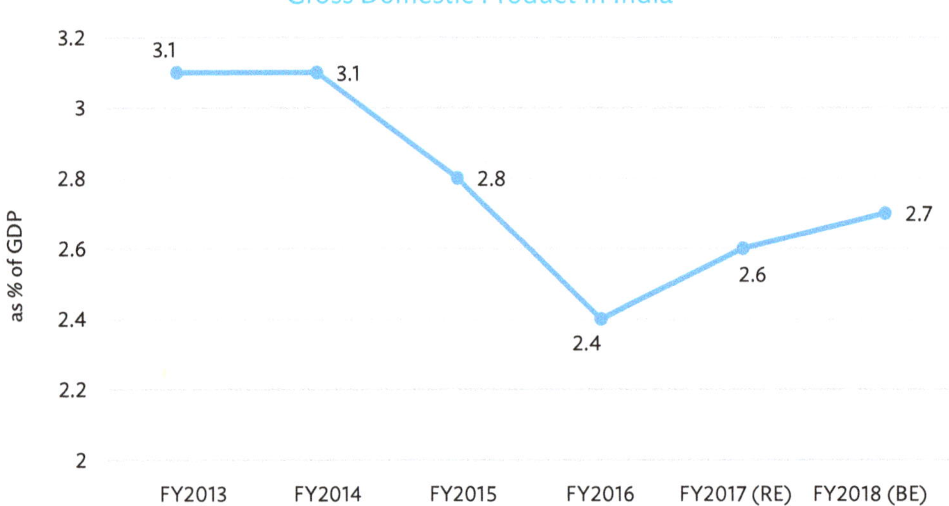

Figure 11   Total Public Expenditure on Education Sector as Percentage of Gross Domestic Product in India

BE = budget estimate, FY = fiscal year, GDP = gross domestic product, RE = revised estimate.
Source: Government of India, Ministry of Finance. 2018. *Economic Survey 2017–18*. New Delhi.

209. Table 10 shows that public spending on education in India is significantly lower than the education expenditure in several developed and developing countries.

210. Public expenditure on education as percentage of GSDP varies significantly across states, from 5.2%

Table 10   Public Spending on Education across the World in 2013

	Per Capita Government Expenditure on Education (PPP $)	Share of Education Expenditures in Total Government Expenditure (%)	Public Education Expenditure as Share of GDP (%)
Argentina	1,096	14.5	5.4
Australia	2,399	14.0	5.3
Brazil	932	15.6	5.8
Ethiopia	55	27.0	4.5
India	187	14.1	3.8
Indonesia	335	17.6	3.4
Japan	1,365	9.5	3.7
Republic of Korea	1,575	–	4.9
South Africa	737	19.2	6.0

– = not applicable, GDP = gross domestic product, PPP = purchasing power parity.
Sources: World Bank. Education Statistics. https://datatopics.worldbank.org/education/; and UNESCO Institute for Statistics. http://uis.unesco.org/.

spent in Bihar to only 1.8% in Tamil Nadu in FY2016. None of the states spent 6% of the GSDP on the education sector (Figure 12).

211. A positive correlation is observed between per capita education expenditure and per capita income of the states (Figure 13), underscoring the fact that public expenditure on education is higher for developed states or alternatively higher-income states can afford to invest more in education. Such trends lead to increasing inequalities in infrastructure levels and human development, causing divergence of incomes across the Indian states.

212. **Education sector performance.** The performance of states in terms of education was assessed based on input, output, and outcome. The following 11 parameters, for which cross state data were available, were chosen for performance assessment:

(i)   Gross enrollment ratio (GER) at primary level

(ii)   GER at upper primary level

(iii)   Dropout rate

(iv)   National Achievement Survey (NAS) scores in English

(v)   NAS scores in Mathematics

Figure 12   Expenditure on Education Sector as a Percentage of Gross State Domestic Product in FY2016

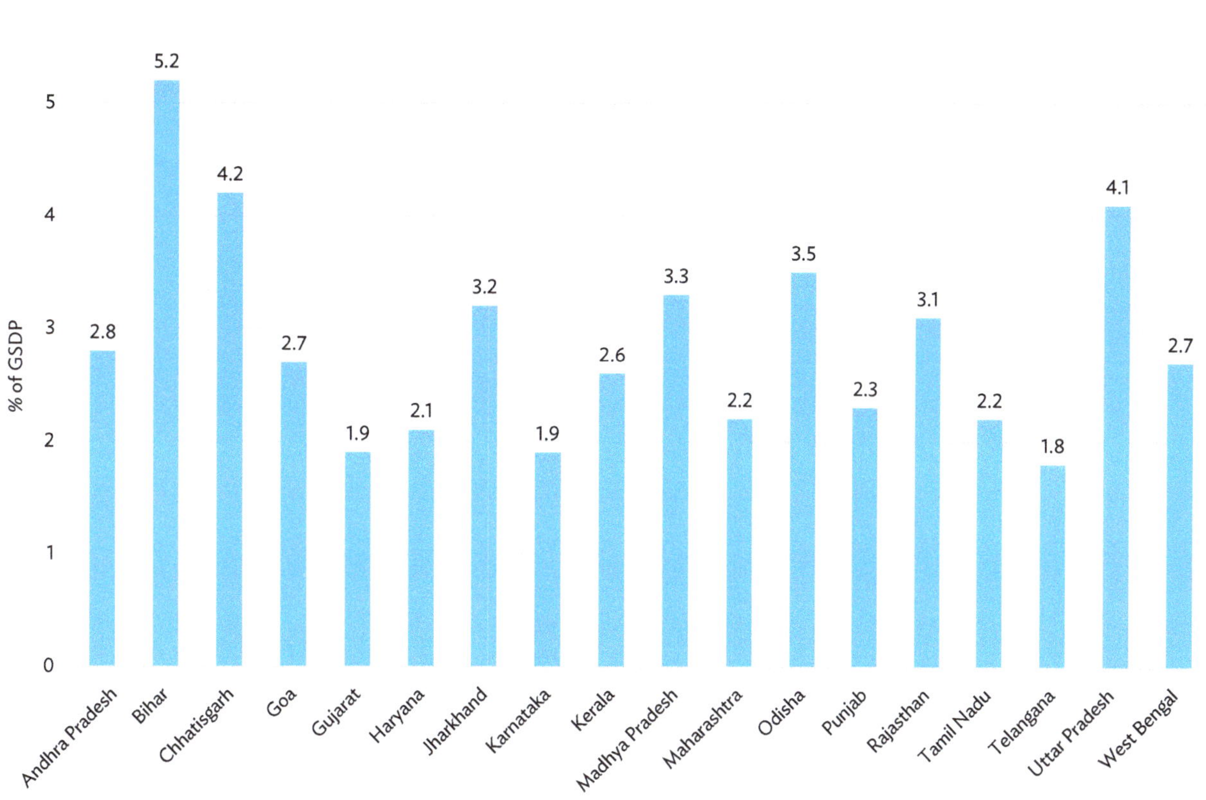

FY = fiscal year, GSDP = gross state domestic product.
Sources: Authors' compilation from the Ministry of Statistics and Programme Implementation for expenditure on the education sector and the Reserve Bank of India for per capita GSDP.

(vi)   NAS scores in Science

(vii)   Percentage of government schools with girls' toilets

(viii)   Percentage of government schools with drinking water facility

(ix)   Percentage of government schools providing mid-day meals and having kitchen sheds

(x)   Percentage of government schools noncompliant with RTE norms for pupil–teacher ratio

(xi)   Percentage of government schools noncompliant with RTE for student classroom ratio

213. A composite rank was given to each state. The state's rank has been calculated by giving equal weightage to each indicator and ranking the state in order of lowest to highest sum of indicator-wise ranks, i.e., the state with the highest sum of ranks has been given an overall ranking of 18, and the state with the lowest sum of rank was given an overall ranking of 1. Appendix 8 provides details on indicator-wise and composite ranking of states. Among 18 states compared, Goa is performing the best with rank 18, while Madhya Pradesh is ranked the worst. As shown in Figure 14, the performance of states is positively correlated with per capita GSDP of the state, i.e., lower income states are expected to have poor education performance.

214. Although India overall has made significant progress in the education sector across indicators such as enrollment levels, completion rates, and other physical infrastructure like construction of school buildings, classrooms, drinking water facilities, toilet facilities, and appointment of teachers, etc., at

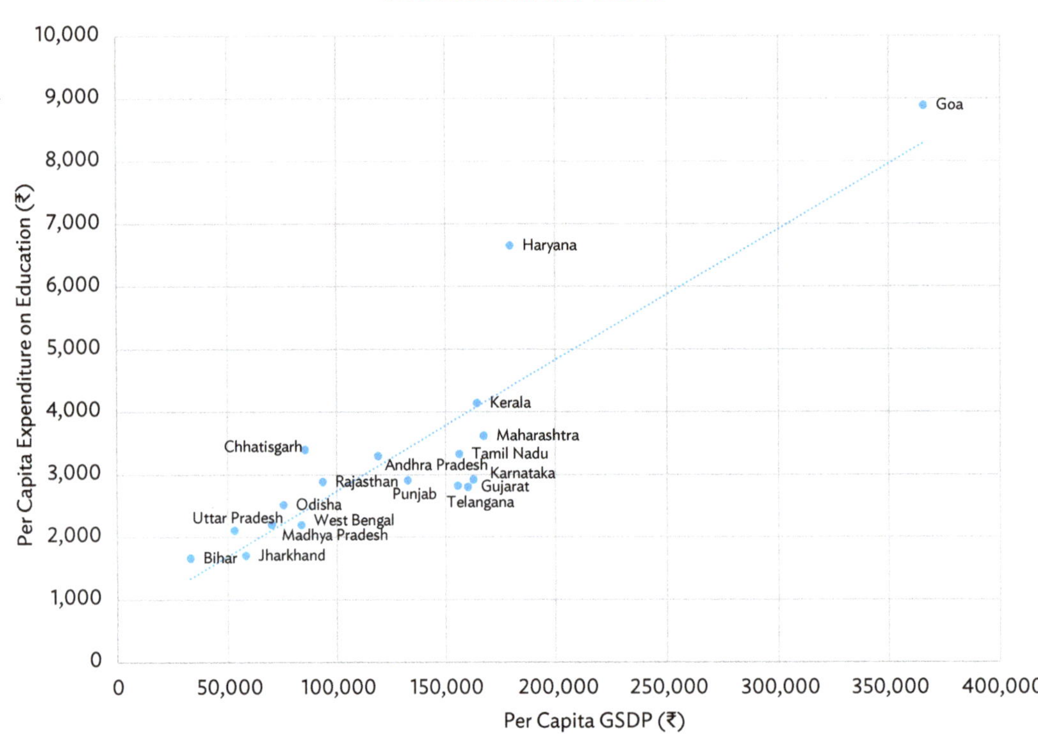

Figure 13   Per Capita Gross State Domestic Product and Per Capita Expenditure on Education in FY2016

FY = fiscal year, GSDP = gross state domestic product.
Sources: Authors' compilation from the Ministry of Statistics and Programme Implementation for per capita expenditure on education; and the Reserve Bank of India for per capita GSDP.

elementary school, there exist significant disparities across states. States with relatively lower per capita GSDP are likely to have lower education sector performance, which can have detrimental effects in the medium to long term, further increasing the disparities across states in human capital, economic growth, and income levels.

C.2. Transfers to Education Sector in India

215. The flagship CSS in the education sector is the Sarva Shiksha Abhiyan (SSA). The GOI also launched the Rashtriya Madhyamik Shiksha Abhiyan (RMSA) scheme in 2009 to assist the states in secondary education. In April 2018, Samagra Shiksha Abhiyan was launched by the government as the umbrella program for school education from preschool to class 12—subsuming the three erstwhile schemes: (i) SSA; (ii) RMSA, and (iii) Teacher Education—with the intention to improve learning outcomes at all levels of schooling.

216. Since specific-purpose grants were not considered by the 14th FC, scheme-based transfers via the central ministries are currently the only medium of transfers specific to the education sector in India. Details on CSS and sector schemes are presented in Appendix 9.

217. With respect to fiscal transfers in the education sector, the three critical issues of (i) insufficient resource allocation by states to social sector; (ii) persistent weaknesses in outcomes pertaining to quality of education; and (iii) continuing challenges in fund allocation and fund transfers through CSS in education sector are discussed below.

218. **Insufficient resource allocation by states.** Successive FCs in India have recommended a higher share of untied transfers to the states. The 14th FC increased the share of states in the central divisible pool from 32% to 42%, while recommending a

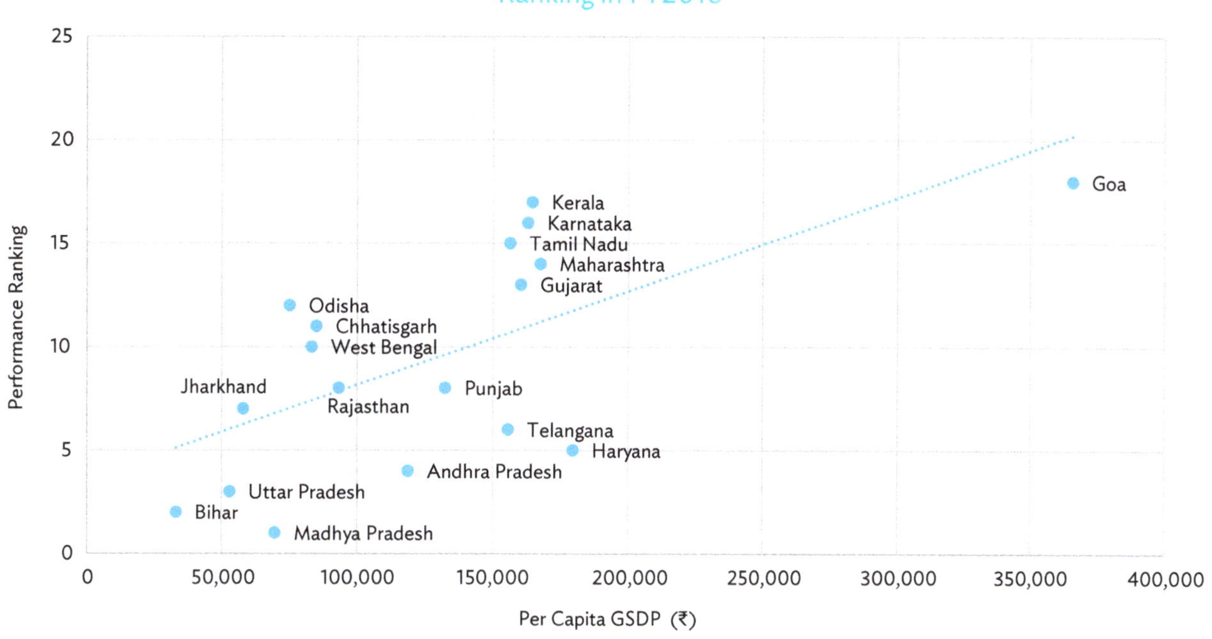

Figure 14   Per Capita Gross State Domestic Product and Education Sector Performance Ranking in FY2016

FY = fiscal year, GSDP = gross state domestic product.
Note: Lower rank implies poor performance.
Sources: Ranking is based on authors' calculation. Per capita GSDP data are compiled from the Reserve Bank of India.

corresponding reduction in transfers through sources such as CSS, most of which went to the health and education sectors, with the intention to grant more autonomy to states in their spending decisions. The consequence of the 14th FC decision is that education expenditure by states as proportion of aggregate expenditure has been declining during the 14th FC period although the ratio of education expenditure to GDP remained stagnant at below 3% in FY2018 (RE) and FY2019 (BE) (Appendix 10). A similar observation is made for health expenditures as well. It appears that increased transfers have been used by state governments for higher allocation in areas other than the social expenditures (World Bank 2019).

219. **Quality of education in government schools.** The quality of education in India is a critical issue across states as per the Annual Status of Education Report 2017 report (ASER Center 2018). While over 50% of students between 14 and 18 years of age struggle with mathematics, less than 55% can read English sentences. Many schools did not have basic infrastructure facilities, with only 68.7% having a usable toilet facility and 74.1% with drinking water facilities. Further, teacher absenteeism in India is significant. The teachers' attendance was 85.4% at primary level and 84.7% at upper primary level.

220. Across India, 78.1% schools were government or government-aided schools in FY2016, while only 19.4% were managed privately, as per the Unified District Information System for Education. However, enrollment in government schools was 66.4% compared with the 31.4% in private schools. Further, the dropout rate at the elementary level in government schools was about 7%, significantly above the average dropout rate of 4.1% across all management schools. Private management schools have had a higher number of well-qualified teachers as compared with government schools. Only 38.6% government schoolteachers in FY2017 had a college graduation degree compared with 49.7% teachers in private schools. The percentage of students that passed Class 10 examinations were higher in private schools than in government schools.

221. **Issues in fund allocation and transfers through CSS.** The fund allocation and transfers through CSS have multiple issues as discussed below. A major portion of the total transfers are under the primary and upper primary education.

(i)   **Input-oriented approach.** The Central Advisory Board on Education (2014), National Achievement Survey (2012), and the Economic Survey 2016–2017 of MOF observed declining learning levels in elementary education even after the implementation of the RTE Act. With 42 interventions under SSA, comprising several sub-schemes with different objectives to be financed, it was noted that resources have been thinly spread and it has become difficult to clearly specify the targets in terms of achievement of minimum standards of services. NITI Aayog in its 3-year action agenda highlighted improvement in learning outcomes as the first action point for school education reform. The Union Budget, 2018–2019 has proposed to treat school education holistically without segmentation from prenursery to Class 12, and consequently SSA has been launched and is intended to address many of the challenges.

(ii)   **Fund allocation is lower than demand.** There is a significant mismatch between funds requested by the Ministry of Human Resource Development (MHRD) for the implementation of SSA and funds that are actually allocated to MHRD for SSA. In FY2017, MHRD estimated a resource requirement of ₹550 billion for SSA. However, it received only ₹225 billion, which is equivalent to 41% of its demand. Similarly, in FY2018, while the funds requested by MHRD remained the same at ₹550 billion, the GOI SSA budget for the year was ₹235 billion (Rao 2018). Thus, there exists a significant funding gap for meeting the education sector requirements.

(iii)   **Lower fund release in comparison with allocation.** There is a considerable difference between the approved allocations and ultimate releases to the states, and this creates difficulties in implementation of the planned activities. This happens primarily due to (i) fiscal constraints with low-income states to provide the matching requirements, and (ii) nonfulfillment with compliances required from the states such as the provision of utilization certificates. The gap between actual allocation and ultimate fund releases to states can be observed by analyzing the data for SSA grants, which constituted about 57% of the total CSS allocation for MHRD during FY2017 (actuals). In 18 out of the 27 states analyzed, the actual release of the center's share did not cross even 50% of the total allocation. The details are presented in Appendix 9.

(iv)   **Non-utilization of SSA fund allocation.** None of the states have been able to utilize 100% of the funds allocated under SSA. This is due to (i) less funds being released as compared with the amount allocated; and (ii) inefficient utilization of the funds by the states, as pointed above (details in Appendix 9).

(v)   **SSA grants are based on incremental plans by states**: The total allocations as well as allocations to each state are based on incremental plans prepared by the respective state governments. Thus, grants are given not necessarily based on the shortfall in the standards of elementary education or the state's economic condition but based on the state's ability to prepare plans.

222. Considering these weaknesses in the existing fiscal transfer arrangements to the education sector in India and the disparities across states in education outcomes, it is imperative to address the performance gaps through an appropriate fiscal transfer mechanism.

C.3. Transfers in Education Sector—Asian Experience

223. Several countries have utilized a combination of specific-purpose grants and performance-based grants for the education sector. The Asian and international experience is summarized below with the details provided in Appendix 3.

224. **Specific-purpose transfers.** They are primarily based on the equalization principle to address regional disparities in education standards. International examples are provided below.

(i) **Australia.** The Australian transfer system provides specific-purpose payments for government schools, distributed as general recurrent grants, capital grants, and targeted programs. The Government of Australia pays 10% of the total public funding for government schools in Australia in general recurrent grants. The remaining 90% of public funding for government schools is provided by the state or territory. Under the Australian Education Act 2013, the capital grants program provides funding to nongovernment primary and secondary school communities for improving school facilities through the responsible Block Grant Authority. Capital grants are additional to funds provided by state and territory governments, nongovernment school authorities, and school communities.

(ii) **Indonesia.** Special Allocation Fund (DAK) is a conditional or earmarked transfer scheme that mainly targets sectors with national priorities but come under the responsibilities assigned to the subnational governments. About 40% of DAK transfers are allocated for education, primarily for school rehabilitation and quality improvement. DAK seeks to equalize a minimum standard of services among certain level of jurisdictions, which are under national priorities. The School Operational Assistance Program (Bantuan Operasional Sekolah, or BOS), which is a special adjustment fund, provides the same per-student amount on a quarterly basis to all government and nongovernment schools. The allocations in the BOS program have been calculated based on operational expenditure needs of schools and the availability of the budget. Schools are given significant flexibility on the use of BOS funds.

(iii) **People's Republic of China.** A wage adjustment grant is provided to provinces having difficulties in paying wages of teachers in rural elementary and middle school. The compulsory education transfer is paid to rural counties. The government also funds special programs to improve education in rural areas. In 2006 and 2015, two different programs targeting teachers were created to attract more qualified teachers to rural and remote areas. In addition, there are over 200 specific-purpose grants, including the education sector, among others, which are earmarked transfers used to subsidize local projects in certain areas subject to matching outlays by local government.

(iv) **South Africa.** The provincial equitable share grant formula includes education as one of the components of transfer, carrying a weight of 48%. The indicators in the formula include size of the school-age population (ages 5–17) and the number of learners enrolled in public schools. National Department of Basic Education grants have supported areas such as curriculum development and monitoring, teacher education, and institutional development.

225. **Performance-based transfers.** Several countries have employed various incentives for better education outcomes.

(i) **Indonesia.** Local incentive grants (Dana Insentif Daerah or DID) reward districts that demonstrate improved education performance. Under a special adjustment fund, Indonesia provides additional allowances such as professional benefits for certified teachers and for uncertified civil service teachers.

(ii) **Uganda.** Under a poverty action fund, school facilities grant (for desks, latrines, and classroom upgrades with specific targets for each) and universal primary education capitation grants are provided to reward schools for increasing enrollments.

(iii)   **United States.** Merit pays for groups of teachers (e.g., specific grade spans or subject areas) and for teachers at the classroom level are performance-based funding mechanisms that align incentives for teachers with outcomes for students.

(iv)   **European Union.** The EU Performance Reserve Fund sets aside 4% of resources to reward projects that achieve predefined goals. The governments are required to evaluate the projects and achievement of their goals to gain access to additional reward funds. The EU Performance Reserve Fund has contributed to capacity building and adoption of good management practices. For example, because of the fund, certain regions incorporated monitoring and evaluation methods into their projects for the first time.

(v)   **Chile.** Established in 1994, the National System of Performance Assessment provides teacher incentive grants to schools based on an index of school excellence measures.

C.4. Education Sector Recommendations for the 15th Finance Commission

226. Lower education sector performance can have detrimental effects on human development indicators and economic growth in the medium to long term. Since higher-income states have been found to spend more on education, the disparities across states in human capital, economic growth, and income levels are likely to increase if education sector performance is not equalized across states in India. The 15th FC may consider an appropriate mix of specific-purpose transfers, as recommended by previous FCs, and performance-based transfers to ensure not only an increase in education expenditure but also more effective outcomes and possibly a certain measure of "catch-up" over time that could also address the horizontal imbalance problem.

227. **Introduce specific-purpose grants in the education sector.** Owing to huge disparities in income among the states in India, it is not feasible to design a general-purpose transfer, which can fully offset the revenue and cost disabilities. Specific-purpose transfers are more efficient for equalization

Table 11   Education Grants Recommended by Finance Commissions in India

Finance Commission	Total Transfers (₹ billion)	Education Grants (₹ billion)	Education Grants as % of Total Transfers	Education Grants as % of Total Grants
10th FC	2,266	6.30	0.30	3.10
11th FC	4,349	5.10	0.12	0.86
12th FC	7,557	101.70	1.35	7.00
13th FC	17,066	240.70	1.41	9.30
14th FC	44,855	0.00	0.00	0.00

FC = Finance Commission.
Source: Authors' compilation from the Finance Commission reports.

than general transfers because they can be designed to match the specific financing requirements of a state. Specific-purpose transfers can play a critical role to ensure that people receive prescribed minimum standards of meritorious public services, irrespective of the jurisdiction they live in (Rao 2017; Rao 2018). Specific-purpose transfers can be quite effective in social sectors such as health and education. These sectors have remained priority sectors for most FCs. The education grants recommended by the 10th FC to the 14th FC are given in Table 11.

228. Table 12 presents the approach of previous FCs on education grants (details in Appendix 11). The 12th FC applied the equalization principle in determining the grants for the education sector. It made a provision of ₹101.72 billion to be distributed among eight states with lower expenditure on education as a proportion of total current expenditure, namely, Assam, Bihar, Jharkhand, Madhya Pradesh, Odisha, Rajasthan, Uttar Pradesh, and West Bengal. The approach was to equalize per capita expenditure on education across states. The commission noted that full equalization was not feasible due to revenue constraints and thus recommended the grants to cover only 15% of the shortfall in achieving per capita education expenditure parity across these states.

229. The 13th FC provided specific grants to 28 states for elementary education (₹240.7 billion) to cover 15% of the estimated SSA expenditure of each state. These grants were subject to the condition that the states

Table 12   Education Grants Provided by the 10th to 13th Finance Commissions

	Basis of Grants

10th FC	• Upgradation grants for
	  o Promotion of girls' education
	  o Additional facilities for upper primary schools
	  o Drinking water facilities in primary schools

11th FC	• Upgradation grants for elementary education based on a composite index worked out by considering the
	  o Number of illiterates in the age group 7–14 as per the 1991 Census
	  o Average per capita expenditure of states under the budget head "2202— General Education" for 3 years, i.e., FY1996, FY1997, and FY1998, giving equal weight to each

12th FC	• Grants based on the principle of equalization of per capita education expenditure across states based on two-stage normative measures • Provided to eight states • Estimated resource requirement computed for equalizing 15% of the distance
13th FC	• Grants for elementary education based on providing a grant of 15% of the estimated SSA expenditure of each state. This amount was to cover the difference between the targeted state share of 50% by the terminal year of the 11th plan and the contribution required to be made in FY2009, i.e., 35% of the individual states' SSA share • Provided to 29 states

FC = Finance Commission, FY = fiscal year, SSA = Sarva Shiksha Abhiyan.
Source: Authors' compilation from the Finance Commission reports.

would maintain the growth of their own expenditure on education at 8% per annum during the award period of the 13th FC, namely, 2010–2015.

230. Appendix 12 shows the suggested methodology for computation of equalization grants to the states performing below all-state average in per capita education sector expenditure if the 15th FC were to adopt an approach similar to the 13th FC in equalizing the gap of a state with the best performing state to the extent of 15%. For the selected states under consideration, it is estimated that over ₹1 trillion will be required during the 15th FC period (2020–2025).

231. The 15th FC can consider specific-purpose transfers based on deficiencies in education levels and conditional on (i) better utilization of the allocated funds under SSA, and (ii) maintaining the trend growth rate in education expenditure. Unutilized SSA grants toward the close of the year can be given to states

fulfilling the performance criteria. It is also important to address the weaknesses of current CSS schemes in planning and utilization, particularly relating to multiplicity of objectives, lack of quality monitoring, and continuing focus on infrastructure rather than on learning outcomes. However, if specific-purpose transfers are considered, this would exhaust the available funds for performance-based transfers. Since education outcomes can best be achieved with performance measures, it is recommended to prioritize performance-based transfers.

232. **Select the right indicator for measuring education sector performance.** The School Education Quality Index (SEQI) can be considered for measuring education outcomes and linking them with performance incentives (Box 9). SEQI has been recently developed by NITI Aayog and MHRD. The 2019 SEQI is a composite index with 30 indicators that critically influence the overall effectiveness, efficiency, equity, and governance of school education (Appendix 13). The composition of SEQI is summarized in Table 13.

233. The main advantage of SEQI is that majority of the indicators related to outcomes, access, and equity are based on published information from NAS and the Unified District Information System for Education. States and union territories also submit their

Table 13   Composition of School Education Quality Index

Category	Domain	Number of Indicators	Weight
1. Outcomes (16 Indicators)	1.1 Learning outcomes	3	360
	1.2 Access outcomes	3	100
	1.3 Infrastructure and facilities for outcomes	3	25
	1.4 Equity outcomes	7	200
2. Governance processes aiding outcomes (14 Indicators)	Student and teacher attendance	2	80
	Teacher adequacy	3	40
	Administrative adequacy	1	20
	Training	3	50
	Accountability and transparency	5	90
Total		30	965

Source: NITI Aayog. https://niti.gov.in/content/school-education-quality-index.

Box 9   Features of the School Education Quality Index

Focus on education outcomes rather than inputs and processes. The School Education Quality Index (SEQI) seeks to institutionalize a focus on improvements in learning levels, access, equity, infrastructure, and governance with the aim of encouraging states to innovate in framing and implementing their own policies to achieve these goals. Instead of focusing on specific schemes for disadvantaged groups to reduce inequality, the index captures the reduction of outcome gaps in access and learning for disadvantaged groups.

Aims to reward continuous improvement. While initial levels vary across states, comparing the changes in the

SEQI with respect to base year will make it possible to track improvement or progress of states relative to their initial level. Hence, states and union territories would be recognized for continuous improvements on key measures of performance.

Transparent comparison of education quality across states. SEQI will serve as a regular and transparent review of quality and delivery of school education. Based on critical indicators, states and union territories will be ranked objectively on their overall performance on the SEQI as well as according to its constituent domains.

Source: NITI Aayog. http://www.social.niti.gov.in/education-index.

information on functioning of education administration at the state level on a dedicated portal with supporting evidence, wherever required. Many indicators under governance and management category are easy to track with government orders and notification.

D. Designing Performance-Based Transfers—Summary of Recommendations

D.1. Proposed Framework on Performance-Based Transfers

234. International best practices (UNCDF 2010; Boadway and Shah 2007) point to the following guiding principles for the design of effective performance-based transfers that could be adopted by the 15th Finance Commission in the context of India.

235. **Measurement of performance.** Performance-based transfers should be based on a few objective criteria or indicators that are transparent and easily measurable. The performance-based grants from the FC can be linked to periodic improvements in the (i) governance index, (ii) health index for the health sector, and (iii) SEQI for education sector. The indices can be measured and assessed by an independent and advisory entity such as NITI Aayog.

236. **Quantum of performance-based grants.** The performance-based transfers should be sizable enough to incentivize change.[29] In this regard, the recommendations by previous FCs could be useful. Previous commissions have, in general, recommended transfers under the following broad categories: (i) tax devolution, (ii) untied current deficit grants, (iii) grants for local governments, (iv) grants for disaster relief, and (v) performance grants. As noted in Table 14, the proportion of total FC grants has ranged from 5% to 7.1% of the divisible pool for the previous four FCs. Out of this, the current deficit grants ranged from 1.1% to 2.8% of the divisible pool, leaving 2.2% to 4.6% of the divisible pool as margin for performance and specific-purpose grants, including disaster relief, and grants to local bodies. The 14th FC did not recommend specific-purpose transfers (except those for local governments and disaster relief) or any performance-based transfers while the 13th FC allocated the highest, i.e., 4.6% equivalent of the divisible pool for this conditional and specific-purpose transfers. We suggest that along the lines of the 13th FC, the total FC grants can be 5.5% of the divisible pool out of which current deficit grants can be targeted at 1%, specific-purpose grants at 2.5% of the divisible pool, and 2% of the divisible pool can be allocated for performance-based grants, which can be divided equally among governance, health, and education improvements.

---

[29]   For example, the European Union Structural Fund dedicates 4% for the performance reserve, including non-commitment of funds in case of poor performance (Mehta and Mehta 2013).

Table 14 Margin for Performance Grants as a Proportion of Divisible Pool

	11th FC	12th FC	13th FC	14th FC
Divisible pool (₹ billion)	12,757	20,102	45,253	94,004
Indicative limit on total transfers (% of gross central revenues)	37.5	38.0	39.5	49.0
Total transfers (% of divisible pool)	34.5	37.6	37.7	47.7
Tax devolution (% of divisible pool)	29.5	30.5	32.0	42.0
FC grants (% of divisible pool)	5.0	7.1	5.7	5.7
Current deficit grant (% of divisible pool)	2.8	2.8	1.1	2.1
Margin for conditional and specific-purpose transfers (% of divisible pool)	2.2	4.3	4.6	3.6
Grants for disaster relief and for local bodies (% of divisible pool)	1.6	2.3	2.5	3.6
Margin for performance grants (% of divisible pool)	0.6	2.0	2.1	0.0

FC = Finance Commission.
Note: The divisible pool consists of all taxes, except surcharges and cess levied for specific-purpose, net of collection charges.
Sources: Authors' compilation from the Finance Commission reports; and authors' calculations.

237. **Mechanism for release of performance-based transfers.** All states should be eligible for performance-based grants. This grant should reward states based on *forward looking criteria,* as it is linked with both *improvement and the quantum of improvement.* The grant may be linked to actual progress in improvement of the underlying index based on a common base year. Annual improvement for each state from this baseline will be measured.

238. The grant may be released in three annual installments from FY2023 to FY2025. This will give the states a period of 2 years to make improvements. The grant allocation can progressively increase for states that make improvements in the underlying index. Actual release of grants to states may depend upon the following:

(i) Initial condition, i.e., condition in the base year, FY2020.

(ii) The incremental improvement (or deterioration) in performance over the base year level, i.e., difference between performance levels in the year of reckoning and in the base year.

(iii) The release of next installment of equalization grants to a state should be contingent on the fact that it exhibits improvement in its performance not only with respect to the base, but also with respect to the previous year.

(iv) Given that improvement over a high base is harder, such improvement will receive higher weightage. Alternatively, the improvement could be measured as a combination of state ranking and annual improvement in the underlying index. High-ranking states can be incentivized for maintaining their respective ranks.

(v) Some states may not be eligible for the grant in case of negative performance, i.e., deterioration in performance in the year of reckoning.

239. **Capacity building.** The performance-based transfers should be stable and predictable over the medium term so that a performance improvement action plan (based on the targeted areas in the underlying index) can be designed and executed by states. A capacity building component can be included as part of the performance improvement action plan and supported under the transfer system to improve the states' organizational and management efficiency.

240. **Monitoring mechanism.** India has no other alternative, but to strengthen provisioning of health and education services given that more than 60% of children

are dependent on the public education system, and the public health system accounts for 44% of inpatient care. Besides direct intervention in these sectors through specific-purpose grants, complementary efforts must be made for governance improvement to ensure more efficient outcomes. A substantially improved monitoring framework can bridge the gaps between resource needs, budget allocation, and actual spending. Building on the monitoring framework adopted by the previous commissions (from the 8th FC to the 14th FC), the following is recommended:

(i)   A High-Level Monitoring Committee (HLMC), which may comprise sector experts, is constituted by each state to ensure proper utilization of grants for their objectives.

(ii)   The HLMC should be responsible for meeting both financial and physical targets and ensuring adherence to the specific conditionalities.

(iii)   In the beginning of the year, the HLMC may approve projects to be undertaken in each sector, quantify both physical and financial targets, and lay down the period for achieving specific milestones.

(iv)   The HLMC should meet periodically to review the utilization of the grants and to issue directions for midcourse correction, if necessary.

241. It is further suggested that the 15th FC may provide some funds to all states for a technology-based monitoring system as a pilot. This will enable states to monitor the schemes efficiently and track the progress in terms of inputs, outputs as well as outcomes and integrate data collection.

D.2. Leveraging Support from International Financial Institutions for Better Results

242. The IFIs have been supporting GOI, state governments, and local bodies in their development and reform agenda. This support could be in the form of grant-based technical assistance, a loan at competitive rates for sector development or direct budget support usually accompanied by grant-based technical assistance, and credit guarantee or partial guarantee products for reducing costs and improving market accessibility for local governments or public-sector enterprises.

243. The policy-based lending programs of IFIs are indeed a model of performance-based lending whereby a state government commits to undertaking some jointly identified benchmarks—in most cases a policy but can also target indicators—and fund transfer is triggered upon attainment of these benchmarks or indicators. These programs can be quite useful to implement international best practices and can be leveraged to further the reform and development agenda recommended by the 15th FC, strengthening governance and capacity of public institutions, increasing expenditure efficiency, improving service delivery, and reducing fiscal burden. In addition, the programs provide a type of third-party monitoring by the IFI, addressing an important gap that could exist otherwise. A few suggested options are as follows:

244. **Capacity development program for urban and rural local bodies.** Starting from the 10th FC, the previous FCs have recommended transfers to the local governments (the third tier), mostly in the form of ad hoc grants (i.e., fixed amounts, percentage of divisible pool). For each year of the 13th FC award period, the grant was computed based on the divisible pool of the previous year.

245. For horizontal distribution of these grants, previous commissions have relied on the following criteria in different combinations and weights: (i) population, (ii) area, (iii) income distance, (iv) scheduled castes and/or scheduled tribes population, (v) index of decentralization, (vi) revenue effort, (vii) index of deprivation, (viii) index of devolution, and (ix) FC grant utilization index. For example, the 14th FC recommended distribution to local bodies based on the recommendation of the respective State Finance Commission (SFC), and if not available then the proportion of population (90%) and area (10%). Further, these grants were divided into two parts: unconditional portion (80% for urban local bodies and 90% for rural local bodies), and performance grant (20% for urban local bodies and 10% for rural local bodies).

246. Through the performance grants, FC recommendations have targeted improvements in budgeting, accounting, auditing, service standard benchmarking, and revenue augmentation at the local

bodies. However, improvements have been slow.[30] As noted on para. 9.60 on p. 110 of the FC report (2015): "…it has been more than twenty years that municipalities and panchayats were sought to be empowered, through a Constitutional amendment, to act as institutions of local self-governance and also to provide certain basic services to citizens. It is inconceivable, and certainly not desirable, that local bodies seek an ever-increasing share of public moneys and yet continue to keep themselves beyond the ambit of accountability and responsibility for the public money placed with them." The FC report (2015) further states in para. 9.75 on p. 113: "Despite the last three FCs raising the issue of reliable data and accounts and providing grants to address the issue, not much has happened."

247. Apart from a few structural issues, a key reason for slow progress in public management reforms at the local level has been the lack of structured capacity building programs. The IFIs have been working with local governments in these areas. Local governments can be encouraged to take support from IFIs for adoption of participatory planning and state-specific GPDP guidelines based on model GOI guidelines, resource mobilization including effective implementation of property taxes, strengthening public asset management (e.g., establishment of asset registries), improvements in budgeting (MTFFs and MTEFs), accounting and audit systems, and adoption of service-level benchmarks. In addition, IFIs can support local governments in synergizing funding under various state and central schemes, state finance commission transfers, and district development fund with FC grants for the most effective utilization of funds.

248. **Issuance of municipal bonds.** Besides helping large corporations directly, IFIs can provide support to set up an intermediary institution that can help small and medium municipalities to access markets and can also help these municipalities to build systems and capacities for bond issuance. In addition, state governments can access the credit enhancement guarantee products of these financial institutions for further cost reduction.

D.2.1. Sustainable Finances through Better Public Expenditure Management

249. **Expenditure rationalization.** As noted earlier in the governance section, state governments have a scope to increase input and output efficiencies of SSEs by almost 30% when compared with the best performing state. Similar efficiency gains can be achieved in other sectors and in the functioning of state public sector units (PSUs). IFI support can be useful for implementation of expenditure and subsidy rationalization strategy, and road map for disinvestment or privatization of state PSUs or closure of nonworking PSUs.

250. **Adoption of MTEFs by the state governments.** The slippage observed in adherence to fiscal targets is mainly because of the disconnect between departmental budget allocations, desired outputs and outcomes, and the medium-term fiscal framework. As discussed earlier, robust MTEFs align these together by bringing top–down and bottom–up budget projections in line with the fiscal trajectory under the state's FRBM Act and/or 15th FC targets. Moreover, the common problem identified above of central programs that cannot be fully realized because of limited absorptive capacity at the subnational level can also be better addressed as capital and recurrent budgets can be better planned and integrated under MTEFs. ADB has introduced MTEFs in its state-level programs in Punjab and West Bengal (see Appendix 5 for details). The 15th FC can consider incentivizing states to adopt MTEFs with support from IFIs.

251. **Quick-disbursing disaster relief.** Disaster relief funding is an important part of FC recommendations. SDRFs have been constituted by all state governments under Section 48 (1) (a) of the Disaster Management Act, 2005. DDRFs have also been created in a few

---

[30] For example, the 13th FC laid out several conditions for states to avail the performance grants. These included putting in place (i) property tax levy by local bodies and a state level Property Tax Board to independently assess the taxes; (ii) electronic transfer of local body grants on a timely basis; (iii) supplementary budget detailing transfers to Panchayati Raj Institutions and urban local bodies; (iv) audit system for all local bodies; and (v) an independent local body for corruption and maladministration cases by officials. The MOF's administrative guidelines stipulated compliance reporting by states every year to be eligible for these grants. A study by Rajaraman and Gupta (2016) showed that several states did not receive the performance grants for urban and rural local bodies during the years of the 13th FC period because of the unmet conditions, mostly related to audit systems, supplementary budget, and accountability mechanisms. This created irregular and unpredictable flow of funds to local bodies, impacting service delivery.

districts. In line with the 14th FC recommendations, the central government has increased its contribution in SDRF to 90% of SDRF allocation with effect from 1 April 2018 (from 75% of SDRF for non-special category states and union territories, and 90% for the Himalayan states and union territories). The 14th FC had recommended that the central government should contribute 90% of the SDRF allocation for all states. It recommended a total contribution of ₹612.19 billion ($8.51 billion) to SDRFs during FY2016–FY2020 out of which 90% or ₹550.97 billion ($7.65 billion) was to be contributed by the central government. The issues in operationalization of disaster relief arise mainly from (i) delays in availability of NDRF's assistance to the states because the SDRF responds first during a severe disaster; (ii) requirements to furnish expenditure details by the state governments to access the disaster relief funds; and (iii) need for strengthening the capacity of state and district disaster management authorities, including transparency in accounting, expenditure reporting, and audit. More critically, in the absence of dedicated "contingency" funds, when an unexpected shock hits the state or local economy, it tends to derail other budgeted spending programs as resources must be subrogated. This ends up undermining planned programs, increasing the overall costs from interrupted spending programs.

252. ADB has structured its disaster relief support in terms of quick disbursing loans contingent on requirement, which has the advantage that governments must pay only the commitment charge on the approved amount until the disbursement happens. This can avoid locking funds for disaster management while ensuring timely release for immediate relief. It can be combined with grant-based funds from the Asia Pacific Disaster Response Fund and grant-based technical assistance for building financial management and reporting standards of state disaster management authorities.

IV. Conclusion

253. The review of the institutional and design aspects of intergovernmental fiscal transfer systems in selected Asian countries in this report shows that decentralization and centralization play complementary roles, and they need to work in tandem. In decentralized systems, central governments have an important role to play in (i) redistribution of public resources in an equitable manner, (ii) setting the regulatory standards and exercising quality control over the use of these resources and provision of services, (iii) providing the right incentives for good governance and performance, and (iv) stimulating competition and innovation among the subnational governments for achieving the desired developmental outcomes. It is also crucial that central governments effectively create integrated markets and a level playing field for all citizens by supporting the disadvantaged regions. The benefits of decentralization occur when all aspects of fiscal, administrative, and political decentralization are strong and when the intergovernmental fiscal transfer systems provide subnational governments with adequate resources and flexibility to carry out their mandates, strengthen their institutional capacity, and ensure their accountability.

254. In line with these learnings, this report draws important lessons relevant for the intergovernmental fiscal transfer system in India. The institutional structure in India is robust and compares quite favorably to other countries across many parameters but it can be further strengthened by setting up a permanent secretariat, which can not only monitor the outcomes during the FC period but also support an incoming commission with ready data, analysis, and observations. Similarly, the SFCs must be further strengthened, and a better alignment with the central FC would enable incorporation of local requirements and improve the overall architecture in line with the subsidiarity principle. Without prodding from the central FCs, state governments do not have the incentive to deepen reforms or further empower SFCs and thereby creating possible distortions in standardizing service delivery across the country.

255. To better address increasing horizontal imbalances across the country and given the absence of forward-looking indicators to track performance at the state level, it is recommended and consistent with international best practices to include only fiscal need and/or cost disability and equalization considerations in the formula design. Specific requirements and performance-based transfers are recommended to be dealt with separately. It has been suggested to add inequality adjusted HDI in the devolution formula to highlight the importance of equalizing disparities in human development and income distribution across states and to reflect effective investment in delegated expenditure assignments including health and education. It is also suggested to strengthen normative measures for assessment of fiscal capacity and needs, including the assessment of deficit grants. Fiscal responsibility legislations by state governments in India with varying degrees of success have encouraged fiscal discipline and transparency at the subnational level. A similar attention needs to be paid to the assessment and reporting of off-budget liabilities of the subnational governments.

256. Other sources of transfers to state governments include CSS. The hitherto large number of CSS have now been rationalized to only 28 schemes with 5 core programs accounting for 66% of total grants under central schemes in FY2017. Further reforms would include reduction of multiple indicators in CSS to focused targets for effectiveness. State governments

can also be encouraged to rationalize their schemes along the same lines as rationalization of CSS. Specific-purpose grants and performance-based transfers are an integral part of effective intergovernmental fiscal transfer system, and they are widely used across several countries. Mechanisms for performance monitoring and adherence of state governments to conditions under these grants should be strengthened in India.

257. Taking a cue from the segregation of fiscal transfers by previous finance commissions, it is recommended to reserve a conservative amount equivalent to 2% of the divisible pool for performance-based grants in line with the earlier recommendations of the 12th and 13th FCs. International review highlights the importance of governance quality as an enabler for effectiveness of other government interventions—health and education in particular. A governance index has been suggested based on selected measurable and quantifiable indicators to assess a state's performance in relation to its peers. Along similar lines, it has been suggested to target health sector and education sector performance improvement using health index and SEQI, respectively. A methodology for incentive transfers for improvements in governance, health, and education has been suggested. The improvement could be measured as a combination of state ranking and annual improvement in the underlying index. High-ranking states can be incentivized to maintain at least their respective ranks. It is proposed to release performance grants in annual installments over the last 3 years of the 15th FC period. A capacity building component can be included as part of the performance improvement action plan and supported under the transfer system to improve the

states' organizational and management efficiency. It is suggested that an HLMC be constituted by each state for ensuring adherence to the specific conditionalities applicable, monitoring proper utilization of grants, and meeting both financial and physical targets.

258. Among measures to strengthen the third tier of government, the 15th FC can consider incentives for local bodies that take steps toward adoption of participatory planning and state-specific GPDP guidelines based on model GOI guidelines, resource mobilization including effective implementation of property taxes, strengthening of public asset management with asset registries, improvements in budgeting, accounting and audit systems, and adoption of service-level benchmarks. The PRC's experience shows that development outcomes can be highly effective if the possibility of civil service career growth and recognition is aligned with successful implementation of progressive reforms. Besides performance-based transfers for the states and/or local bodies, a recognition program for the best performing states and/or local bodies and the concerned department officials can also be initiated.

259. Support from IFIs can be effectively leveraged to (i) further the reform and development agenda recommended by the 15th FC, (ii) strengthen governance and capacity of public institutions, (iii) increase expenditure efficiency, (iv) improve service delivery, and (v) reduce fiscal burden on the state governments. The support could include, among other options, capacity building of local governments, outcome-based budgeting and expenditure management using MTFFs and MTEFs, expenditure rationalization measures, and quick-disbursing disaster relief.

Institutional Structure of Fiscal Transfers to Subnational Governments— International Case Studies

A. Australia

1. The Council of Australian Government (COAG) is an apex intergovernmental forum and key decision-making body in vertical fiscal devolution. The COAG is chaired by the Australian Prime Minister and comprises state and territory premiers and chief ministers and the President of the Australian Local Government Association. The COAG was set up in 1992, following an agreement by the then Prime Minister (Paul Keating), state premiers, and chief ministers. The current institutional arrangement for the fiscal devolution mechanism in Australia is largely based on the Intergovernmental Agreement on Federal Financial Relations (IGA FFR), signed by COAG and effective on 1 January 2009.

2. Australia's fiscal devolution has evolved since the late 1800s when then six self-governing colonies of New South Wales, Queensland, South Australia, Tasmania, Victoria, and Western Australia united to form the Commonwealth of Australia. In 1933, the Commonwealth Grants Commission (CGC) was set up under Section 96 of the Australian Constitution, which stipulates that the Commonwealth "may grant financial assistance to any state on such terms and conditions as the Parliament thinks fit." After the Commonwealth was given an effective monopoly over the levying of income tax in 1942, state expenditure started to exceed their revenues, and the Commonwealth compensated by transferring general financial assistance grants and specific-purpose payments to the states through negotiations. Since 1976, a system of grant sharing has evolved from one based upon negotiation and agreements to one based upon a complex formula that consider all revenues earned by a state and its expenditure needs.

3. The Commonwealth Grants Commission Act 1973 provides that the CGC is a small independent agency. The Commission is responsible for horizontal fiscal devolution, measuring the states' relative fiscal capacities and deciding on how to allocate the goods and services tax (GST) revenues among the states. A Secretariat supports the Commission and its members, and collects and assesses data, and undertakes research to provide advice to the Commission. The Commission members (i) consider the advice they receive from all stakeholders as well as the Secretariat, (ii) decide how the GST pool is distributed and other policy issues, and (iii) direct the Secretariat.

4. The Commission consists of a Chairperson and not less than two other members. Advised by the Federal Executive Council[1] and following the Commonwealth Grants Commission Act 1973, the Governor-General of the Commonwealth of Australia, appoints CGC commissioners on a full-time or part-term basis. Their term is not less than 1 year or more than 5 years, but they are eligible for reappointment.

5. The Secretariat consults widely and draft reports for the consideration of the Commission members. The Secretariat employees are civil servants, hired under the Public Service Act 1999. A Secretary heads the Secretariat employees and is the Chief Executive Officer and Accountable Authority. The Secretary

---

[1] The Federal Executive Council is established by the Constitution. It is the legal body responsible for advising the Governor-General and comprises all current and former Commonwealth Ministers and Assistant Ministers.

is assisted by two assistant secretaries and a chief operating officer. In FY2018, the Secretariat had 30 staff with an annual budget of A$6.2 million.

6. The CGC has well-established processes that involve consultation with the states every 5 years and regular methodology reviews. The CGC considers the submissions of the states before it finalizes its recommendations to the Commonwealth Treasurer on the updated relativities among the states. The Commission presents to the federal and state treasurers with public release of the Report on GST Revenue Sharing among the states, usually in March before the Commonwealth and states release their budgets. The federal treasurer would accept those recommendations and uses them in the forthcoming Commonwealth budget to share the estimated GST for that year among the states.

7. Australia's federal–state financial relations are based on IGA FFR and the Commonwealth, and the states collaborate in developing policies and delivering services. The Council on Federal Financial Relations, comprising the federal and state treasurers, was set up to oversee the implementation of IGA FFR. The Council generally meets biannually and is supported by the Commonwealth-State Relations Division in the Department of Treasury of the Federal Government.

8. The COAG Reform Fund Act, 2008 sets up the COAG Reform Fund to make grants to the states. This Act also stipulates that the terms and conditions of financial assistance grants should be in written agreements between the Commonwealth and the states.

9. The Federal Financial Relations Act, 2009 specifies that the Commonwealth provides financial support to the states through national specific purpose payments (including National Health Reform funding), and the Treasurer determines distributions of GST revenues to the states based on the advice from the CGC. It also provides that the Commonwealth Treasurer determines National Partnership payments and general revenue assistance to the states from the COAG Reform Fund.

B. Indonesia

10. Indonesia is a unitary republic and is divided into five layers of government: central, provinces, *kabupaten* (districts) and *kota* (municipalities), *kecamatan* (subdistricts), and *kelurahan/desa* (villages) (Nasution 2016).

11. Indonesia followed a highly centralized system of governance and fiscal structure prior to 1998. The central government played a dominant role in (i) appointment of officials at the subnational level; (ii) planning of projects; and (iii) providing funds to the subnational governments for administration, production of public goods, and service delivery. This changed in 1999 when Indonesia implemented a wide range of reforms such as adoption of a multiparty democratic political system, move toward market-based and globalized economy, and decentralization by providing greater budget and responsibilities to the subnational government (Nasution 2016).

12. Under the decentralization, the provincial governments have limited powers, while districts and municipalities at the sub-provincial level have greater involvement in governance and provision of public goods for local service delivery. Nearly three-fourths of the budget of the local governments belonged to districts and municipalities while provinces get only one-fourth.

13. The Ministry of Finance is the key government department that manages the public finances of the country with three main divisions that focus on public finance. The Directorate General (DG) Budget is responsible for budget preparation while DG Treasury focuses on budget execution, cash management and accounting, and DG Fiscal Balance is responsible for fiscal transfers across the various levels of government (World Bank 2018).

14. The DG Fiscal Balance prepares the Presidential Decree covering the allocation of various intergovernmental transfers to the different levels of subnational government and manages the disbursement of these transfers. The Ministry of Home

Affairs facilitates implementation of transfers. The DG Fiscal Balance is further subdivided into directorates, one of which covers the Balancing Funds (Dana Perimbangan), i.e., the funds that are transferred from the central government to subnational government. Balancing Funds cover the Revenue Sharing Fund (DBH), General Allocation Fund (DAU), and Specific Allocation Fund (DAK). The allocations of these funds are largely based on a predetermined formula and the Parliament endorses the allocation based on the Presidential Decree.

15. Despite the decentralization, the process continues to be mostly top–down with central government wielding most of the power in determining the volume and composition of the transfers. The reluctance of the central bureaucracy to devolve greater powers and jurisdictions has resulted in the mechanism of intragovernmental transfers being a combination of objectivity and arbitrariness (Sen et al. 2014). The overwhelming role played by the central government line ministries in many of the decentralized areas like health and education also points to continuing dominance of the central government. In many instances the sub-provincial governments lack the technical capacity to evaluate and undertake expenditures due to lack of experienced personnel, resulting in dilution of service delivery. Even on the revenue side, the current system does not provide incentives to the sub-provincial governments for raising their own revenues.

C. Japan

16. Japan is a unitary country. The Prime Minister is responsible to the National Diet (Japan's bicameral legislature) and must resign en masse with his ministers if a motion of no confidence is adopted by the Diet. The Ministry of Internal Affairs and Communications (MIC) and the MOF are part of the Cabinet and are headed by ministers appointed and dismissed by the Prime Minister.

17. The MIC oversees the administrative system, manages local governments and governmental statistics. The scope of its functions includes the administration of local autonomy (regional decentralization reforms and regional vitalization). The MIC represents the local governments during the national budget allocation process to ensure (i) the availability of vertical fiscal transfers from the central government, and (ii) the equitability through the horizontal fiscal transfers among local governments. (Aoki 2008; Mochida 2001). The Local Public Finance Bureau and the Local Tax Bureau under MIC are responsible for the planning, implementation, and supervision of the local finance system and the local tax system.

18. The MOF coordinates resource allocation between the central and local governments. In general, the central government deals with matters relating to (i) Japan's position in the international community; (ii) basic rules on national activities or local autonomy that should be standardized nationally; and (iii) policies and programs to be implemented on a national level or from a national viewpoint. Japan's budget is compiled by the MOF based on estimates from other ministries and guidance from the Cabinet, before being approved by the Diet.

19. Each fiscal year, the preparation of the annual budget requires negotiations between national and local officials. In these negotiations, budget officials in each ministry evaluate the requests for funding by local governments and then prepare their own budget for submission to the MOF, which has final authority before the cabinet considers the overall budget. Since expenditures of local governments typically exceed revenue, local governments must rely on national government transfers. If they can persuade the national government ministries of their necessities and urgencies, then they receive more money.

20. In the budgeting process, the Local Public Finance Program (LPFP) estimates, including revenue, expenditure, and intergovernmental transfers for all local governments, are combined with estimates for national policies and programs, e.g., the Fiscal Investment and Loan Program (FILP) (Aoki 2008). While compiling the national budget, MIC and MOF negotiate to secure revenue to balance the LPFP. A draft budget is then prepared by MOF and is presented to each ministry and agency. After

necessary add-ons and adjustments, the draft budget is approved by the Cabinet and is finalized for submission to the Diet.

21. The Constitution guarantees "local autonomy" to the local governments, meaning that the central government cannot abolish and create local governments at will within the national government structure (ADBI 2017). The Local Autonomy Law stipulates the basic framework for the organization and operation of local governments and specifies the relationship between central and local governments, as well as among local governments. The executive heads of the local governments are the governors and mayors. Prefectures are administratively headed by governors, while cities, towns, and villages are headed by mayors. The legislative organs are the local assemblies composed of elected members. Among their functions, these assemblies establish or abolish local ordinances, determine local government budgets, and approve settlements of accounts. Both the local government heads and the members of the local assemblies are elected by local citizens to serve for 4 years.

22. The Local Allocation Tax (LAT) Grant, which is the largest transfer from the central government to local governments to cover local revenue shortfall is governed by the LAT Law. The Local Tax Law is a national law that provides for prefecture taxes and municipal taxes. It provides standard tax rates used to calculate standard fiscal revenue of the LAT Grant (Aoki 2008). The local governments in Japan must establish taxation bylaws and taxation regulations that are in accordance with the stipulations of the Local Tax Law and must levy and collect taxes based on these bylaws and regulations. According to Uda (2015), except for the local consumption tax, which has a uniform tax rate, local governments are not bound by the standard tax rates if their fiscal conditions so require. They can decide on matters such as taxation criteria and tax rates in accordance with their bylaws on levying and collecting local taxes (Local Tax Law, Article 3, Clause 1).

23. Local governments can also introduce taxes not stipulated in the Local Tax Law if they have special needs. However, they must seek first the approval of MIC (Uda 2015). MIC usually gives its consent unless

the tax (i) imposes a heavy burden on citizens, (ii) significantly impedes the distribution of goods across municipalities or prefectures, or (iii) is contrary to national economic policy. Although the local tax laws provide flexibility in setting tax rates, except for high corporate tax rates, local governments have rarely taken advantage of this (Aoki 2008). According to Bessho (2017), excess revenue from such taxes is barely 1.5% of total tax revenue.

24. The Local Finance Law specifies the financial and political relationship between central and local governments. Article 282 of the law provides that "the central government shall endeavor to promote the self-dependence and soundness of local finance, and refrain from any action prejudicial to the financial autonomy of local government or from shifting its burden upon local governments" (Ichimura and Bahl 2009).

25. Expenditure responsibilities determined by national legislation (e.g., local finance law, local autonomy law, LAT law) cannot be changed at the discretion of the central government since the central government has no legal right to issue unfunded mandates on local governments (Mochida 2001). With the LPFP, overlapping functions, conflicting interests, lobbying, and preferential allocations are diminished if not avoided, lessening the tensions between central and local governments.

D. People's Republic of China

26. Despite a high degree of fiscal decentralization, particularly on the expenditure side, the PRC is a unitary country and a one-party state. The Communist Party of China (CPC) plays an increasing role in economic policy making both at the strategic and operational level. The government works under the direction of the CPC. All senior government officials hold CPC positions. The implementation of CPC decisions on fiscal policy are monitored by the Central Committee of the CPC and Leading Small Groups. CPC decisions are binding. Their enforcement has been strengthened over recent years in conjunction with efforts to strengthen party discipline and the "leading role of the party in all areas of policy making and social life." This undercuts the leeway

subnational governments have had in many policy areas over recent decades.

27. The MOF deals with the fiscal policy and central–local fiscal relations even though its autonomy is limited. The MOF is under the State Council, i.e., the Cabinet, comprising the Premier and Vice-Premiers. Two Vice-Premiers, both senior to the MOF, are responsible for economic policy. The MOF submits recommendations to the State Council or the CPC. New governments are approved by the National People's Congress (i.e., the Parliament) every 5 years. In practice, the Congress just endorses a prior decision made by the Central Committee of the CPC. Various party organizations and meetings formulate economic policy and provide directions to the MOF, which also has a Party Secretary. The Party also establishes "Leading Small Groups," which are top-level steering committees that detail policies, including on subnational finances, and coordinate their implementation.

E. Republic of Korea

28. The Ministry of Economy and Finance (MOEF)[2] coordinates resource allocation between the central and local governments from the annual budget approved by the National Assembly. The Ministry of Interior and Safety (MOIS) works with 244 local governments in formulating local fiscal affairs, promoting sound local fiscal management, supporting the operation of local state-owned enterprises, drafting mid- to long-term plans such as the 5-year medium-term local government finance plans, research on local tax systems, and overseeing tax compliance. MOIS also inspects the implementation of government-subsidized projects.

29. Both the MOEF and MOIS are created by law under the Government Organization Act headed by cabinet-level ministers appointed by the President. The ministers of both are coterminous with the President (whose term of office is 5 years) and may be removed by the President, as recommended by the Prime Minister. The Budget Office and Local

Fiscal and Economic Policy Office of the MOEF and MOIS, are each headed by a deputy director-general, a member of the Senior Civil Service, complemented by permanent government staff. In 2012, there were about 400 full-time MOEF staff.

30. A 15-member Committee for Deliberation on Local Financial Obligations headed by the Prime Minister, was established in 2014 to decide on financial burdens of local governments. Local governments are granted local autonomy under the 1948 Constitution. The system allows for the right to autonomous legislation and right to autonomous finance. However, autonomous entities have not been guaranteed complete autonomy and have been controlled by the central government. Fiscal roles of central and local governments are stipulated under both the National Public Finance Act and Local Finance Act.

31. The Subsidy Management Committee under the MOEF is headed by the Second Vice-Minister with both government and 12 NGO members. Local subsidy is provided under the Local Subsidy Act, local education subsidy stipulated under the Local Education Subsidy Act, and the subsidy from National Treasury under the Act on Budgeting and Management of Subsidy.

32. MOIS issues the annual budget preparation manual for local governments (top–down process). Heads of local governments request subsidies and/or national funding from heads of line ministries which in turn, consults with MOEF. Line ministries report the results of the grants to MOEF and to the National Assembly Budget Office (National Finance Act, Local Finance Act). Participatory budgeting is being implemented.

33. To facilitate local governments' dealings with central government on common fiscal interests, there are four civil society organizations in the ROK, namely, Governors' Association of Korea, National Association of Mayors, Association of Chairpersons of Metropolitan and Provincial Councils, and National Association of Chairpersons of Municipal Councils.

---

[2]   Formerly the Ministry of Strategy and Finance (MOSF) and was renamed in August 2018.

APPENDIX 2
Evolution of India's Fiscal Devolution Formula

Table A2.1   Indicators under the Fiscal Devolution Formulas in India

OBJECTIVE	FISCAL NEED / COST DISABILITY							EQUALIZATION					PERFORMANCE			
INDICATORS (Weight in %)	Shareable Pool	Population (1971)	Population (2011)	Area	Forest Cover	Infrastructure Index Distance	Income Distance	Inverse Income	Poverty Ratio	Index of Backwardness	Revenue Equalization	Gap Filling	Tax Collection	Tax Effort	Fiscal Discipline	Other Factors
1st FC (1952–1957)	Income Tax	80.00											20.00			
	Excise	100.00														
2nd FC (1957–1962)	Income Tax	90.00											10.00			
	Excise	90.00														10.00 Discretionary adjustments
3rd FC (1962–1966)	Income Tax	80.00											20.00			
	Excise	Major factor (weight unspecified)								Economic backwardness (weight unspecified)						
4th FC (1966–1969)	Income Tax	80.00											20.00			
	Excise	80.00								20.00						
5th FC (1969–1974)	Income Tax	90.00											10.00			
	Excise	80.00 + 16.66 for states with per capita income below the states' average								3.33						
6th FC (1974–1979)	Income Tax	90.00											10.00			
	Excise	75.00						25.00								
7th FC (1979–1984)	Income Tax	90.00											10.00			
	Excise	25.00						25.00	25.00		25.00					

continued on next page

Table A2.1   continued

OBJECTIVE	INDICATORS (Weight in %)	FISCAL NEED / COST DISABILITY						EQUALIZATION						PERFORMANCE			
		Shareable Pool	Population (1971)	Population (2011)	Area	Forest Cover	Infrastructure Index Distance	Income Distance	Inverse Income	Poverty Ratio	Index of Backwardness	Revenue Equalization	Gap Filling	Tax Collection	Tax Effort	Fiscal Discipline	Other Factors
8th FC (1984–1989)	90% of Shareable Pool of Income Tax		25.00					50.00	25.00								
	10% of Shareable Pool of Income Tax													100.00 As-sessment/ Contribution			
	40% of Union Excise Duties		25.00					50.00	25.00								
	5% of Union Excise Duties												Assessed deficits				
9th FC (1) (1989–1995)	Shareable Pool of Income Tax		25.00					50.00	12.50		12.50						
9th FC (2) (1989–1995)	90% of Shareable Pool of Income Tax		25.00					50.00	12.50	12.50							
	10% of Shareable Pool of Income Tax													100.00 Assessment/ Contribution			
	37.575% of Union Excise Duties		29.94					40.12	14.97		14.97						
	7.425% of Union Excise Duties												Assessed deficits				

continued on next page

Table A2.1   *continued*

OBJECTIVE		FISCAL NEED / COST DISABILITY							EQUALIZATION					PERFORMANCE			
INDICATORS (Weight in %)		Shareable Pool	Population (1971)	Population (2011)	Area	Forest Cover	Infrastructure Index Distance	Income Distance	Inverse Income	Poverty Ratio	Index of Backwardness	Revenue Equalization	Gap Filling	Tax Collection	Tax Effort	Fiscal Discipline	Other Factors
10th FC (1995–2000)	Income Tax		20.00		5.00		5.00	60.00							10.00		
	47.5% of Union Excise Duties		20.00		5.00		5.00	60.00							10.00		
	7.5% of Union Excise Duties																
	Alternative Scheme (sharing of all union taxes after constitutional amendment)		20.00		5.00		5.00	60.00							10.00		
11th FC (2000–2005)	Divisible Pool*		10.00		7.50		7.50	62.50							5.00	7.50	
12th FC (2005–2010)	Divisible Pool*		25.00		10.00			50.00							7.50	7.50	
13th FC (2010–2015)	Divisible Pool*		25.00		10.00			47.50								17.50	
14th FC (2015–2020)	Divisible Pool*		17.50	10.00	15.00	7.50		50.00									

FC = Finance Commission.

Note: The term "tax collection" used by earlier commissions refers to the relative income tax collection by a state government as these commissions treated income tax and excise separately for devolution. The term "tax effort" covers both income tax and excise for the 10th FC, and combined taxes from 11th FC onward. "Tax effort" has generally been defined as a function of own-tax revenue to gross state domestic product ratio.

* The divisible pool consists of all taxes, except surcharges and cess levied for specific-purpose, net of collection charges.

Sources: Authors' compilations from various Finance Commission reports; and D. K. Srivastava and B. C. Rao. 2009. *Review of Trends in Fiscal Transfers in India*. Madras School of Economics.

Intergovernmental Fiscal Transfers—International Case Studies

A. AUSTRALIA	
Type of Government: Federation	**Tiers of Government:** • Federal Government • State Governments • Municipal Governments

Overview of types of transfers from the center

The Commonwealth Grants Commission (CGC) is responsible for the intergovernmental transfer system. There are two main transfers to the state and territorial governments, provisioned by the federal government:
- General Purpose Transfers (Equalization Transfer)
- Specific Purpose Payments (SPPs)

<u>**General Purpose Transfers (Equalization Transfer)**</u>
- They address the horizontal fiscal imbalance among the state and territorial governments.
- They are based on the revenue capacity and expenditure needs of the states. Factors such as (i) interstate cost variation, (ii) the economic and socio-demographic feature of the state population, and (iii) the impact of other Commonwealth transfers are also considered for determining fiscal capacity.
- The goods and service tax (GST) is collected by the Commonwealth and constitutes the main revenue source for transfers. For calculating general purpose transfers, first, the entire GST revenue pool is divided into all states on an equal per capita basis. Then, the revenue is added (subtracted) for the state having the fiscal capacity below (above) the average fiscal capacity of all states, to (from) its share received on equal per capita basis.

<u>**Specific Purpose Payments (SPPs)**</u>
- SPPs are the earmarked grants from the Commonwealth to the states and territories for specific services such as **education, health,** roads, housing, transport, social security etc. to achieve national policy objectives. There are three types of SPPs:
    - (i) direct payment to the state governments,
    - (ii) payments to local governments through state governments, and
    - (iii) direct payments to the local governments.
- SPPs are determined based on the cost-sharing principle and distributed to the states according to the population share on equal per capita basis. They are subject to conditions such as (i) general policy requirement, (ii) matching funds, and (iii) performance reporting.
- The SPPs are deducted for each recipient state while deriving the equalization grants.
- There are three types of PSPs:
    - (i) **National specific purpose payments (NSPPs)** to support the key sectors of service delivery, such as **health care, schools, skill development,** disability services, housing, etc.
    - (ii) **National partnership payments (NPPs)** for facilitation and reward payments so that the specific state or territory receives benefits which are not redistributive to other states or territories.
    - (iii) **National Health Reform Funding** follows activity-based funding based on outcomes.

Do central transfers give specific priority to education? The Australian transfer system provides specific grants for the development of education in Australia.

Specific Purpose Grants for Schools
This funding is distributed among (i) general recurrent grants, (ii) capital grants, and (iii) targeted programs.

The contribution for general recurrent grants by the Commonwealth and respective state government or territory is in the ratio 10:90.

Under the Australian Education Act 2013, capital grants are provided through the Block Grant Authority to nongovernment primary and secondary school communities for improving infrastructure. Capital grants are in addition to the funds provided by state and territory governments, nongovernment school authorities and school communities, which are responsible for maintaining nongovernment school facilities.

Sources: R. Boadway and A. Shah. 2007. Intergovernmental Fiscal Transfers: Principles and Practice. *Public Sector Governance and Accountability Series 38077*. World Bank; J. Clemens and N. Veldhuis. 2013. *Federalism and Fiscal Transfers: Essays on Switzerland, Germany, Australia and United States*. Fraser Institute; K. R. Panta. 2017. *Study on Intergovernmental Fiscal Transfers for Federal Nepal*. Government of Nepal, Ministry of Federal Affairs and Local Development. Local Body Fiscal Commission; and A. Shah. 2012. *Lessons from Worldwide Practices of Intergovernmental Fiscal Transfers*. Presentation at Seminar on Fiscal Federalism. Azores. 5–6 July 2012.

B. CANADA

Type of Government:	Tiers of Government:
Federal	• Federal Government • Provincial Governments • Local Governments

Overview of types of transfers from the center
The four types of federal transfers in Canada and their shares in FY2015 are as follows:
- **Canadian Health Transfers – 49%**
- Canadian Social Transfers –19%
- Equalization Transfers – 26%
- Territorial Formula Financing – 5%

Canadian health transfers and social transfers are specific-purpose grants to minimize the vertical imbalances. Equalization transfers and territorial formula financing are unconditional grants to minimize horizontal fiscal imbalances among provinces.

<u>Canadian Health Transfers</u>
- These are block grants to the provinces and regions for improving their **health services.**
- Provinces utilize this fund according to their need, complying with the Canada Health Act criteria such as universality, comprehensiveness, accessibility, portability, and conditions like no extra billing by physicians and no extra user charges by the hospital.

<u>Canadian Social Transfers</u>
- They may be in the form of cash transfer or tax point transfer.
- These are block transfers to provinces and territories for (i) **post-secondary education**, (ii) social assistance and social services, and (iii) early childhood development and early learning and childcare in accordance with the Federal Provincial Fiscal Arrangement Act.
- The value of the cash transfer is determined by a legislated funding formula, in which payments to provinces and territories are provided on an equal per capita basis and are set to grow by 3% annually since FY2015 according to an automatic escalator.

<u>Equalization Transfers</u>
- Equalization transfers are unconditional transfers to enable all provinces to finance minimum national standard of public services.
- This type of transfer is the only constitutional transfer among the four major transfers.
- It is a formula-based transfer considering fiscal capacity criteria such as per capita income, tax capacity, and national average level of tax and focuses on representative tax bases for different revenue sources.

continued on next page

<u>**Territorial Formula Financing**</u>
- This transfer is given to three territorial governments to address their high cost of public service delivery.
- It is an unconditional grant provided to **hospitals, schools**, and to fund other infrastructures and social services for the large number of small and isolated communities in the north.
- The formula for transfer is the difference between expenditure need and revenue capacity where expenditure need is determined based on large area, extreme weather conditions, and small population.

Do central transfers give specific priority to education?
- Free public education is provided to all Canadian citizens and permanent residents until the end of secondary school (age 18).
- There are no federal transfers for free public education. The elementary and secondary education is entirely funded by provincial or territorial government or through a mix of provincial and territorial transfers and local government taxes or by school boards that have the power to impose taxes.
- In the 1950s and 1960s, federal transfers were "conditional" cost-sharing grants that encouraged the establishment of national programs.
- Over the years, federal support has evolved from cost-sharing programs to block funding transfers such as support for post-secondary education under Canadian social transfers based on acceptance of broad principles and shared objectives.

Sources: J. Clemens and N. Veldhuis. 2013. *Federalism and Fiscal Transfers: Essays on Switzerland, Germany, Australia and United States.* Fraser Institute; K. R. Panta. 2017. *Study on Intergovernmental Fiscal Transfers for Federal Nepal.* Government of Nepal, Ministry of Federal Affairs and Local Development. Local Body Fiscal Commission; and Government of Canada. Department of Finance. Federal Transfers to Provinces and Territories. https://www.canada.ca/en/department-finance/programs/federal-transfers.html.

C. INDONESIA

Type of Government:	**Tiers of Government:**
Unitary	• Central Government • Provincial Governments • Local Governments

Overview of types of transfers from the center
Intergovernmental transfers in Indonesia are as follows:
- (i)   Revenue Sharing
- (ii) General Allocation Fund
- (iii) Specific Allocation Fund
- (iv) Discretionary Specific Purpose Grants

<u>**Revenue Sharing**</u>
There are three types of taxes shared between the central and subnational governments:
- Natural resource taxes (the most significant type of transfer)
- Personal income tax
- Property taxes

<u>**General Allocation Fund – DAU (Dana Alokasi Umum)**</u>
- It is the most important transfer, financing over 50% of subnational government expenditures.
- The DAU is a general-purpose block grant, giving full discretion to local governments to spend the funds according to their priorities.
- It is allocated based on a national formula, which is the sum of a basic allocation (a portion of the subnational budget for public servant salaries) and the "fiscal gap" (the difference between the estimated fiscal needs and fiscal capacity) of the subnational government.
- Fiscal needs are based on regional variables such as population, area, per capita gross domestic product, construction price index, and the human development index. Fiscal capacity is measured by a region's own-source revenue and a fraction of total revenue-sharing.

continued on next page

<u>**Specific Allocation Fund – DAK (Dana Aokasi Khusus)**</u>
- DAK is a conditional or earmarked transfer scheme allocated to specific regions and certain sectoral programs.
- DAK seeks to equalize the minimum standard of services of national priority among certain levels of jurisdictions.
- DAK allocation areas include **education, health,** agriculture, forestry, trade, and various infrastructure sectors (road, irrigation, water, sanitation, rural electricity, housing and local government, and remote areas infrastructure).
- DAK transfers are determined based on
  - **General fiscal position.** Subnational governments that are below the average fiscal position, net of employee compensation and benefits, are deemed eligible.
  - **Specific criteria** are determined by relevant line ministries. Some specific criteria include regions providing preferential access to local governments in Papua and West Papua, coastal areas and islands, areas that border other countries, regions of interest for food security or tourism reasons, disaster-prone areas, and less-developed areas.
  - **Technical criteria** are set by line agencies, in consultation with the Ministry of Finance, the Ministry of Home Affairs, and the Ministry of Planning. These criteria include macroeconomic, service-related, administrative, and needs-based indicators.
  - **Matching requirements.** The region is obliged to allocate a minimum of 10% of the total DAK they receive as co-funding.

These criteria are used by progressively combining them and setting cutoffs to eliminate some of the local governments at each stage.

<u>**Discretionary Specific Purpose Grants**</u>
Discretionary grants constitute two parts:
- *Special Autonomy Fund* is provided to the three jurisdictions—Aceh, Papua, and West Papua.
- The remaining portion is completely discretionary and distributed on ad hoc basis.

Do central transfers give specific priority to education?
The 12 years of compulsory education consists of 6 years at elementary level and 3 each at middle and high school levels. The details on education-related funding are given below:

Revenue Sharing
Local governments use 0.5% of their revenue sharing receipts from the natural resources on basic education.

DAK Allocation
- Out of the 19 sectors funded under DAK in 2011, **education** is a key priority.
- Weightage to **education**: About 40% of DAK transfers is allocated for education and used primarily for school rehabilitation and quality improvement.

DAK allocation is earmarked for capital spending, but routine maintenance expenditure is also allowed.

Special Autonomy and Adjustment Funds
- Specific grants for Papua, Papua Barat, and Aceh
- Special Adjustment Funds include additional allowances for teachers, such as professional benefits for certified teachers and for uncertified civil service teachers.
- Local incentive grants (Dana Insentif Daerah or DID) reward districts that demonstrate improved education performance. These funds used to be earmarked but since 2015 local governments have been free to use them according to local needs.
- School Operational Assistance Program (Bantuan Operasional Sekolah) provides the same per-student amount on a quarterly basis to all government and nongovernment schools. The amount is determined based on operational expenditure needs of schools as well as the availability of the budget. Schools have flexibility on the use of funds.

Sources: Asian Development Bank Institute (ADBI). 2017. Central and Local Government Relations in Asia. Edited by N. Yoshino and P. Morgan. Elgar Publishing, Inc.; B. Lewis and P. Smoke. 2017. Intergovernmental Fiscal Transfers and Local Incentives and Responses: The Case of Indonesia. *Fiscal Studies*; K. R. Panta. 2017. *Study on Intergovernmental Fiscal Transfers for Federal Nepal.* Government of Nepal, Ministry of Federal Affairs and Local Development. Local Body Fiscal Commission; and P. Smoke and Y. Kim. 2002. *Intergovernmental Fiscal Transfers in Asia: Current Practice and Challenges for the Future.* Asian Development Bank.

D. JAPAN

Type of Government: Unitary	**Tiers of Government:** • Central Government • Prefectures • Municipalities

Overview of types of transfers from the center

The Ministry of Finance coordinates resource allocation between the central and local governments. The ratio of central to local government expenditure in Japan is about 40:60 while the ratio of central to local tax collection is the reverse (60:40). Three types of funds are transferred to local governments: (i) the local allocation tax (LAT) grants, and (ii) local transfer tax (LTT) grants, both of which are general-purpose transfers; and (iii) central government subsidies (CGSs) and national treasury disbursements, which are specific-purpose transfers.

Local allocation tax (LAT) grants
- The LAT grants are legally linked to the amount of five national taxes (corporate tax, consumption tax, income tax, liquor tax, and tobacco tax) and constitute the largest transfer from the central government to the local governments; and 32% of revenues from corporate tax, income tax, and liquor tax; 29.5% of revenues from consumption tax; and 25% of revenues from tobacco excise are allocated to the LAT grants. These percentages are periodically amended to ensure the adequacy of LAT.
- If the LAT turns out to be insufficient, the central government sometimes tops up supplementary grants from the general budget to the LAT before allocation to the local bodies.
- The LAT is provided each year to the local governments as a general-purpose transfer. It is separated into two components: an "ordinary" LAT, accounting for 94% of the total, and a "special" LAT, comprising the remaining 6%. The ordinary LAT covers local services and has also an equalization function. The special LAT covers emergency expenses such as those for natural disasters. These two funds are calculated separately for each local body.
- The ordinary LAT grants that each prefecture and municipality receives is set as the difference between estimated expenditures and the sum of local tax revenues, the CGS, and local borrowing.

Local transfer tax (LTT)
- The LTT includes local gasoline transfer tax and other taxes that are collected at a national level and then transferred directly to local governments. Each local government receives an amount based on its population and the number of employed people in its jurisdiction.

Central government subsidies (CGS)
- The CGS is composed of purpose-specific categorical grants directly disbursed from the budgets of central ministries. The use of CGS is decided by the national government. The CGS allows local governments to maintain uniform services required by national laws and adopt projects that contribute to national objectives.

Do central transfers give specific priority to education?
- Central government transfers support local governments in key social sectors. Local government expenditures include social welfare, public **health** and sanitation, agriculture, forestry and fisheries, commerce and industry, civil engineering, **education,** and debt services. The breakdown of local government expenditure shows social welfare (24.1%) is followed by **education** (16.5%) and civil engineering works (12.4%).
- Social welfare services include the development and operation of welfare facilities for children, the elderly, and people with disabilities.
- Funds support various **public health and mental health programs** and sanitation services to promote health of the residents.
- **Education** is one of the basic administrative areas of local governments. Expenditure is made toward schools and social education programs.

Source: S. Bessho. 2017. A Study of Central and Local Government Finance in Japan. In N. Yoshino and P. Morgan, eds. *Central and Local Government Relations in Asia*. US: Edward Elgar Publishing, Inc.

E. PEOPLE'S REPUBLIC OF CHINA (PRC)

Type of Government:	Tiers of Government:
Unitary	<ul><li>Central</li><li>Provincial</li><li>Prefectural</li><li>County Level</li><li>Township</li></ul>

Overview of types of transfers from the center

As of 2011, there are three types of transfers from the center to provinces in the PRC:

General Transfers – 46%
- Equalization transfer – 19%
- Pension and social security – 9%
- Wage adjustment and civil service – 7%
- Compulsory Education – 3%
- Others – 10%

Earmarked Transfers – 42%
- Agriculture, forestry, and water – 12%
- Transportation – 9%
- Affordable housing – 4%
- Energy saving and pollution abatement – 4%
- Social security and employment – 4%
- Others – 9%

Compensation Transfers – 12%

<u>General Transfers</u>

General transfers are used to lower disparities in expenditure. There are five types of general transfers, of which two are discussed below:
- **Equalization transfers** lower spending inequality across the country.
  - <u>Basis of calculation:</u> The revenue capacity is estimated using the tax bases and standard tax rates, while the current expenditure is calculated based on per capita spending for categories of outlays adjusted for cost factors such as altitude, population density, temperature, transport distance, and the proportion of the population belonging to minority groups.
  - <u>Categories of spending:</u> The categories of spending include administration services, public safety, **education,** urban maintenance, **health care,** environmental protection, and social assistance.
  - <u>Provision of performance-based rewards:</u> Additional grants are given to provinces that achieve better fiscal equalization results at sub-provincial levels.
- **Wage adjustment grant** fills the fiscal gap caused by the central policy mandate of increasing wages of public sector employees. Provinces facing difficulties in paying wages of teachers in rural elementary and middle schools are compensated under this transfer.

<u>Earmarked Transfers</u>
- These transfers are used to subsidize local projects subject to matching outlays by local government.
- As of 2013, there were 220 specific-purpose grants, delivered on an ad hoc negotiated basis.
- These grants range from infrastructure development, basic construction, **education,** and **health care,** to disaster relief as well as general operating funds for government administration and public service.

<u>Compensation Transfers</u>
- These are designed to reduce the revenue losses accruing to local governments following the 1994 tax reform. The compensation payment declines with rising income.

continued on next page

Do central transfers give specific priority to education?
- The compulsory education transfer is only paid to rural counties to compensate for the abolition of the agricultural tax, previously used for funding education.
- Spending on basic education in the PRC is a prime responsibility of county-level governments.
- In 2006 and 2015, two special programs targeting teachers were created to improve education and attract more qualified teachers to rural and remote areas.

Sources: Asian Development Bank Institute (ADBI). 2017. Central and Local Government Relations in Asia. Edited by N. Yoshino and P. Morgan. Elgar Publishing Inc.; J. Martínez-Vázquez et al. 2006. Local Public Finance in China: Intergovernmental Transfers. *CEMA Working Papers 552*. China Economics and Management Academy, Central University of Finance and Economics; and K. R. Panta. 2017. *Study on Intergovernmental Fiscal Transfers for Federal Nepal*. Government of Nepal, Ministry of Federal Affairs and Local Development. Local Body Fiscal Commission.

F. REPUBLIC OF KOREA

Type of Government:
Unitary

Tiers of Government:
- Central Government
- Metropolitan City
- Province
- Municipality

Overview of types of transfers from the center
There are two major grant sources: (i) Local Shared Tax (LST), and (ii) National Treasury Subsidy.

Local Shared Tax
- It includes distribution of a fixed portion of domestic tax revenue. The local shared tax is further divided into Ordinary LST and Special LST.
- Equalization formula for distribution of Ordinary LST calculates standardized fiscal needs, revenue, and their difference for each local government.
- Special LST is used to finance fiscal emergency of local governments, projects of national interests, recovery of natural disasters, and regional development. It is based on government discretion.

National Treasury Subsidy
- National treasury subsidy includes discretionary categorical grants provided by the central governments for specific projects such as social welfare and fiscal needs of local autonomy. They vary every year.
- The system was reformed in 2005 with implementation of a block-grant called Special Account for Balanced National Development, which uses a distribution formula factoring population, area, the ratio of old aged people, fiscal capacity index, and regional income. It includes over 100 specific grants.

Do central transfers give specific priority to education?
- Public spending for primary and secondary education is managed by local education offices. The central government provides major financing using local education subsidy that is based on estimated differences between standard fiscal demand and standard fiscal revenue of local governments. Under Article 5 of the Local Education Subsidy Act, special subsidies support local governments in operating local educational administration. The education tax is distributed based on population of the province.
- The revenue of education tax, a national tax, is transferred to a special account for Local Education Transfer Fund, managed by the Ministry of Education and Human Resource Development. The fund is then sent to the Local Education Special Account. The revenue of local education tax, collected by local governments, is also sent to the Local Education Special Account.
- Education expenditures are financed by central government general grants for education (76%), transfers from local governments (18%), and tuition and fees (6%). Local education subsidies, composed of 20.27% of internal taxes and 100% of education taxes, are granted to 17 city and provincial education offices. This grant is divided into general subsidies (total amount of education tax and 96% of the 20.27% of internal taxes) provided to education units whose standard fiscal income falls below the standard fiscal demand; and special subsidies (4% of the 20.27% of internal taxes) for special fiscal demands of local education offices.

Sources: H. Kim. 2018. Fiscal Decentralization and Inclusive Growth: Considering Education. In J. Kim and S. Dougherty, eds. *Fiscal Decentralization and Inclusive Growth*. Chapter 6. pp. 127–151. OECD and Korean Institute of Public Finance; and Government of the Republic of Korea, Ministry of Strategy and Finance (MOSF). 2014. *Budget System of Korea*.

G. SOUTH AFRICA

Type of Government: Quasi Federal	**Tiers of Government:** • Central Government • Provincial Governments • Local Governments

Overview of types of transfers from the center

The Financial and Fiscal Commission provides recommendations on the intergovernmental fiscal relations. The transfers in South Africa are (i) Equitable Share Grants (80%), and (ii) Conditional Grants (20%).

Equitable Share Grant
- **Provincial Equitable Share Grant** is a formula-based transfer system for unconditional grants to provincial governments, consisting of six components—**education, health,** poverty, economic activity, institutional, and basic (share of population).
- Each province decides how to divide its lump sum between the different provincial social services (**education, health,** welfare, housing, and community development).
- **Local Government Equitable Share Grant** is an unconditional transfer to local governments determined based on poverty, access to service, basic services, quality of services, population growth, municipal size, projected own-revenue of wealthier local governments and poor local governments.

Conditional Grants

The national government provides four types of conditional grants:
- Supplementary grant
- Financing for specific program of national interest
- Specific purpose in-kind grant for special program
- Grant for disaster management for the basic services to achieve the uniformity among all citizens

Do central transfers give specific priority to education?

The Constitution of South Africa provides everyone the right to basic education. The National Treasury allocates funds to the provinces and it is at the discretion of the provincial government to allocate funds for public welfare like **education, health,** agriculture, rural development, etc. For FY2017, the total basic education budget of the country can be categorized into following:
- Provincial Equitable Share Grant – 89.7%
- National Department of Basic Education Expenditure – 2.8%
- Conditional Grants – 7.5%

Provincial Equitable Share Grant
- The equitable share formula includes **education** as one of the components of transfer. It carries a weightage of 48% in the formula.
- The indicators used are size of the school-age population (ages 5 to 17) and the number of learners enrolled in public schools.
- The percentages allocated to **education** consider the proportion of expenditure on this sector from the historical provincial allocation.
- The equitable share formula only serves to calculate each province's share of the overall provincial allocation. It does not prescribe the method of expenditure by the province. Each province decides on the division of its lump sum between different social services (**education, health,** welfare, and housing).

Conditional Grants
- Curriculum policy, support, and monitoring
- Teacher education, human resources, and institutional development
- Planning information and assessment
- Educational enrichment services

Source: K. R. Panta. 2017. *Study on Intergovernmental Fiscal Transfers for Federal Nepal.* Government of Nepal, Ministry of Federal Affairs and Local Development. Local Body Fiscal Commission.

Medium-Term Expenditure Framework Preparation Methodology

1. A medium-term expenditure framework (MTEF) is prepared for a medium term of 3 years, which includes the budget year as the first year, and then estimates for the next 2 years. The years following the budget year are referred to as the outer years of the MTEF and the estimates for these years are technically called "forward estimates." The process of MTEF preparation is presented below and illustrated in Figure A4.1:

A. Top–Down Budgeting

2. This involves estimating the "resource envelope" for a department by projecting the likely multiyear availability of resources for expenditures to better prioritize resources and their optimal utilization among various schemes. A three-step methodology is used:

3. **Step I: Estimating fiscal policy resource envelope for state total expenditure.** This step involves projection of affordable resource envelope available for state total expenditure for the next 3 years consistent with the state's medium-term fiscal framework (MTFF) and its Fiscal Responsibility and Budget Management (FRBM) Act.

4. **Step II: Estimating sectoral state plan resource envelope available to state.** This step involves projection of total state plan expenditure in the sector for the next 3 years consistent with the state's explicit sectoral priorities in its long-term planning exercise (five-year plan and/or state annual plan). State plan spending includes expenditure under both state plan schemes and centrally sponsored schemes (CSS). To arrive at the sectoral resource envelope, the past share of sector plan spending in total state plan spending is applied for future projections.

5. **Step III: Estimating MTEF resource envelope for the department.** This stage involves estimating total budget resources available for departmental expenditure during MTEF period. After estimating the past share of departmental spending in the concerned sector, resource availability from the center for the departmental schemes and non-plan expenditure are projected based on the historical trend.

B. Bottom–Up Budgeting

6. Expenditure requirements to sustain current level of performance in service delivery under the trend scenario are estimated, followed by estimating the required additional cost for achieving desired targets under suggested interventions. The methodology is explained below:

7. **"Baseline Budget" or "Trend Scenario".** This entails estimation of expenditure requirement for maintaining and sustaining current or baseline level of performance in service delivery by a department. Projections are made at detailed head level for all schemes at their historical rates (i.e., utilization of the allocated budget observed in the past, pay commission rates or inflation growth rate for committed expenses, and/or past trend growth rates).

8. **"Above the Baseline Budget" or "Costed Reform Interventions".** A logical framework is constructed to show the connections between outputs of the schemes, department objectives and/or outcomes, and long-term sectoral and societal government goals. This helps identify scope for (i) convergence of programs and/or schemes that have similar objectives, (ii) group the schemes for better

Figure A4.1   Medium-Term Expenditure Framework Preparation Methodology

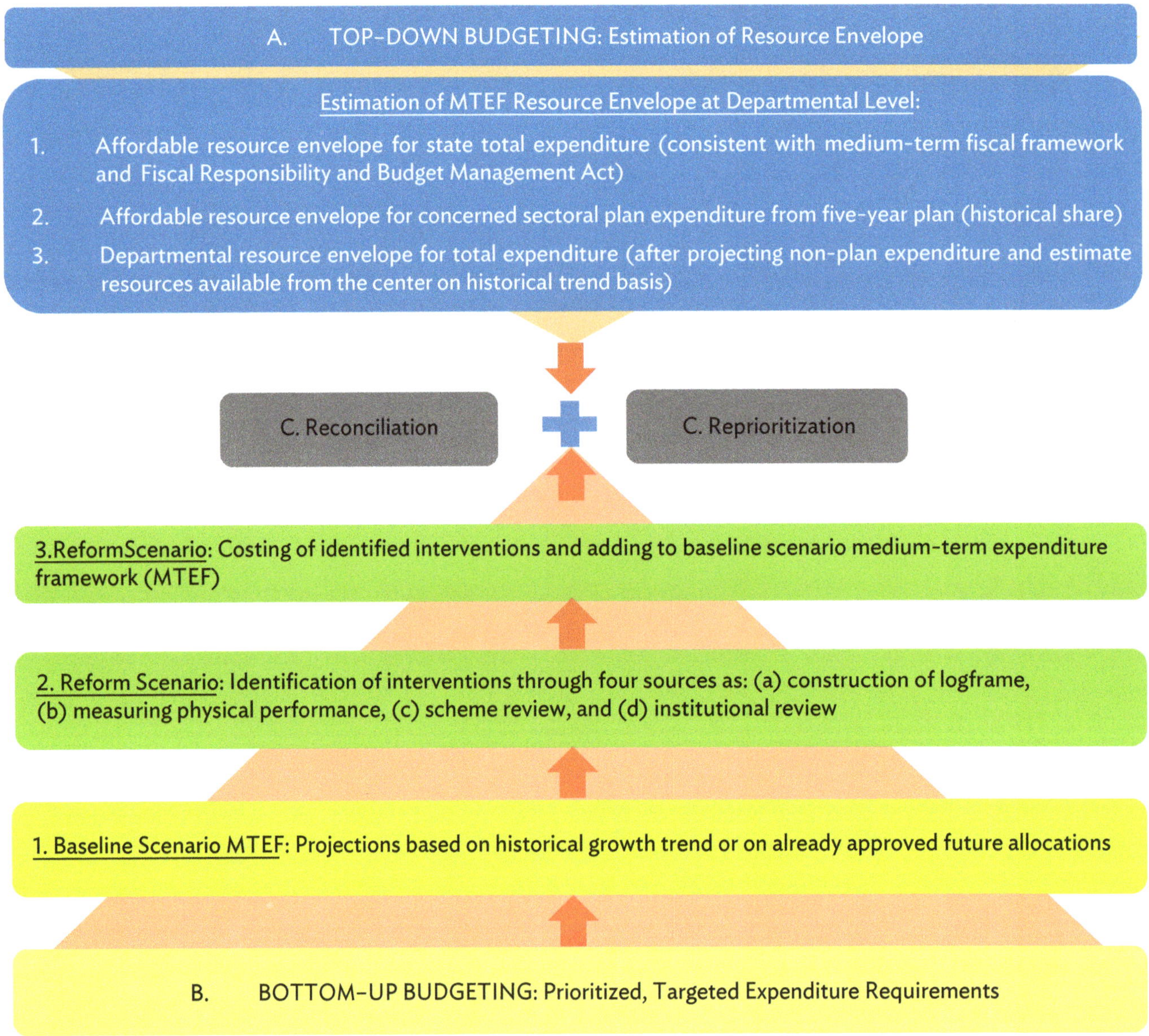

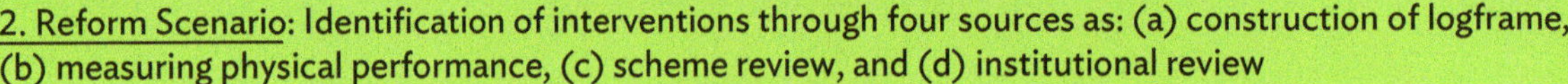

Source: Asian Development Bank.

targeting and administrative efficiency, and (iii) focus areas not targeted in a structured manner. After establishing the results chain for each scheme of the department, performance indicators for monitoring and measuring progress or change are identified for result-orientation in MTEF. The performance indicators provide the evidence-based updating of MTEF projections in the next cycle. An assessment of the status of the department's performance on performance indicators at both scheme output level and outcome (results of department objective) level is undertaken as compared with the national average and other progressive states. Scheme reviews and/or evaluations are undertaken based on past expenditure analysis and examination of design and implementation. Finally, institutional review of the department is undertaken to study effectiveness of service delivery and identify areas of improvement.

9. Once the interventions that will achieve the targeted performance level are identified, the additional funding requirement over the trend scenario expenditure projections is estimated. The methodology for costing of these interventions include, among others, (i) estimating the per unit per input cost based on norms set at the national level or at states, which have already implemented such interventions; and (ii) costing inputs using existing scheme guidelines and/or inflation indexation.

10. Following the costing of interventions, the respective head of accounts under which the expenditure is made are identified by mapping the targeted performance indicator under each intervention to the schemes via the logical framework.

C. Reconciliation and Reprioritization

11. This involves matching of estimated expenditure requirements under bottom–up budgeting with anticipated resource availability, and if the resource constraint is binding, then suggesting prioritization of expenditure.

12. In case of surplus funds, additional interventions can be proposed to utilize the excess. In case of deficit, the department may (i) request more funds from the central schemes, (ii) gather additional resources from the Finance Commission grants, (iii) identify savings and potential efficiency gains through scrutiny of existing spending, or (iv) identify low priority programs to reduce allocation. A lower budget can be allocated to the schemes, which are relatively inefficient in attainment of the outputs and objectives of department and/or contribute to the bottom 10% of total departmental expenditure. The MTEF as a budgeting tool can help states consolidate the state schemes and CSS and improve monitoring and audit.

D. Update of MTEF Exercise

13. The departmental MTEF is updated annually by rolling over into the next (overlapping) 3-year period. The MTEF provides evidence-based feedback for subsequent rounds of budgeting and decision-making. While measuring performance, the reasons explaining the gaps observed, i.e., underspending or cost and time overruns, will accordingly inform the target setting and budgeting when the 3-year MTEF is rolled over in the next year. However, non-attainment of performance need not invariably lead to lower outlay in the subsequent round. Officials can be made accountable to explain the reasons for the outcomes.

Case Studies in the Implementation of Medium-Term Expenditure Framework in India

1. **West Bengal.** Under the West Bengal Development Finance Program of the Asian Development Bank (ADB) poverty-focused and gender-responsive medium-term expenditure frameworks (MTEFs) were prepared and linked to the actual budget allocations for the Health and Family Welfare Department (HFWD), School Education Department (SED), and Public Works Department (PWD). The HFWD's MTEF for FY2014–FY2016 included interventions such as (i) construction of primary health care infrastructure catering to rural areas, and (ii) improved public education and communication promoting the delivery of babies in health care institutions to reduce the maternal and infant mortality rates. Greater coverage of health care facilities across the state, and accessibility for women and children helped improve the effective delivery of health care services. The SED's MTEF included interventions such as monthly stipends to all secondary and higher-secondary school students living below the poverty line, the universalization of elementary and secondary education, and ensuring 100% enrollment of female students, especially those from backward and minority communities. For the PWD, construction work on district roads and enhanced transport services improved the connectivity of underserved communities.

2. **Punjab.** The Government of Punjab approved its state-level FRBM rules in 2018, pursuant to the Punjab Fiscal Responsibility and Budget Management (FRBM) Act (2003 and amended 2011). A new requirement under the FRBM rules is the preparation of a medium-term fiscal policy statement with fiscal targets for the next 2 years in addition to current year revised estimates and ensuing year target budget estimates. Thus, 3-year rolling targets are introduced in line with the amended FRBM rules of the Government of India

for effective and credible fiscal programming. Under ADB's Punjab Development Finance Program, the Finance Department prepared a multiyear medium-term fiscal framework (MTFF) for FY2017, FY2018, and FY2019, and estimates of FY2017 were closely reflected in the budget.

3. Another new feature of the FRBM rules is that the state government is granted the authority to issue directives to any or all its departments to prepare and implement MTEFs, incorporating expenditure growth for 3–5 years, expenditure rationalization measures, and gender- and poverty-based budget prioritization. If a department fails to implement the MTEF by the stipulated deadline, it must provide a report before the state legislature, explaining the reasons for failure and present a plan to achieve the targets within 1 year of the completion of the MTEF. Implementation of MTEF paves the way for effectively linking macro-fiscal targets with department-wise budgetary allocations and performance targets as well as more focused use of resources. The Finance Department approved MTEFs for FY2017, FY2018, and FY2019 for the SED, HFWD, PWD, and the Power Department consistent with MTFF, and the estimates for FY2017, closely aligned with the MTEF projections, were reflected in state budget allocations.

4. The MTEF projections incorporated allocations for gender-responsive programs. The SED identified 20 schemes, targeting reduction of gender disparity, increase in female literacy, and female (secondary) school attendance as performance indicators. The HFWD identified 12 rural and urban health care schemes, targeting increase in pregnant women receiving antenatal care visits, institutional delivery of babies, immunization, reductions in maternal mortality rates, and eradication of malnutrition.

Ayushman Bharat Scheme

1. In India, 86% of rural households and 82% of urban households do not have access to health care insurance (National Sample Survey Office 2015). More than 17% of India's population spends at least 10% of their household budget for health care services. Catastrophic health care expenditures push families into debt with more than 24% of rural households and 18% of urban population having met their health care expenses through borrowings. In order to address these structural weaknesses in the health care system and fulfill the vision of *Health for All* and *Universal Health Coverage* as envisaged under the National Health Policy 2017, the Government of India conceived the Ayushman Bharat Scheme (ABS). The ABS adopts a continuum of care approach by moving away from sectoral and segmented health service delivery to a comprehensive need-based health care services (Ministry of Health and Family Welfare [MOHFW] 2018a). It has two interrelated components:

2. **Health and Wellness Centers (HWCs)**. The first component of ABS is the creation of 150,000 HWCs, which will provide comprehensive primary health care, accessible by the community within 30 minutes of walking distance. The scope of existing services from primary health centers is proposed to be broadened, and a package of 12 services will be implemented, such as free essential drugs and diagnostics, services for maternal and child health care, screening for noncommunicable diseases, and follow-up of hospitalization cases, among others. The HWCs will play a critical role in creating awareness about the Pradhan Mantri Jan Arogya Yojana (PM-JAY).

3. **Pradhan Mantri Jan Arogya Yojana (PM-JAY)**. The second component of ABS is the PM-JAY, which will help reduce catastrophic expenditure for hospitalizations and mitigate the financial risk arising out of catastrophic health episodes through cashless and paperless access to services at the point of health care delivery (MOHFW 2018b). The PM-JAY will provide up to ₹500,000 per family per year for secondary and tertiary care hospitalization. As per the latest socioeconomic caste census data for both rural and urban areas and the active families under the Rashtriya Swasthya Bima Yojana, the PM-JAY will benefit over 107.4 million vulnerable families (approximately 500 million people).

4. The National Health Agency under the Ministry of Health and Family Welfare is the apex body, responsible for the design, rollout, and implementation of PM-JAY. The state governments will set up the state health agencies on similar lines.

5. For HWCs, funding is released in the ratio of 60 (center): 40 (state) by GOI to the treasury in the state, and from there to state health societies, which are autonomous. For PM-JAY, funds will flow from the central government to a separate designated escrow account in a Ministry of Finance approved bank and it will have a contribution from the state governments in the ratio of 60 (center): 40 (state).

The Health Index

Table A7.1   Indicators under the Health Index

No.	Indicator	Definition
DOMAIN 1—HEALTH OUTCOMES		
SUB-DOMAIN 1.1—KEY OUTCOMES (Weight: Larger States – 500, Smaller States and Union Territories – 100)		
1.1.1	Neonatal mortality rate	Number of infant deaths of less than 29 days per thousand live births during a specific year
1.1.2	Under-five mortality rate (U5MR)	Number of child deaths of less than 5 years per thousand live births during a specific year
1.1.3	Total fertility rate (TFR)	Average number of children that would be born to a woman if she experiences the current fertility pattern throughout her reproductive span (15–49 years), during a specific year
1.1.4	Proportion of low birth weight among newborns	Proportion of low birth weight (<=2.5 kg) newborns out of the total number of newborns weighed during a specific year born in a public health facility
1.1.5	Sex ratio at birth	The number of girls born for every 1,000 boys born during a specific year
SUB-DOMAIN 1.2—INTERMEDIATE OUTCOMES (Weight: Larger and Smaller States – 300, Union Territories – 250)		
1.2.1	Full immunization coverage (%)	Proportion of infants 9–11 months old who have received Bacillus Calmette-Guerin (BCG); 3 doses of diphtheria, tetanus, and pertussis (DPT); 3 doses of oral polio vaccine (OPV); and one dose of measles against estimated number of infants during a specific year
1.2.2	Proportion of institutional deliveries	Proportion of deliveries conducted in public and private health facilities against the number of estimated deliveries during a specific year
1.2.3	Total case notification rate of tuberculosis	Number of new and relapsed tuberculosis cases notified (public + private) per 100,000 population during a specific year
1.2.4	Treatment success rate of new microbiologically confirmed tuberculosis cases	Proportion of new cured and their treatment completed against the total number of new microbiologically confirmed tuberculosis cases registered during a specific year
1.2.5	Proportion of people living with human immunodeficiency virus (HIV) (PLHIV) on antiretroviral therapy (ART)	Proportion of PLHIVs receiving ART treatment against the number of estimated PLHIVs who needed ART treatment for the specific year
1.2.6	Out of pocket expenditure per delivery in public health facility	Average out of pocket expenditure per delivery in public health facility (in rupees)

continued on next page

Table A7.1   *continued*

No.	Indicator	Definition
DOMAIN 2—GOVERNANCE AND INFORMATION		
SUB-DOMAIN 2.1—HEALTH MONITORING AND DATA INTEGRITY (Weight: 70)		
2.1.1	Data integrity measure: a. Institutional deliveries b. Antenatal care (ANC) registered within first trimester	Percentage deviation of reported data from standard survey data to assess the quality/integrity of reported data for a specific period
SUB-DOMAIN 2.2—GOVERNANCE (Weight: 60)		
2.2.1	Average occupancy of an officer (in months), combined for following three posts at state level for last 3 years	Average occupancy of an officer (in months), combined for following posts in last 3 years
2.2.2	Average occupancy of a full-time officer (in months) in last 3 years for all districts—district chief medical officers (CMOs) or equivalent post (heading district health services)	Average occupancy (in months) of a CMO in last 3 years for all the districts
DOMAIN 3—KEY INPUTS / PROCESSES		
SUB DOMAIN 3.1—HEALTH SYSTEMS/SERVICE DELIVERY (Weight: 200)		
3.1.1	Proportion of vacant health care provider positions (regular + contractual) in public health facilities	Vacant health care provider positions in public health facilities against total sanctioned health care provider positions for following cadres (separately for each cadre) during a specific year
3.1.2	Proportion of total staff (regular + contractual) for whom an e-pay slip can be generated in the information technology (IT)-enabled Human Resource Management Information System (HRMIS).	Availability of a functional IT-enabled HRMIS measured by the proportion of staff (regular + contractual) for whom an e-pay slip can be generated in the IT-enabled HRMIS against total number of staff (regular + contractual) during a specific year
3.1.3	a. Proportion of specified type of facilities functioning as first referral units (FRUs)	Proportion of public sector facilities conducting specified number of C-sections* per year (FRUs) against the norm of 1 FRU per 500,000 population during a specific year
	b. Proportion of functional 24x7 primary health centers (PHCs)	Proportion of PHCs providing all stipulated health care services** round the clock against the norm of one 24x7 PHC per 100,000 population during a specific year
3.1.4	Proportion of districts with functional cardiac care units (CCUs)	Proportion of districts with functional CCU [with desired equipment (ventilator, monitor, defibrillator, CCUs bed, portable ECG machine, pulse oxymeter, etc.), drugs, diagnostics, and desired staff as per program guidelines] against total number of districts
3.1.5	Proportion of ANC registered within first trimester against total registrations	Proportion of pregnant women registered for ANC within 12 weeks of pregnancy during a specific year.
3.1.6	Level of registration of births (%)	Proportion of births registered under the Civil Registration System against the estimated number of births during a specific year
3.1.7	Completeness of Integrated Disease Surveillance Programme reporting of P and L form	Proportion of reporting units reporting in stipulated time period against total reporting units, for P and L forms during a specific year

continued on next page

Table A7.1   *continued*

No.	Indicator	Definition
3.1.8	Proportion of community health centers (CHCs) with grading above 3 points	Proportion of CHCs that are graded above 3 points against total number of CHCs during a specific year
3.1.9	Proportion of public health facilities with accreditation certificates by a standard quality assurance program (National Quality Assurance Standards / National Accreditation Board for Hospitals and Health Care Providers / International Organization for Standardization / Association of Health Care Providers [India])	Proportion of specified type of public health facilities with accreditation certificates by a standard quality assurance program against the total number of following specified type of facilities during a specific year
3.1.10	Average number of days for transfer of central National Health Mission fund from state treasury to implementation agency based on all tranches of the last financial year	Average time taken (in number of days) by the state treasury to transfer funds to implementation agencies during a specific year

Source: NITI Aayog. 2019. *Healthy States, Progressive India: Report on the Ranks of States and Union Territories. June 2019 Health Index.* Ministry of Health and Family Welfare and World Bank. New Delhi. http://social.niti.gov.in/uploads/sample/health_index_report.pdf. Table is available at http://social.niti.gov.in/health-index.

Education Sector in India

A. Institutional Mechanism for Education in India

1. At the national level, the Ministry of Human Resource Development (MHRD) regulates the education sector and is in charge of the overall education policy planning. At the state level, education departments in each state administer the schools and state regulatory bodies. In higher education, the state departments work with central bodies and councils such as the University Grants Commission and the All India Council of Technical Education. Table A8.1 presents the summary of institutions at each level of education in India. Figure A8.1 provides the level-wise education expenditure in FY2015 (budget estimate [BE]).

Figure A8.1   Level-Wise Total Education Expenditure in FY2015

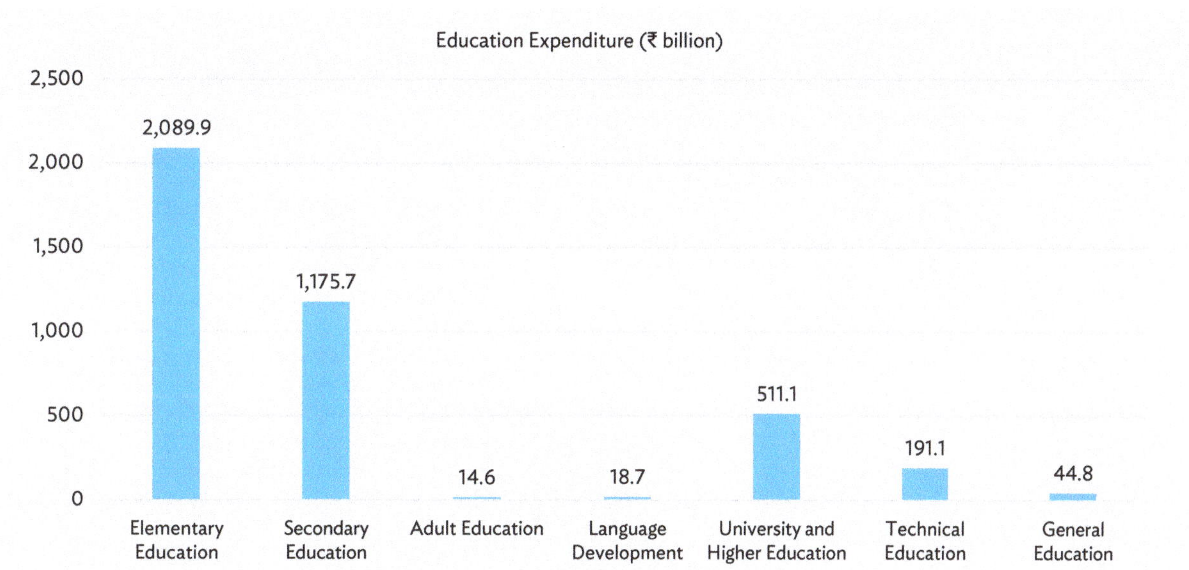

FY = fiscal year.
Source: Authors' compilation from the Analysis of Budget Expenditure FY2013 to FY2015 (budget estimate), Planning, Monitoring and Statistics Bureau, Ministry of Human Resource Development.

Table A8.1   Education Levels and Institutions

Elementary Education	Class 1 to Class 8 divided into two parts: • Primary which consists of Class 1 to Class 5 • Upper primary from Class 6 to Class 8	• National Council of Educational Research and Training • State Government Boards of Education • Central Board for Secondary Education • Council for Indian School Certificate Exam • National Institute of Open Schooling
Secondary Education	Class 9 and Class 10	
Higher Secondary	Class 11 and Class 12	
University Education	• 45 central universities, of which 40 are under the purview of MHRD • 318 state universities • 185 state private universities • 129 deemed universities • 51 institutions of national importance (established under Acts of Parliament) under MHRD (Indian Institutes of Technology [IITs]—16, National Institutes of Technology [NITs]—30, and Indian Institutes of Science Education and Research [IISERs]—5) • 4 institutions (established under various state legislations)	• University Grants Commission (UGC)
Adult Education	Aims at extending educational options to adults, who have crossed the age of formal education, but feel a need for learning of any type, including literacy, basic education, skill development (vocational education), and equivalency	• Ministry of Human Resource Development (MHRD)
Technical Education	Covers programs in engineering, technology, management, architecture, town planning, pharmacy, applied arts and crafts, hotel management, catering technology	• All India Council for Technical Education (AICTE) • Indian Council for Agriculture Research (ICAR) • National Council for Teacher Education (NCTE) • Rehabilitation Council of India (RCI) • Medical Council of India (MCI) • Indian Nursing Council (INC) • Dentist Council of India (DCI) • Central Council of Homeopathy (CCH) • Central Council of Indian Medicine (CCIM), etc.
Language Development	Promotion and development of Hindi and other 21 languages listed in schedule VIII of the Constitution, including Sanskrit and Urdu. In fulfilling the constitutional responsibility, the Department of Higher Education is assisted by autonomous organizations and subordinate offices.	UGC funds the following institutions: 1. Shri Lal Bahadur Shastri Rashtriya Sanskrit Vidyapeetha, New Delhi 2. Rashtriya Sanskrit Vidyapeetha, Tirupati 3. English and Foreign Languages University, Hyderabad 4. Mahatma Gandhi Antarrashtriya Hindi Vishwavidyalaya, Maharashtra 5. Maulana Azad National Urdu University, Hyderabad 6. Rashtriya Sanskrit Sansthan, New Delhi

Source: Authors' compilation from the Indian Standard Classification of Education, Ministry of Human Resource Development.

B. Analysis of Education Performance Indicators across Non-Special Category States

2. **Gross enrollment ratio (GER).** Class enrollment has been consistently increasing from FY2003 to FY2012 at both the primary and upper primary level. However, between FY2013 and FY2016, while enrollment increased at the upper primary level, it decreased at the primary level. In FY2016, 129.12 million students enrolled in primary school, and 67.59 million students enrolled at the upper primary school. The all-India average GER stood at 99.21 at the primary level and 92.81 at the upper primary level in FY2016. There exists a disparity across states (Figure A8.2).

3. The GER in Bihar, Jharkhand, Odisha, Punjab, Tamil Nadu, and West Bengal has been higher than the all-India average at both the primary and upper primary level. With the high rate of enrollment, these states require relatively more infrastructure facilities and funds.

4. The Supreme Court of India has also ruled that certain basic facilities, like separate toilets for boys and girls, and drinking water should be available in all schools, including those run by minority communities. However, many states have not yet fully achieved these targets. While Goa, Punjab, Tamil Nadu, Gujarat, Rajasthan, and Telangana were the only states to have achieved separate girls' toilets in all schools by FY2016; Jharkhand, Madhya Pradesh, and Bihar had lower achievement in this parameter as compared with the all-states average. Bihar was the only state with a separate girls' toilet in less than 90% of government schools.

5. **Dropout rate.** The average dropout rate in India has been increasing between FY2015 and FY2017 across each education level. The all-India average dropout rate at the upper primary level in FY2016 stood at 4.03%, with significant disparity among states (Figure A8.3). While the dropout rates in some states, such as Madhya Pradesh and Jharkhand, are almost double of the all-India average, they are negligible in other states such as Goa.

6. The Supreme Court of India has also ruled that certain basic facilities, like separate toilets for boys and girls, and drinking water should be available in all

Figure A8.2   State-Wise Gross Enrollment Ratio in FY2016

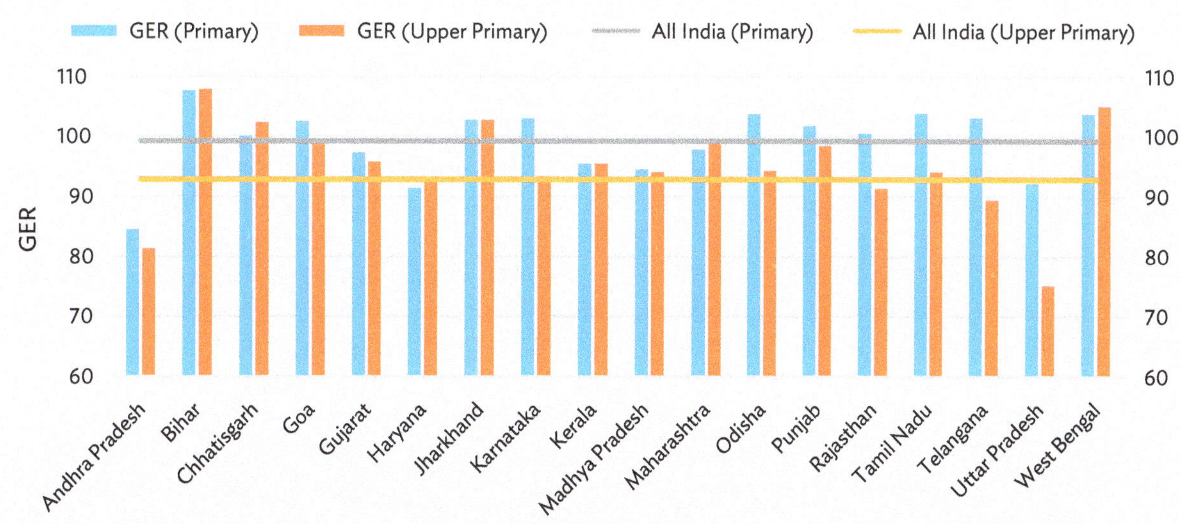

FY = fiscal year, GER = gross enrollment ratio.
Source: Authors' compilation from the Unified District Information System for Education (U-DISE 2015-16).

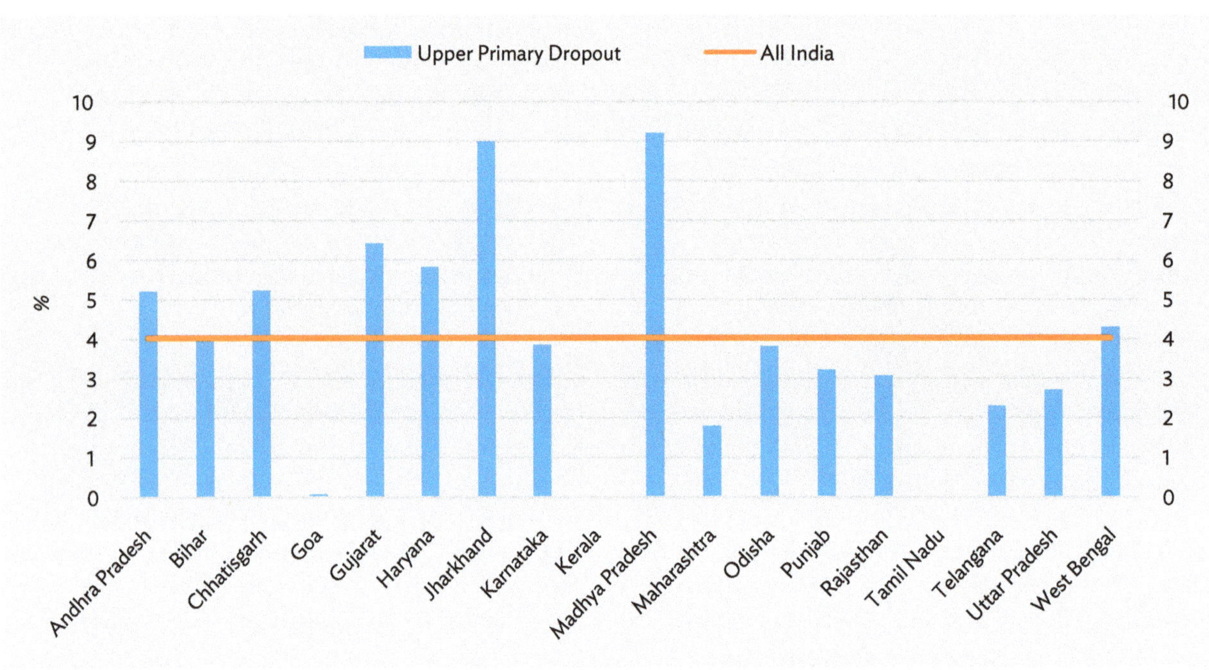

Figure A8.3   Dropout Rate at the Upper Primary Level in FY2016

FY = fiscal year.
Note: U-DISE 2015-16 did not report the states with negative dropout rates (Kerala and Tamil Nadu).
Source: Authors' compilation from the Unified District Information System for Education (U-DISE 2015-16).

schools, including those run by minority communities. However, many states have not yet fully achieved these targets. While Goa, Punjab, Tamil Nadu, Gujarat, Rajasthan, and Telangana were the only states to have achieved separate girls' toilets in all schools by FY2016, Jharkhand, Madhya Pradesh, and Bihar had lower achievement in this parameter as compared with the all-states average (Figure A8.4). Bihar was the only state with a separate girls' toilet in less than 90% of government schools.

7. On similar lines, Figure A8.5 shows that Goa, Punjab, Tamil Nadu, Karnataka, and Gujarat were the only states with drinking water facilities in all the government schools in FY2016. In Rajasthan, Madhya Pradesh, Bihar, Andhra Pradesh, Jharkhand, and Telangana, the availability of drinking water facilities is lower than the all-India average.

8. As seen in Figure A8.6, Kerala is the only state, providing mid-day meals cooked in school kitchen sheds in almost 100% of government schools. While other states are relatively close to the target, in states such as Bihar, Gujarat, Punjab, and Telangana mid-day meals are provided in schools less than the all-India average of 97.61%. As per Right to Free and Compulsory Education Act, 2009 (RTE) norms, the meals must be cooked in kitchen sheds in schools. However, in states such as Andhra Pradesh, Gujarat, Haryana, Karnataka, Madhya Pradesh, Maharashtra, and Telangana the number of schools with kitchen sheds is lower than the all-India average of 90.77%. In Goa, only 0.54% of schools providing mid-day meals have their own kitchen sheds.

9. **Quality of education.** The quality of education depends upon the quality and availability of teachers

Figure A8.4   Government Schools with Separate Girls' Toilet Available in FY2016

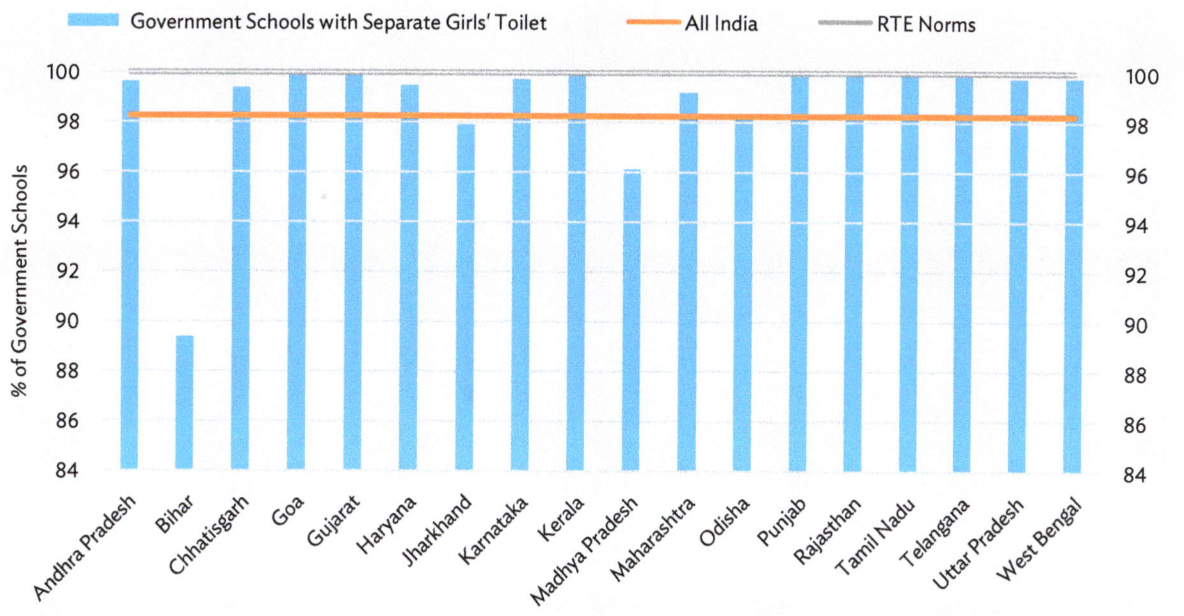

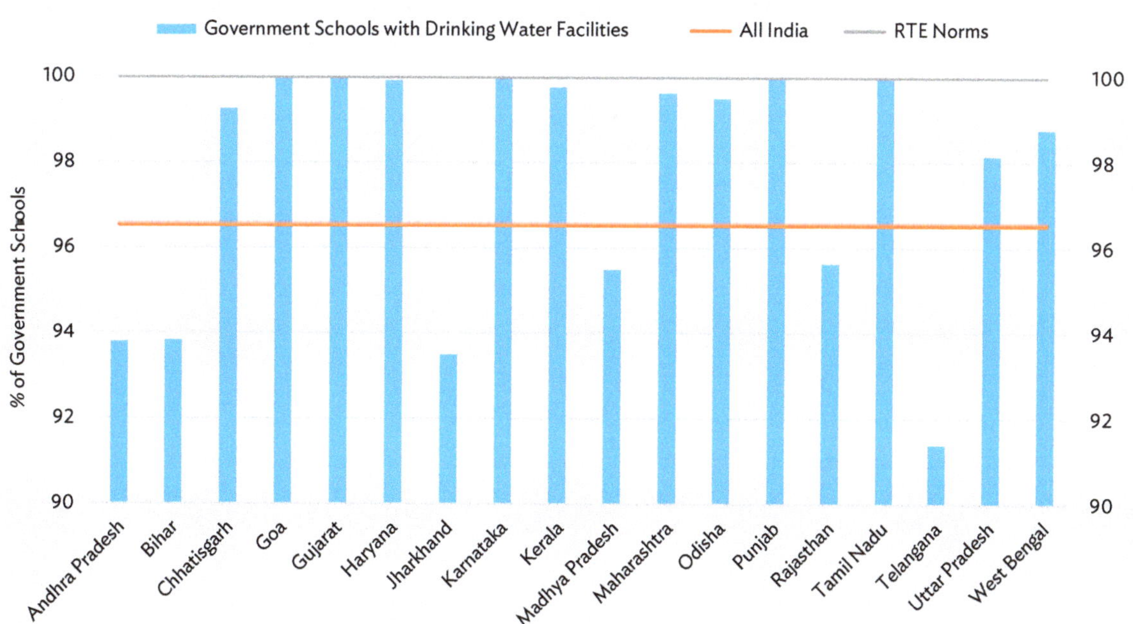

FY = fiscal year, RTE = Right to Free and Compulsory Education Act, 2009.
Source: Authors' compilation from the Unified District Information System for Education (U-DISE 2015-16).

Figure A8.5   Government Schools with Drinking Water Facilities in FY2016

FY = fiscal year, RTE = Right to Free and Compulsory Education Act, 2009.
Source: Authors' compilation from the Unified District Information System for Education (U-DISE 2015-16).

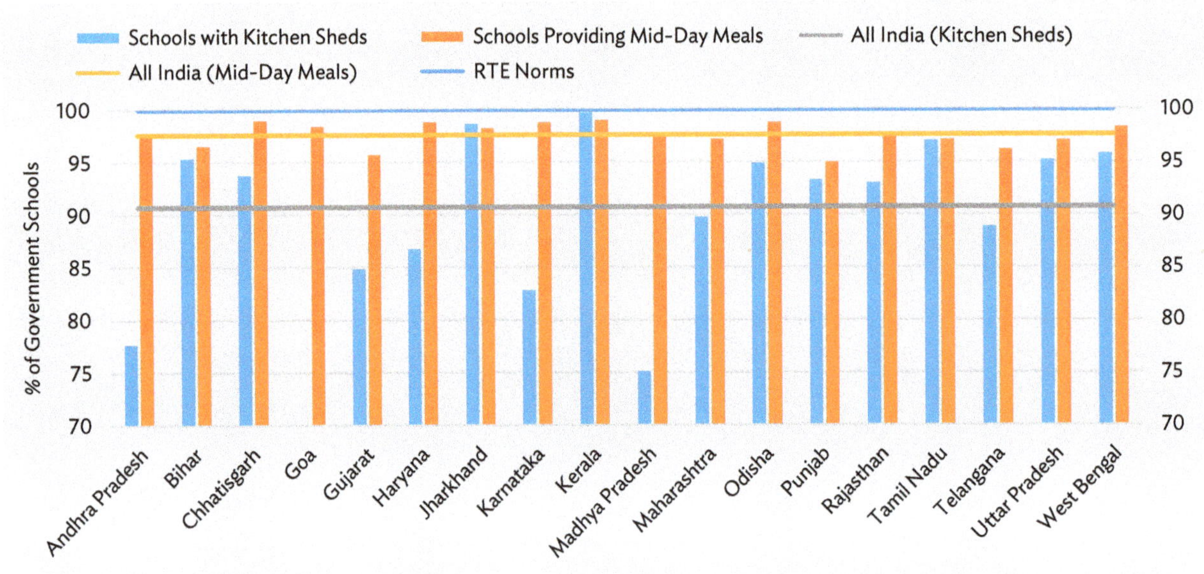

Figure A8.6   Provision of Mid-Day Meals and Kitchen Sheds in FY2016

FY = fiscal year, RTE = Right to Free and Compulsory Education Act, 2009.
Source: Authors' compilation from the Unified District Information System for Education (U-DISE 2015-16).

and classrooms, among others. It can also be evaluated based on dropout, transition, and retention in schools. As per RTE, pupil–teacher ratio (PTR) is recommended to be 30 at the primary level and 35 at the upper primary level.

10. The percentage of government schools in select Indian states, which do not meet this norm vis-à-vis the all the India average, is provided in Figure A8.7.

11. All states in Figure A8.7 have government schools that are not in line with the RTE norms for primary as well as upper primary levels. The percentage of noncompliant government schools are particularly high in Bihar, Haryana, Jharkhand, and Uttar Pradesh at the primary level. While the percentage of noncompliant government schools at the upper primary level is lower than that at the primary level in most states, a high percentage of schools in Bihar, Chhattisgarh, Madhya Pradesh, Uttar Pradesh, and West Bengal have a PTR greater than 35 at the upper primary level.

12. In Figure A8.8, the percentage of noncompliant schools with a student classroom ratio greater than 30 at the primary level is particularly high in Bihar and Uttar Pradesh. A high percentage of schools in Bihar, Odisha, and West Bengal have a student classroom ratio greater than 35 at the upper primary level. Bihar has the most need for teachers and classrooms.

13. **Learning outcomes.** The National Achievement Survey (NAS) evaluates the learning outcomes in English, Mathematics, and Science in government and government-aided schools.

14. The average score for Class 8 students in 2014 in each subject area is provided in Figures A8.9, A8.10, and A8.11. The scores of the survey vary state-wise as well as subject-wise. Overall, Kerala is one of the better performing states when compared with Andhra Pradesh and Tamil Nadu.

15. Based on the parameters above, except the learning outcomes, the states analyzed have been provided a

Figure A8.7   Pupil–Teacher Ratio in Government Schools in FY2016

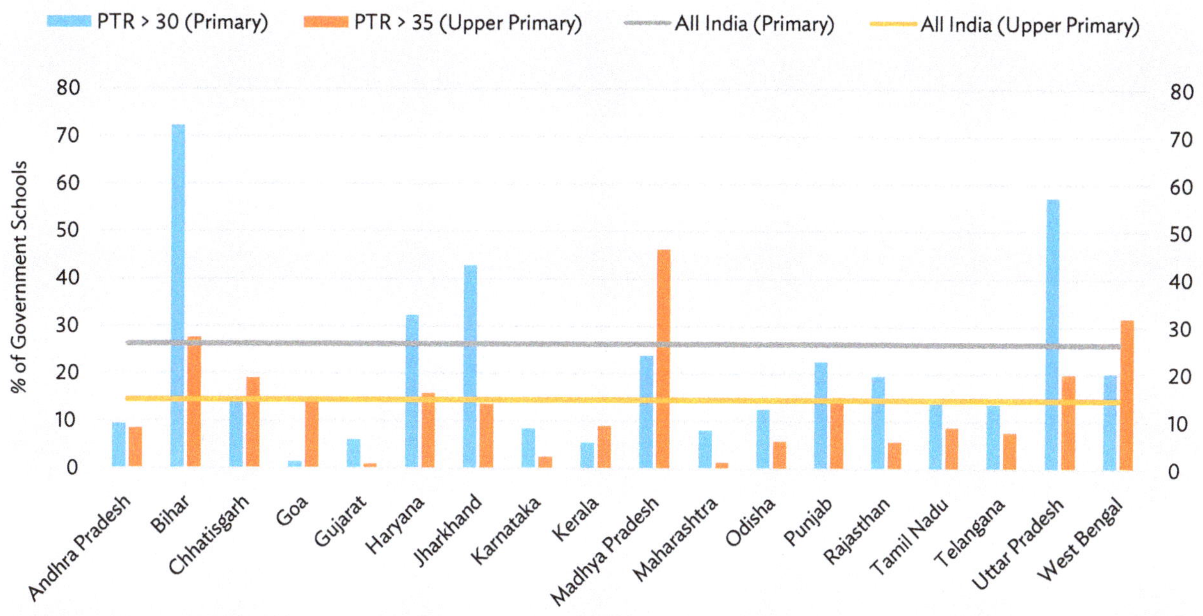

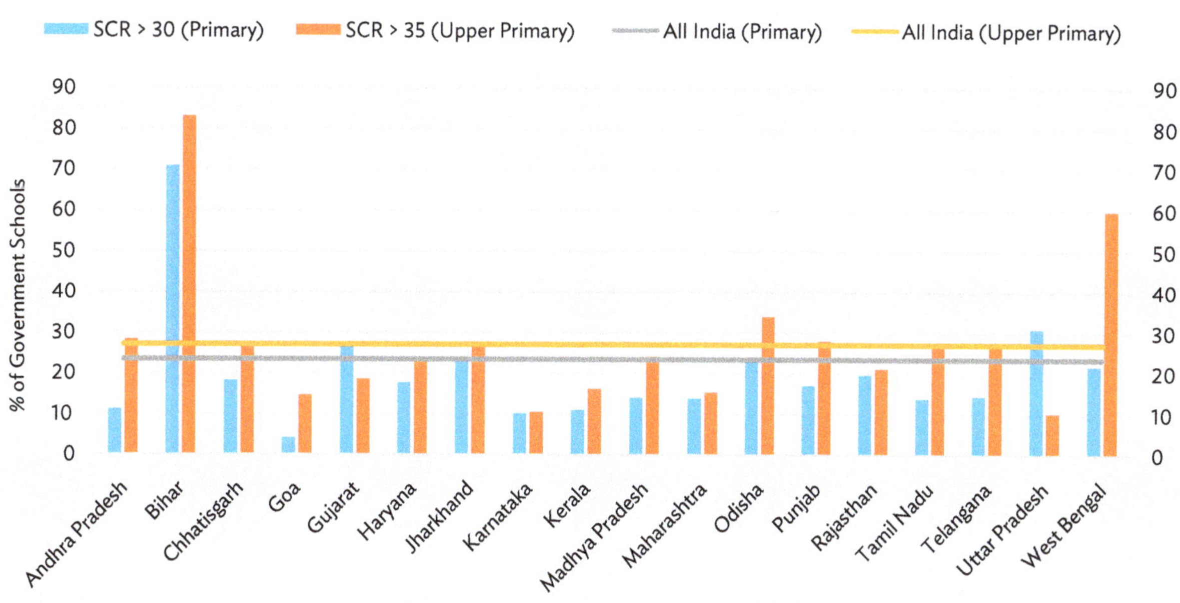

FY = fiscal year, PTR = pupil–teacher ratio.
Source: Authors' compilation from the Unified District Information System for Education (U-DISE 2015-16).

Figure A8.8   Student Classroom Ratio in FY2016

FY = fiscal year, SCR = student classroom ratio.
Source: Authors' compilation from the Unified District Information System for Education (U-DISE 2015-16).

Figure A8.9   National Achievement Survey Score for English in 2014

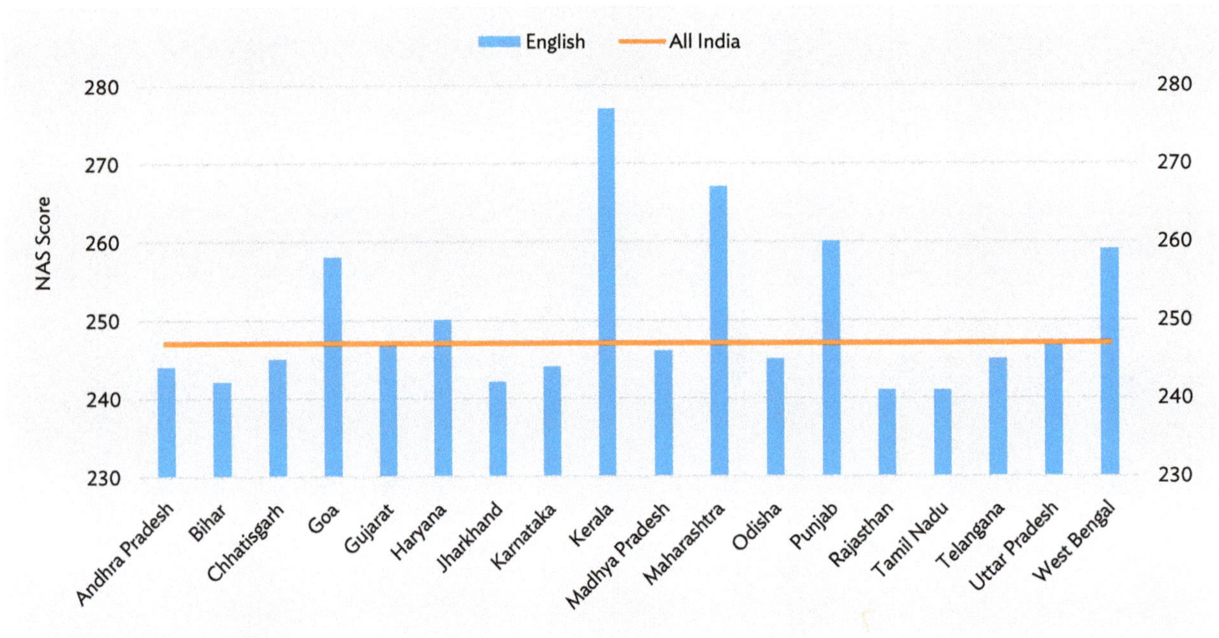

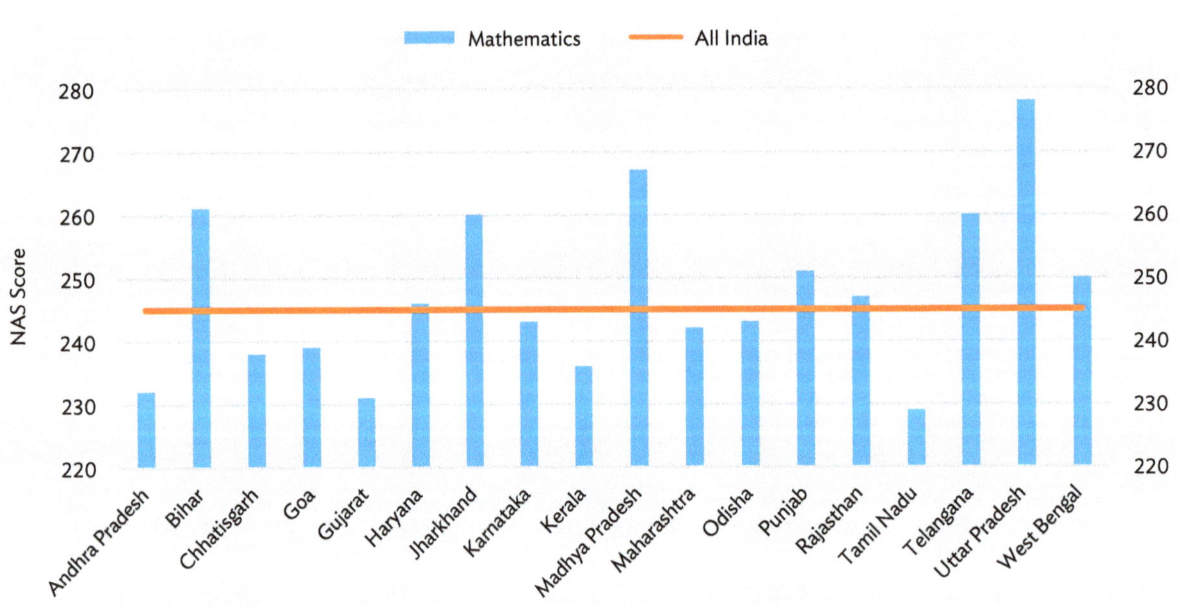

NAS = National Achievement Survey.
Source: Authors' compilation from the National Achievement Survey, National Council of Educational Research and Training.

Figure A8.10   National Achievement Survey Score for Mathematics in 2014

NAS = National Achievement Survey.
Source: Authors' compilation from the National Achievement Survey, National Council of Educational Research and Training.

Figure A8.11   National Achievement Survey Score for Science in 2014

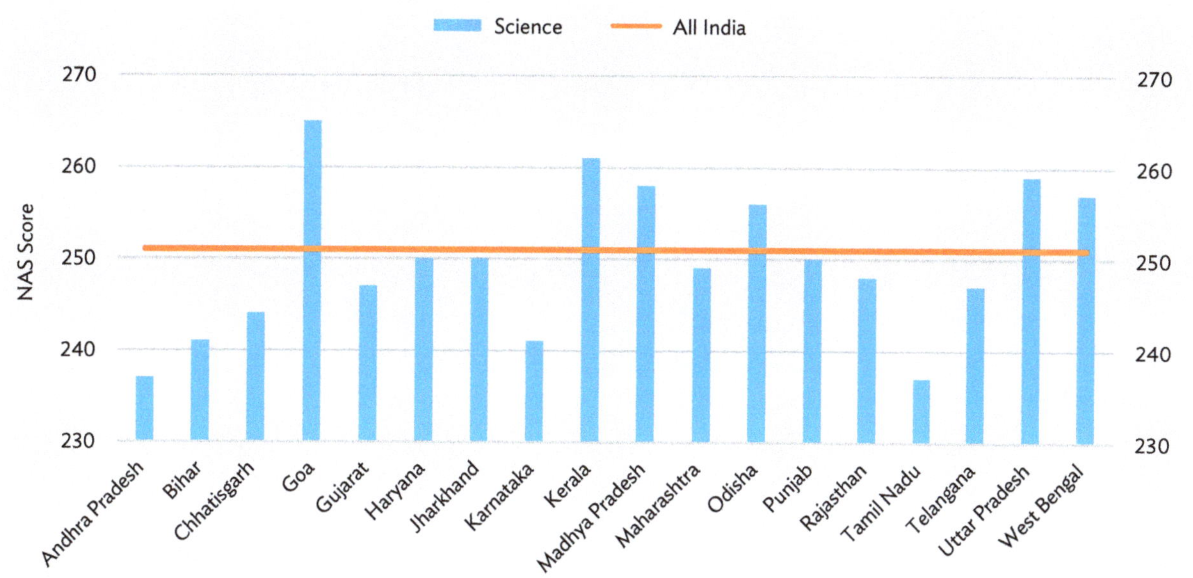

NAS = National Achievement Survey.
Source: Authors' compilation from the National Achievement Survey, National Council of Educational Research and Training.

ranking in Table A8.2. Relatively well performing states have a ranking of 18 while the worst performing state for that parameter received a rank of 1. Thereafter, an overall ranking, taking equal weights for each parameter is provided for the states. Overall, while Goa, Kerala, and Maharashtra are the best performing states, Uttar Pradesh, Bihar, and Madhya Pradesh have poor performance.

16. Figure A8.12 shows that the education sector performance ranking of states has a strong positive correlation with the states' per capita expenditure on education. Well-performing states, such as Goa and Kerala, tend to have a higher per capita expenditure on education as compared with relatively poor performing states such as Bihar and Madhya Pradesh.

Table A8.2   Ranking Analysis of the Non–Special Category States

States	Gross Enrollment Ratio (GER) Primary	Gross Enrollment Ratio (GER) Upper Primary	Mid-Day Meal (MDM)	Kitchen Sheds	Girls' Toilet	Drinking Water	Student Classroom Ratio (SCR) Noncompliant (Primary)	Student Classroom Ratio (SCR) Noncompliant (Upper Primary)	Pupil–Teacher Ratio (PTR) Noncompliant (Primary)	Pupil–Teacher Ratio (PTR) Noncompliant (Upper Primary)	Overall Rank
Andhra Pradesh	1	2	9	3	8	3	15	4	13	12	4
Bihar	17	18	4	14	1	4	1	1	1	3	2
Chhattisgarh	8	15	17	11	6	9	8	9	9	5	11
Goa	11	13	13	1	16	17	18	16	18	8	18
Gujarat	6	11	2	5	15	14	3	13	16	18	13
Haryana	2	5	16	6	7	13	9	11	4	6	5
Jharkhand	18	16	11	17	3	2	4	7	3	9	7
Karnataka	12	6	15	4	9	15	17	17	14	16	16
Kerala	5	10	18	18	12	12	16	14	17	10	17
Madhya Pradesh	4	7	10	2	2	5	12	10	5	1	1
Maharashtra	7	14	7	8	5	11	13	15	15	17	14
Odisha	15	9	14	12	4	10	5	3	12	14	12
Punjab	10	12	1	10	13	17	10	5	6	7	8
Rajasthan	9	4	8	9	13	6	7	12	8	15	8
Tamil Nadu	16	8	6	16	16	16	14	6	10	11	15
Telangana	13	3	3	7	16	1	11	8	11	13	6
Uttar Pradesh	3	1	5	13	10	7	2	18	2	4	3
West Bengal	14	17	12	15	11	8	6	2	7	2	10

Source: Authors' calculation.

Figure A8.12   Per Capita Expenditure on Education and Education Sector Performance Ranking in FY2016

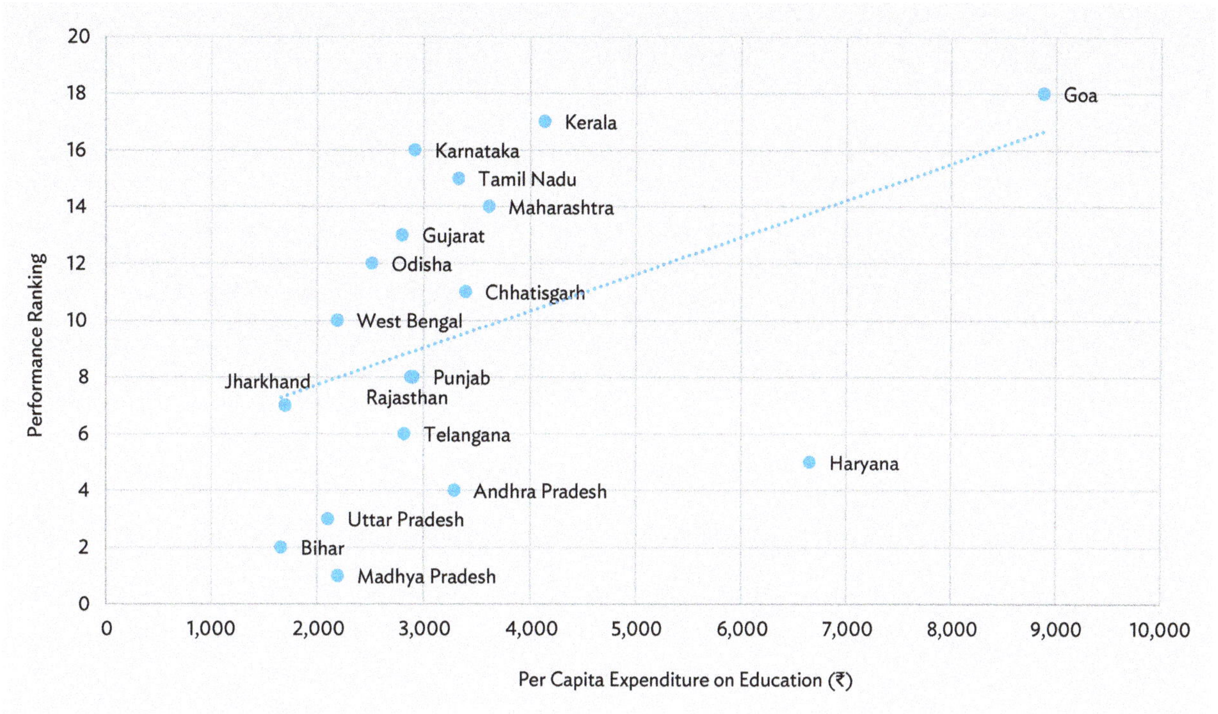

Source: Authors' calculation.

Centrally Sponsored and Central Sector Schemes in Education

1. Details of the key centrally sponsored schemes (CSS) of the Ministry of Human Resource Development (MHRD) are presented in Table A9.1. The CSS administered by the MHRD's Department of Higher Education are as follows:

1. National Education Mission: Rashtriya Uchchatar Shiksha Abhiyan (RUSA)
2. Interest subsidy and contribution for guarantee funds
3. Scholarship for college and university students
4. Technical Education Quality Improvement Programme (TEQIP) (externally aided project)
5. Higher Education Financing Agency
6. e-Shodh Sindhu Consortium
7. National Mission in Education through Information and Communication Technology (NMEICT)
8. Pandit Madan Mohan Malaviya National Mission on Teachers and Teaching
9. National Apprenticeship Training Scheme (NATS)
10. Start-Up India Initiative in higher education institutes
11. Impacting Research Innovation and Technology (IMPRINT) Initiative
12. Prime Minister's Research Fellowship Scheme
13. Setting up of virtual classrooms and massive open online courses (MOOCs)
14. Ucchatar Avishkar Abhiyan
15. World Class Institutions
16. Support to skill-based higher education including Community Colleges
17. M. Tech. Programme Teaching Assistantship
18. National Initiative for Design Innovation
19. Global Initiative for Academic Networks (GIAN)
20. Girls' Hostels Scheme
21. Unnat Bharat Abhiyan
22. Centers for Training and Research in Frontier Areas of Science and Technology (FAST)
23. Higher Education Statistics and Public Information
24. Establishment of multidisciplinary research universities including Central University of Himalayan Studies (CUHS), creation of Centers of Excellence and National Centers for Excellence in Humanities
25. National Academic Depository
26. National Institutional Ranking Framework
27. National initiative on inclusion of person with disabilities in higher education

Table A9.1   Details of Key Centrally Sponsored Schemes in Education

No.	Name of Scheme	Objectives	Key Interventions	Funding Pattern
1.	Sarva Shiksha Abhiyan	Ensuring universal access and retention Inclusiveness by bridging gender and social category gaps in education Enhancement of the learning levels of children	• Building of school infrastructure, and provisioning for teachers • Periodic teacher training and academic resource support • Provisioning of learning resources like textbooks, computers, and libraries to children • Setting up residential schools for girls known as the Kasturba Gandhi Balika Vidyalayas • Provisioning of support to identified children with special needs including aids and appliances • Monitoring effectiveness of schools • Engagement with community-based organizations to build local capacity for accountability	60 (center): 40 (state) for non-special category states; 90 (center): 10 (state) for special category states
2.	Mid-Day Meal Scheme	Enhancement of enrollment, retention, and attendance Improving nutritional levels among children	• Provision of mid-day meals to children • Meals cooked in kitchen sheds within school premises	60 (center): 40 (state) for non-special category states; 90 (center): 10 (state) for special category states
3.	Rashtriya Madhyamik Shiksha Abhiyan	Enhancement of access to secondary education and improving its quality	• Provisioning of classrooms, laboratories, libraries, toilet blocks, drinking water, and residential hostels for teachers in remote areas • Appointment of additional teachers to reduce pupil-teacher ratio to 35:1 at the upper primary level • Focus on science, math, English, and information technology-enabled education • In-service training of teachers, curriculum reforms, and teaching-learning reforms • Special focus in micro planning • Preference to Ashram schools for upgradation • Opening schools in areas with concentration of scheduled castes, scheduled tribes, and minorities • Promotion of female teachers and separate toilet blocks for girls	60 (center): 40 (state) for non-special category states; 90 (center): 10 (state) for special category states

Source: Authors' compilation from the Government of India, Ministry of Human Resource Development.

2. **Sarva Shiksha Abhiyan.** Since the Government of India intends to implement the Right to Free and Compulsory Education Act, 2009 (RTE) through the Sarva Shiksha Abhiyan (SSA), as per the Anil Bordia Committee Report, 2010, the utilization of funds for SSA in FY2017 is presented in Table A9.2. Figure A9.1 shows the expenditure as a share of total fund allocation under SSA.

Table A9.2   Utilization of Funds for Sarva Shiksha Abhiyan for Selected States in FY2017

States	Amount Allocated by the Center (₹ million)	Amount Released by the Center (₹ million)	Release / Allocated (%)
Andhra Pradesh	15,822.0	6,330.2	40.0
Assam	15,092.0	8,765.2	58.1
Bihar	57,991.0	27,068.8	46.7
Chhattisgarh	14,106.0	5,926.3	42.0
Gujarat	174.0	86.9	50.0
Haryana	15,548.0	7,774.1	50.2
Jharkhand	6,374.0	3,200.1	54.2
Karnataka	3,841.0	1,282.5	48.3
Kerala	9,399.0	5,094.6	35.8
Madhya Pradesh	11,273.0	5,449.6	49.3
Maharashtra	3,164.0	1,131.7	43.8
Manipur	31,339.0	15,445.5	17.7
Meghalaya	13,778.0	6,037.0	49.4
Mizoram	2,487.0	440.5	61.9
Odisha	4,061.0	2,006.7	53.0
Punjab	1,766.0	1,093.4	47.2
Rajasthan	2,707.0	1,072.5	51.9
Tamil	13,295.0	7,042.3	51.5
Tripura	6,355.0	3,000.3	72.8
Uttar Pradesh	35,199.0	18,257.8	44.3
Uttarakhand	616.0	347.9	46.2
West Bengal	15,936.0	8,211.1	29.2

FY = fiscal year.
Source: Authors' compilation from the Ministry of Human Resource Development, Education Statistics.

Figure A9.1   Expenditure by Non-Special Category States under Sarva Shiksha Abhiyan

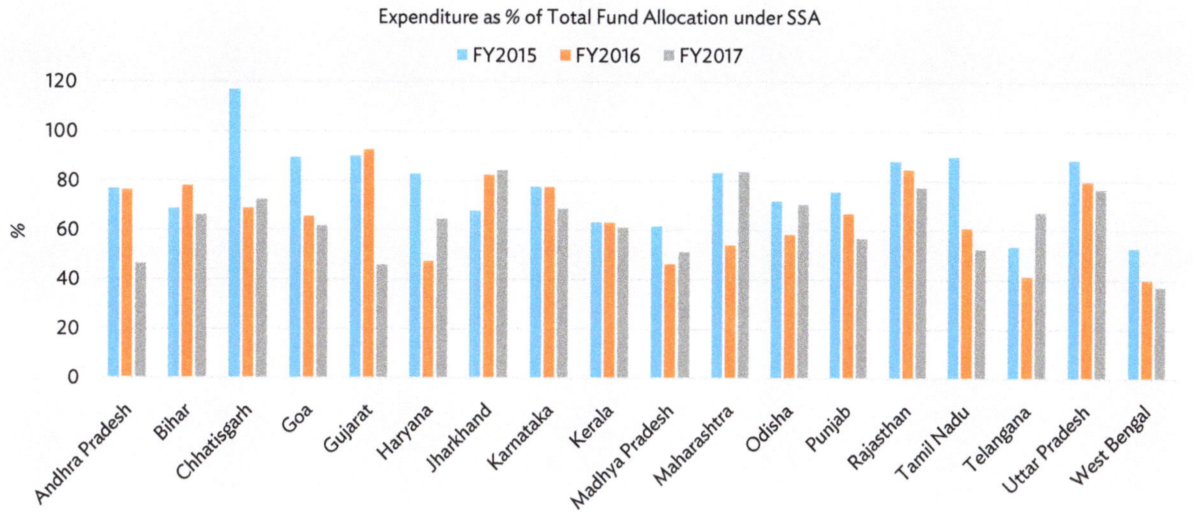

FY = fiscal year, SSA = Sarva Shiksha Abhiyan.
Source: Authors' compilation from the Education Statistics of the Department of School Education and Literacy, Ministry of Human Resource Development.

Impact of 14th Finance Commission Recommendations on Education Expenditure

1. In Figure A10.1, a state-wise analysis of the spending priorities reveals that among the non-special category states, except for Andhra Pradesh and Uttar Pradesh, the share of education sector expenditure in aggregate expenditure has declined in FY2016 (first year of 14th Finance Commission [FC]) as compared with FY2015 (last year of 13th FC).

Figure A10.1   Education Expenditure in Selected Non-Special Category States

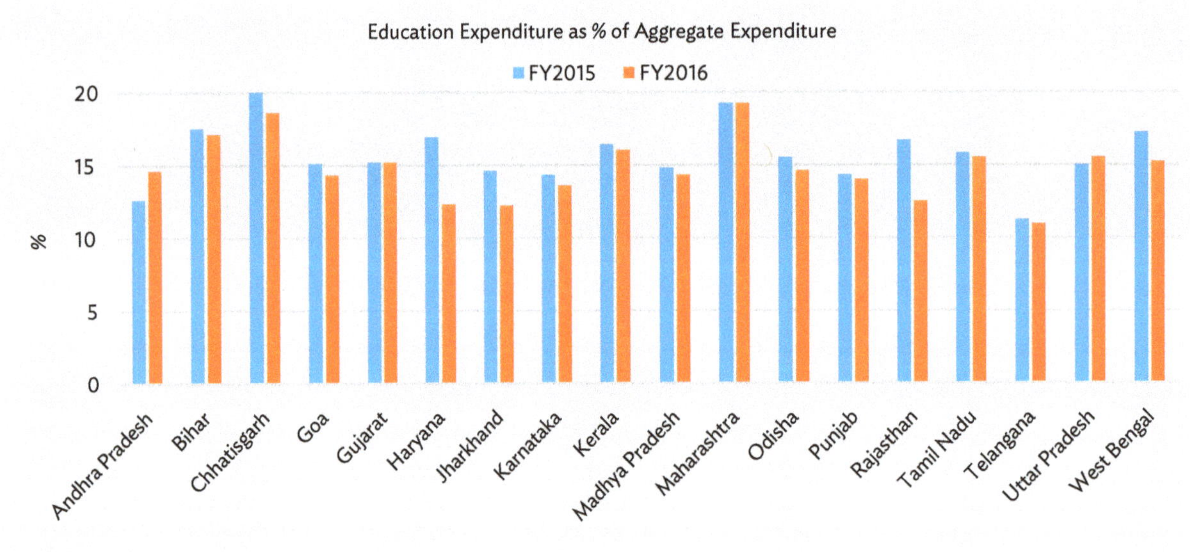

FY = fiscal year.
Source: Authors' compilation from the Reserve Bank of India. State Finances: Study of Budgets (includes expenditure on sports, art, and culture under current expenditure and capital outlay).

2. In case of special category states, the trend is unclear. Education expenditure as a percentage of aggregate expenditure has fallen in some states as shown in Figure A10.2.

Figure A10.2   Education Expenditure in Selected Special Category States

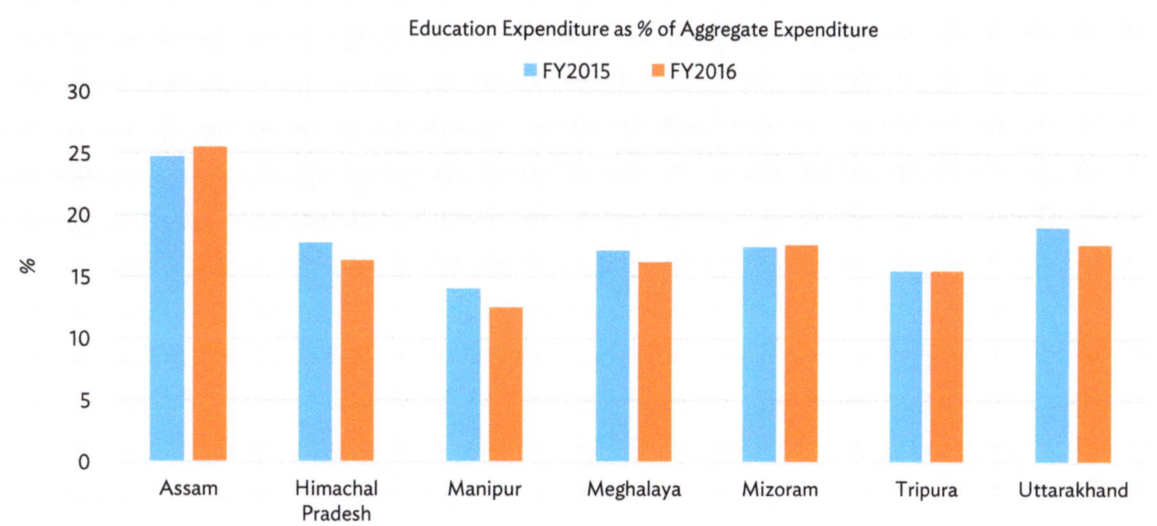

FY = fiscal year.
Source: Authors' compilation from the Reserve Bank of India. State Finances: Study of Budgets (includes expenditure on sports, arts, and culture under current expenditure and capital outlay).

Education Grants by Previous Finance Commissions

1. The details and methodology of the grants provided by the previous Finance Commissions (FCs) are presented below.

A. Upgradation Grants for Education by the 10th FC

2. Based on the report of the 10th FC (1995), grants for education were provided under the following categories:

(i) **Promotion of girls' education.** The states with very low female literacy rates were assisted with upgradation grants. Thus, 83 districts with female literacy rates below 20% and 199 districts with rates between 20%–40% in 1991 were provided upgradation grants. The assessment was made based on ₹2 million and ₹1 million, respectively, per district per year.

(ii) **Additional facilities for upper primary schools.** Basic amenities such as drinking water and toilets were considered for support under this category. Grant was provided to achieve at least 75% satisfaction in provision of basic amenities. The unit cost for drinking water facility and sanitation was taken to arrive at the total cost.

(iii) **Drinking water facilities in primary schools.** The commission provided upgradation grants for providing drinking water facility in all primary schools by applying the ratio obtained in the All India Educational Survey (1986) to the number of schools in 1992–1993 in each state, taking the average unit cost of ₹15,000 for a hand pump.

3. The FC proposed to retain the monitoring mechanism of the upgradation grants, as was introduced by the 8th FC and continued by the 9th FC. The recommended arrangement included an interministerial empowered committee at the Government of India level, consisting of representatives of the concerned central ministries. They had the power to alter the physical targets or transfer grants across schemes in the same sector. A similar state-level committee was constituted, chaired by the chief secretary or a senior officer.

B. Upgradation Grants for Elementary Education by the 11th FC

4. The 11th FC prioritized the construction of the school buildings and related infrastructure for the elementary education sector, i.e., classes 1–8, particularly in rural areas and provided ₹5.06 billion for this purpose (Finance Commission 2000). The amount was distributed among the states based on a composite index, comprising (i) the number of illiterates in the age group 7–14 as per the 1991 Census; and (ii) the average per capita expenditure of the states under the budget head "2202—General Education" for 3 years—1995–1996, 1996–1997, and 1997–1998, giving equal weight to each.

5. **Conditionalities attached for utilization.** The construction of buildings and classrooms was prioritized in areas where the schools were running in the open. After meeting this basic requirement, the remaining amount was utilized for provision of toilet and drinking water facilities in the existing schools.

C. Equalization Grant by the 12th FC

6. The 12th FC determined the grants for the education sector based on the equalization principle and made a provision of ₹101.7 billion for distribution among eight states, namely, Assam, Bihar, Jharkhand, Madhya Pradesh, Odisha, Rajasthan, Uttar Pradesh, and West Bengal (Finance Commission 2004). A two-step procedure was followed to equalize per capita expenditure on education across states:

- **Step 1:** States with lower expenditure on education as a proportion of total current expenditure were identified and benchmarked to average expenditure on education incurred by respective groups (special category and general).

- **Step 2**: States with lower per capita expenditure than the group average were identified, and grants to the extent of 15% of the difference between per capita expenditure of the state on this sector and average per capita expenditure of the group were provided.

7. Given that providing transfers to bridge the entire gap in per capita expenditure on education (full equalization) across states was not feasible due to the revenue constraints, the 12th FC recommended the grants to cover only 15% of the shortfall.

8. The 12th FC's conditionality for grants-in-aid for education (budget head 2202) indicated that

(i)   the grant should be utilized only for meeting the non-plan current expenditure under the budget head; and

(ii)   the grant may be allocated in two equal installments in each financial year. While there will be no precondition for release of the first installment in any year, the second installment will be released on the fulfillment of certain conditions for each successive year.

D. Grant for Elementary Education by the 13th FC

9. The 13th FC recommended grants specifically for elementary education and provided ₹240.7 billion to all the 28 states based on the following arguments (Finance Commission 2009):

(i)   The Ministry of Human Resource Development (MHRD), in its memorandum dated 16 March 2009, requested the FC to provide grants for "elementary education," based on actual estimation of resource requirements and gaps in each state, instead of the earlier methodology of equalization by MHRD.

(ii)   The Sarva Shiksha Abhiyan (SSA) began with a matching fund requirement of 15% from states in FY2002. While the matching fund requirement was 25% until FY2007, it progressively increased to 35% in FY2008 and FY2009 and to 40% in FY2010. It was expected to go up to 45% in FY2011 and to 50% in FY2012, the terminal year of the Eleventh Five-Year Plan. Assuming the same ratio in the remaining years of the award period, various states have expressed difficulties in providing this matching share, especially since the size of their annual plans has increased over the years.

(iii)   SSA had an "equalizing" effect as the disadvantaged states and districts have received proportionately more funds than relatively better states and districts.

10. Thus, a grant of 15% of the estimated SSA expenditure by each state was provided to cover the difference between the targeted state share of 50% by the terminal year of the Eleventh Plan and the contribution required in FY2009, i.e., 35% of the individual states' SSA share.

11. As per the conditionality of grants, states had to maintain growth of their own expenditure on education at 8% per annum during the award period of the 13th FC namely, 2010–2015.

E. Analysis of Education Grants by the 12th and 13th FCs

12. Table A11.1 captures the quantum of education grant awarded to selected states by the 12th FC and 13th FC and education expenditure of states as a percentage of aggregate expenditure.

Table A11.1   Education Grants Recommended by the Finance Commissions

States	Education Grants (₹ million)		Education Expenditure as % of Aggregate Expenditure	
	12th FC	13th FC	Average of Ratios 2005–2010	Average of Ratios 2010–2015
Andhra Pradesh	0	9,420	9.98	12.94
Bihar	26,837	40,180	18.70	18.08
Chhattisgarh	0	8,570	13.96	18.16
Gujarat	0	4,830	12.84	15.24
Haryana	0	2,290	13.90	16.20
Jharkhand	6,517	15,280	16.02	14.92
Karnataka	0	6,670	14.32	15.02
Kerala	0	1,400	16.62	17.10
Madhya Pradesh	4,595	22,160	11.90	14.00
Maharashtra	0	7,440	17.08	20.28
Odisha	3,233	10,160	15.38	16.14
Punjab	0	2,240	10.80	14.06
Rajasthan	10,000	17,660	16.86	14.06
Tamil Nadu	0	7,000	13.36	14.06
Uttar Pradesh	44,540	50,400	14.20	14.06
West Bengal	3,918	23,590	14.98	14.06
Assam	11,073	2,380	19.30	22.04
Himachal Pradesh	0	1,130	15.22	17.70
Manipur	0	150	13.08	11.96
Meghalaya	0	520	14.54	16.58
Mizoram	0	50	13.88	16.16
Tripura	0	230	15.38	16.40
Uttarakhand	0	1,970	18.74	21.12

FC = Finance Commission.
Source: Authors' compilation from the 12th and 13th Finance Commission Reports.

Approach for Calculation of Equalization Grants for Education

The ratios of education expenditure of each state with respect to their aggregate current expenditure are calculated for FY2017. The data on the states' finances and budgets are obtained from the Reserve Bank of India. For each state, current expenditure under the head "Education, Sports, Arts and Culture" is used. The detailed procedure and calculations are as follows:

A. Calculation using Per Capita Education Expenditures

Step 1: For estimation of grants, attention is given to the states with allocation on education as measured in relation to their current expenditure that is below the group average.

Step 2: For each group, namely, non-special category and special category, average ratio is calculated and normatively assigned to states with less than average ratios for FY2017.

Step 3: After the correction, the per capita education expenditure is calculated for each state.

Step 4: The group-wise normative average expenditure is calculated.

Step 5: The state with normative per capita expenditure that is lesser than the normative average in the group is classified as needing financial assistance.

Step 6: The amount of grant covers 15% of the difference between the per capita expenditure of the below-average state and the group average.

Step 7: To calculate the amount of grant for base year, namely, FY2020, a trend growth rate of 12.82% (for current expenditure of all states) is applied. Grants for the 15th Finance Commission (FC) period are estimated based on annual growth of 10% from the base year value (Table A12.1).

Table A12.1   Estimated Education Grants Using per Capita Expenditures in Selected States (2020–2025)

Non-Special Category States	(₹ million)
Bihar	281,960
Gujarat	49,610
Jharkhand	60,340
Madhya Pradesh	76,420
Odisha	47,640
Punjab	2,830
Rajasthan	10,910
Uttar Pradesh	314,550
West Bengal	126,120
Special Category States	**(₹ million)**
Assam	132,610
Manipur	8,390
Meghalaya	8,190
Tripura	10,020
Uttarakhand	24,700

Source: Authors' calculation.

B. Calculation Using per Child Education Expenditures

Step 1: For estimation of grants, attention is given to the states with allocation on education as measured in relation to their current expenditure that is below the group average.

Step 2: For each group, namely, non-special category and special category, average ratio is calculated and normatively assigned to states with less than average ratios for FY2017.

Step 3: After the correction, the per capita education expenditure is calculated for each state.

Step 4: The group-wise normative average expenditure is calculated. The per child expenditure is calculated by dividing the expenditure by each state's children population between ages 6–13 years. Data are obtained from the 2011 census.

Step 5: The state with per child expenditure that is lesser than the group average is classified as needing financial assistance.

Step 6: The amount of grant covers 15% of the difference between the per student expenditure of the below-average state and the group average.

Step 7: To calculate the amount of grant for base year, namely, FY2020, a trend growth rate of 12.82% (for current expenditure of all states) is applied. Grants for the 15th FC period are estimated based on annual growth of 10% from the base year value (Table A12.2).

Table A12.2   Estimated Education Grants Using per Child Education Expenditures in Selected States (2020–2025)

Non-Special Category States	(₹ million)
Bihar	483,080
Gujarat	58,320
Jharkhand	95,540
Madhya Pradesh	163,340
Odisha	49,890
Rajasthan	89,140
Uttar Pradesh	722,320
West Bengal	84,610
Special Category States	**(₹ million)**
Assam	165,380
Manipur	3,130
Meghalaya	13,010
Tripura	5,950
Uttarakhand	40,410

Source: Authors' calculation.

APPENDIX 13
School Education Quality Index

Table A13.1   Indicators under School Education Quality Index

No.	INDICATORS	DATA SOURCE	WEIGHT
	CATEGORY 1: OUTCOMES		
	DOMAIN 1.1. LEARNING OUTCOMES		**360**
1.1.1	**Average score in Class 3**	National Achievement Survey (NAS)	200
a	Language		100
b	Mathematics		100
1.1.2	**Average score in Class 5**	NAS	100
a	Language		50
b	Mathematics		50
1.1.3	**Average score in Class 8**	NAS	60
a	Language		30
b	Mathematics		30
	DOMAIN 1.2. ACCESS OUTCOMES		**100**
1.2.1	**Adjusted net enrollment ratio (NER)**	Unified District Information System for Education (U-DISE)	40
a	Elementary level		20
b	Secondary level (Class 9 to 10)		20
1.2.2	**Transition rate**	U-DISE	40
a	Primary to upper primary level		20
b	Upper primary to secondary level		20
1.2.3	**Percentage of identified out-of-school children mainstreamed in last completed academic year (Class 1 to 8)**	Ministry of Human Resource Development (MHRD)'s ShaGun Management Information System (MIS) / States	20
	DOMAIN 1.3. INFRASTRUCTURE AND FACILITIES FOR OUTCOMES		**25**
1.3.1	**Computer-related learning**	U-DISE	10
a	Percentage of schools having computer-aided learning at elementary level		5
b	Percentage of secondary schools with computer lab facility		5

continued on next page

Table A13.1   *continued*

No.	INDICATORS	DATA SOURCE	WEIGHT
1.3.2	**Percentage of schools having book banks / reading rooms / libraries (Class 1 to 12)**	U–DISE	5
1.3.3	**Percentage of schools covered by vocational education (Class 9 to 12)**	U–DISE	10
	DOMAIN 1.4. EQUITY OUTCOMES		**200**
1.4.1	**Difference (absolute value) in performance between scheduled castes and general category students**	NAS	30
a	Language		
	Class 3		5
	Class 5		5
	Class 8		5
b	Mathematics		
	Class 3		5
	Class 5		5
	Class 8		5
1.4.2	**Difference (absolute value) in performance between scheduled tribes and general category students**	NAS	30
a	Language		
	Class 3		5
	Class 5		5
	Class 8		5
b	Mathematics		
	Class 3		5
	Class 5		5
	Class 8		5
1.4.3	**Difference (absolute value) in performance between students studying in rural and urban areas**	NAS	30
a	Language		
	Class 3		5
	Class 5		5
	Class 8		5
b	Mathematics		
	Class 3		5
	Class 5		5

continued on next page

Table A13.1   *continued*

No.	INDICATORS	DATA SOURCE	WEIGHT
	Class 8		5
1.4.4	**Difference (absolute value) in student performance between boys and girls at elementary level**	NAS	30
a	Language		
	Class 3		5
	Class 5		5
	Class 8		5
b	Mathematics		
	Class 3		5
	Class 5		5
	Class 8		5
1.4.5	**Difference (absolute value) in transition rate in all schools from upper primary to secondary level**	U-DISE	40
a	Scheduled castes and general category		10
b	Scheduled tribes and general category		10
c	Other backward class and general category		10
d	Boys and girls		10
1.4.6	**Percentage of entitled children with special needs receiving aids and appliances (Class 1 to 10)** (Note: This is measured against targets set in the Project Approval Board minutes where the number of students receiving aids / appliances is specified.	MHRD's ShaGun MIS / States	30
1.4.7	**Percentage of schools with toilet for girls (Class 1 to 12)**	U-DISE	10
	CATEGORY 2: GOVERNANCE PROCESSES AIDING OUTCOMES		
	ATTENDANCE		
2.1	**Student Attendance**	MHRD's ShaGun MIS / States	50
a	Percentage of children whose unique ID is seeded in student data management information system (SDMIS)		20
b	Percentage of average daily attendance of students in SDMIS / electronic / digital database updated at least every month (Class 1 to 12) (Note: Data are collected monthly and aggregated)		30
2.2	**Teacher Attendance**	MHRD's ShaGun MIS / States	30

continued on next page

Table A13.1   *continued*

No.	INDICATORS	DATA SOURCE	WEIGHT
a	Percentage of teachers whose unique ID is seeded in any electronic database of state government / union territory administration (Class 1 to 12)		10
b	Percentage of average daily attendance of teachers recorded in the electronic attendance system (Note: Data are collected monthly and aggregated)		20
	TEACHER ADEQUACY		
2.3	**Percentage of single teacher schools**	U-DISE	10
2.4	**Percentage of schools meeting teacher norms as per Right to Free and Compulsory Education (RTE) Act**	MHRD's ShaGun MIS / States	20
a	Percentage of elementary schools meeting teacher norms		10
b	Percentage of upper primary schools meeting subject-teacher norms		10
2.5	**Percentage of secondary schools with teachers for all core subjects (Class 9 to 10)**	MHRD's ShaGun MIS / States	10
	ADMINISTRATIVE ADEQUACY		
2.6	**Percentage of schools with headmaster / principal**	U-DISE	20
	TRAINING		
2.7	**Percentage of academic positions filled in state and district academic training institutions at the beginning of the given academic year** (Note: Measured against number of positions approved / sanctioned by MHRD)	MHRD's ShaGun MIS / States	15
a	State Council of Educational Research and Training or equivalent		5
b	District Institute for Education and Training		10
2.8	**Percentage of teachers provided with sanctioned number of days of training in the given financial year (Class 1 to 10)**	MHRD's ShaGun MIS / States	20
2.9	**Percentage of headmasters / principals who have completed school leadership training in the given financial year (Class 1 to 12)**	MHRD's ShaGun MIS / States	15
	ACCOUNTABILITY AND TRANSPARENCY		
2.10	**Percentage of schools that have completed self-evaluation and made school improvement / development plans in the given financial year**	MHRD's ShaGun MIS / States	20
a	Percentage of schools that have completed self-evaluation		5

continued on next page

Table A13.1   *continued*

No.	INDICATORS	DATA SOURCE	WEIGHT
b	Percentage of schools that have made school improvement / development plans (Note: Includes only those self-evaluation systems that are approved by the Department of School Education and Literacy-MHRD).		15
2.11	**Timely release of funds** (Note: Includes funds for both Sarva Shiksha Abhiyan and Rashtriya Madhyamik Shiksha Abhiyan. On release of central share of funds, the central share is supposed to be transferred to state implementation societies within 15 days and the state share is supposed to be released to state implementation societies within 30 days).	MHRD's ShaGun MIS / States	10
a	Average number of days taken by state / union territory to release total central share of funds to societies (during the previous financial year).		5
b	Average number of days taken by state to release total state share due to state societies (during the previous financial year) (Note: This indicator is not applicable for union territories. Most union territories do not contribute a state / union territory share and this reduces the ability to compute and compare scores).		5
2.12	**Number of new teachers recruited through a transparent online recruitment system as a percentage of total number of new teachers recruited in the given financial year** (Note: The transparent recruitment system should include (a) annual assessment of the teacher demand—displayed online; (b) written test (may or may not be online); (c) online advertisement for recruitment; (d) online display of marks secured by all applicants; (e) online display of objective, merit-based criteria for selection; and (f) transparent, online counseling for teachers.)	MHRD's ShaGun MIS / States	20
2.13	**Number of teachers transferred through a transparent online system as a percentage of total number of teachers transferred in the given year (Class 1 to 12)** (The transparent online transfer system should (a) include a regular and annual transfer; (b) be done on an electronic and transparent online system; (c) include teacher preferences; and (d) be based on an objective transfer policy.)	MHRD's ShaGun MIS / States	20
2.14	**Number of headmasters / principals recruited through a merit-based selection system as a percentage of total number of headmasters / principals recruited (in the given financial year) (Class 1 to 12)**	MHRD's ShaGun MIS / States	20

Source: NITI Aayog. 2019. *The Success of Our Schools: School Education Quality Index (SEQI)*. New Delhi. https://niti.gov.in/sites/default/files/2019-09/seqi_document.pdf.

Bibliography

A. Abbott and P. Jones. 2012. Intergovernmental Transfers and Procyclical Public Spending. *Economics Letters.* Volume 115. pp. 447–451.

C. D. Agustina et al. 2012. Political Economy of Natural Resource Revenue Sharing in Indonesia. *Asia Research Centre Working Papers.* No. 55. London: The London School of Economics & Political Science. http://eprints.lse.ac.uk/57962/.

C. Akın et al. 2017. Fiscal Responsibility and Budget Management Act in India: A Review and Recommendations for Reform. *ADB South Asia Working Paper Series.* No. 52. Manila. https://www.adb.org/sites/default/files/publication/337306/swp-52.pdf.

I. Aoki. 2008. Decentralization and Intergovernmental Finance in Japan. *Policy Research Institute Discussion Paper Series.* No. 08A—04. June. Ministry of Finance. http://www.eaber.org/system/tdf/documents/PRI_Aoki_2008.pdf?file=1&type=node&id=23074&force=.

ASER Center. 2018. *Annual Status of Education Report 2017 "Beyond Basics" (Rural).* http://img.asercentre.org/docs/Publications/ASER%20Reports/ASER%202017/aser2017fullreportfinal.pdf.

Asian Development Bank (ADB). 2014. *Money Matters—Local Government Finance in the People's Republic of China.* Manila. https://www.adb.org/sites/default/files/publication/151515/money-matters-local-government-finance-peoples-republic-china.pdf.

Asian Development Bank Institute (ADBI). 2018. *Tax and Development—Challenge in Asia and the Pacific.* Edited by S. Araki and S. Nakabayashi. Tokyo. https://www.adb.org/publications/tax-and-development-challenges-in-asia-pacific.

ADBI. 2017. Central and Local Government Relations in Asia. Edited by N. Yoshino and P. Morgan. Elgar Publishing, Inc. https://www.adb.org/sites/default/files/publication/376606/adbi-central-local-government-relations-asia.pdf.

Australian Institute of Health and Welfare. 2012. Australia's Health 2012. *Australia's Health Series.* No. 13. Canberra. https://www.aihw.gov.au/getmedia/5fd0fcfe-bac9-4a4c-8128-1152d0ae9d8d/14178.pdf.aspx?inline=true.

Badan Pusat Statistik Indonesia. 2018. Statistical Yearbook of Indonesia. Jakarta. https://www.bps.go.id/publication/2018/07/03/5a963c1ea9b0fed6497d0845/statistik-indonesia-2018.html.

R. Bahl. 2019. Rebalancing the Economy and Reforming the Fiscal System of the People's Republic of China. *The Governance Brief Issue 34.* Manila: ADB. https://www.adb.org/sites/default/files/publication/488946/governance-brief-034-prc-economy-fiscal-system.pdf.

I. Beazley et al. 2019. Decentralization and Performance Measurement Systems in Health Care. *OECD Working Papers on Fiscal Federalism.* No. 28. Paris. https://www.oecd-ilibrary.org/taxation/decentralisation-and-performance-measurement-systems-in-health-care_6f34dc12-en.

P. Berman et al. 2010. Government Health Financing In India: Challenges in Achieving Ambitious Goals. *Health, Nutrition and Population (HNP) Discussion Paper 59886*. World Bank. https://openknowledge.worldbank.org/bitstream/handle/10986/13597/59886 0WP0Box351ving0Ambitious0Goals.pdf?sequence=1&isAllowed=y.

S. Bessho. 2017. A Study of Central and Local Government Finance in Japan. In N. Yoshino and P. Morgan, eds. *Central and Local Government Relations in Asia*. US: Edward Elgar Publishing, Inc. https://www.adb.org/sites/default/files/publication/376606/adbi-central-local-government-relations-asia.pdf.

A. Biggs. 2018. Recent Developments in Federal Government Funding for Public Hospitals: A Quick Guide. *Research Paper Series 2018–19*. Parliament of Australia. https://parlinfo.aph.gov.au/parlInfo/download/library/prspub/6180516/upload_binary/6180516.pdf.

A. Biggs. 2016. Hospital Funding. *Budget Review 2016–17*. Parliament of Australia. https://www.aph.gov.au/About_Parliament/Parliamentary_Departments/Parliamentary_Library/pubs/rp/BudgetReview201617/Hospital.

R. Bird. 1993. Threading the Fiscal Labyrinth: Some Issues in Fiscal Decentralization. *National Tax Journal* 46 (?). pp. 207–227.

R. Bird and M. Smart. 2002. Intergovernmental Fiscal Transfers: International Lessons for Developing Countries. *World Development*. 30 (6). pp. 899–912. http://www1.worldbank.org/publicsector/pe/pfma07/BirdSmart2002.pdf.

O. Blanchard and A. Shleifer. 2000. Federalism with and without Political Centralization: China versus Russia. *NBER Working Paper* No. 7616. https://www.nber.org/papers/w7616.

M. Blaxter. 1981. *The Health of Children: A Review of Research on the Place of Health in Cycles of Disadvantage*. London: Heinemann Educational.

D. Bloom and V. Y. Fan. The Value of Vaccination: Concepts, Measures, Evidence, and Policy Implications. Unpublished Working Paper.

R. Boadway and L. Eyraud. 2018. Designing Sound Fiscal Relations across Government Levels in Decentralized Countries. *IMF Working Paper* WP/18/271. International Monetary Fund. https://www.imf.org/en/Publications/WP/Issues/2018/12/10/Designing-Sound-Fiscal-Relations-Across-Government-Levels-in-Decentralized-Countries-46425.

R. Boadway and A. Shah. 2007. Intergovernmental Fiscal Transfers: Principles and Practice. *Public Sector Governance and Accountability Series 38077*. World Bank. https://openknowledge.worldbank.org/bitstream/handle/10986/7171/380770Fiscal0t101OFFICIAL0USE0ONLY1.pdf?sequence=1&isAllowed=y.

J. Boex et al. 2000. Multi-Year Budgeting: A Review of International Practices and Lessons for Developing and Transitional Economies. *Public Budgeting and Finance*. 20 (2). pp. 91–112. https://onlinelibrary.wiley.com/doi/pdf/10.1111/0275-1100.00013.

H. Brixi et al. 2013. Engaging Sub-National Governments in Addressing Health Equities: Challenges and Opportunities in China's Health System Reform. *Health Policy and Planning*. 28 (8). December. pp. 809–824. https://doi.org/10.1093/heapol/czs120.

D. Cantarero and M. Pascual. 2008. Analyzing the Impact of Fiscal Decentralization on Health Outcomes: Empirical Evidence from Spain. *Applied Economics Letters*. 15. pp. 109–111.

Central Bureau of Health Intelligence (CBHI). 2018. *National Health Profile 2018*. 13th Issue. New Delhi: Directorate of General Health Services, Government of India. https://cbhidghs.nic.in/index1.php?lang=1&level=2&sublinkid=88&lid=1138.

P. Chakraborty et al. 2018. Will UDAY Brighten Up Rajasthan's Finances? *Economic and Political Weekly.* 53 (31). pp. 31–35. https://www.researchgate.net/publication/326826644_Will_UDAY_brighten_up_Rajasthan's_finances.

M. Choudhury and R. Mohanty. 2018. Utilisation, Fund Flows and Public Financial Management under the National Health Mission. *NIPFP Working Paper Series 227.* New Delhi: National Institute of Public Finance and Policy. https://www.nipfp.org.in/media/medialibrary/2018/05/WP_2018_227.pdf.

M. Choudhury and A. Nath. 2012. *An Estimate of Public Expenditure on Health in India. National Institute of Public Finance and Policy.* New Delhi. https://nipfp.org.in/media/medialibrary/2013/08/health_estimates_report.pdf.

B. Clements et al. 2012. The Challenge of Health Care Reform in Advanced and Emerging Economies. In *The Economics of Public Health Care Reform in Advanced and Emerging Economies.* Chapter 1. pp. 3–21. Washington, DC: International Monetary Fund. https://www.elibrary.imf.org/doc/IMF071/12275-9781616352448/12275-9781616352448/Other_formats/Source_PDF/12275-9781475559514.pdf.

J. Clemens and N. Veldhuis. 2013. *Federalism and Fiscal Transfers: Essays on Switzerland, Germany, Australia and United States.* Fraser Institute. https://www.fraserinstitute.org/sites/default/files/federalism-and-fiscal-transfers-rev.pdf.

Commonwealth of Australia. 2018. Horizontal Fiscal Equalization. *Productivity Commission Inquiry Report* No. 88. Australian Government Productivity Commission. https://www.pc.gov.au/inquiries/completed/horizontal-fiscal-equalisation/report/horizontal-fiscal-equalisation.pdf.

Commonwealth of Australia. 2018. *Federal Financial Relations Budget Paper.* No. 3. 2018–19. https://parlinfo.aph.gov.au/parlInfo/download/library/budget/2018_19/upload_binary/budget%20paper%203.pdf;fileType=application%2Fpdf#search=%22library/budget/2018_19%22.

B. Crane et al. 2018. China's Special Economic Zones: An Analysis of Policy to Reduce Regional Disparities. *Regional Studies, Regional Science.* 5 (1). pp. 98–107.

S. Dougherty. 2019. *Comparing Fiscal Equalisation Systems Looking at 2019 Data.* Presentation made at the 15th Annual Meeting of the OECD Network of Fiscal Relations Across Levels of Government. December 2019. https://www.oecd.org/tax/federalism/annual-meeting-oecd-fiscal-network.htm.

Fadliya and R. McLeod. 2010. Fiscal Transfers to Regional Governments in Indonesia. *Working Papers in Trade and Development.* No. 2010/14. Arndt-Corden Department of Economics, Crawford School of Economics and Government, ANU College of Asia and the Pacific. Canberra: Australian National University. https://acde.crawford.anu.edu.au/sites/default/files/publication/acde_crawford_anu_edu_au/2016-12/wp_econ_2010_14_fadliya_mcleod.pdf.

V. Fan et al. 2018. Fiscal Transfers Based on Inputs or Outcomes? Lessons from the Twelfth and Thirteenth Finance Commission in India. *The International Journal of Health Planning and Management.* 33 (1). pp. e210–e227. https://www.ncbi.nlm.nih.gov/pmc/articles/PMC5901023/pdf/HPM-33-e210.pdf.

A. Feltenstein and S. Iwata. 2005. Decentralization and Macroeconomic Performance in China: Regional Autonomy Has Its Costs. *Journal of Development Economics.* 76 (2). pp. 481–501. http://dept.ku.edu/~empirics/Research/feltenstein-iwata_jde05.pdf.

S. Fung and B. McAuley. 2020. Cambodia's Property Tax Reform: Policy Considerations Toward Sustained Revenue Mobilization. *The Governance Brief.* Issue 38. Manila: ADB. https://www.adb.org/sites/default/files/publication/561136/governance-brief-038-cambodia-property-tax-reform.pdf.

C. Garg and A. Karan. 2009. Reducing Out-of-Pocket Expenditures to Reduce Poverty: A Disaggregated Analysis at Rural-Urban and State Level in India. *Health Policy and Planning*. 24 (2). pp. 116–128. https://academic.oup.com/heapol/article/24/2/116/590631.

P. Gertler et al. 2014. Rewarding Provider Performance to Enable a Healthy Start to Life: Evidence from Argentina's Plan Nacer. *Policy Research Working Paper*. No. 6884. World Bank. https://www.rbfhealth.org/sites/rbf/files/Rewarding%20provider%20performance%20to%20enable%20a%20healthy%20start%20to%20life%20-%20evidence%20from%20Argentina's%20Plan%20Nacer_1.pdf.

A. Glassman and Y. Sakuma. 2014. *Intergovernmental Fiscal Transfers for Health: Overview Framework and Lessons Learned.* Centre for Global Development. https://www.cgdev.org/sites/default/files/CGD-Consultation-Draft-Glassman-Sakuma-IGFT-Health.pdf.

Government of Australia. 2011. Part 2: Payment for Specific Purposes—Health. Australia's Federal Relations 2011–12. *Budget Paper No. 3.* https://archive.budget.gov.au/2011-12/index.htm.

Government of India, Ministry of Finance (MOF). 2018. *Economic Survey 2017–18.* New Delhi. https://mofapp.nic.in/economicsurvey/economicsurvey/index.html.

—————. 2017. *Economic Survey 2016–17.* New Delhi. https://www.indiabudget.gov.in/budget2017-2018/es2016-17/echapter.pdf.

—————. 2017. Responsible Growth: A Debt and Fiscal Framework for 21st Century India. *FRBM Review Committee Report.* Volume 1. FRBM Review Committee. New Delhi. https://dea.gov.in/sites/default/files/Volume%201%20FRBM%20Review%20Committee%20Report.pdf.

—————. 2016. *Indian Public Finance Statistics, 2015–2016.* New Delhi. https://dea.gov.in/sites/default/files/IPFS%20English%202015-16.pdf.

Government of India, Finance Commission. 2015. *Recommendations of the Fourteenth Finance Commission.* New Delhi. http://www.thehinducentre.com//multimedia/archive/02321/14th_Finance_Commi_2321247a.pdf.

—————. 2009. Report of the Thirteenth Finance Commission, 2010–2015. New Delhi. https://fincomindia.nic.in/writereaddata/html_en_files/oldcommission_html/fincom13/tfc/13fcreng.pdf.

—————. 2004. Report of the Twelfth Finance Commission (2005–10). New Delhi. https://fincomindia.nic.in/ShowContent.aspx?uid1=3&uid2=0&uid3=0&uid4=0&uid5=0&uid6=0&uid7=0.

—————. 2003. *Fifty Years of Fiscal Federalism: Finance Commissions of India.* 12th Finance Commission. New Delhi.

—————. 2000. *Report of the Eleventh Finance Commission (for 2000–2005).* New Delhi. https://fincomindia.nic.in/writereaddata/html_en_files/oldcommission_html/fcreport/11threport.pdf.

—————. 1995. *Report of the Tenth Finance Commission.* New Delhi. https://fincomindia.nic.in/writereaddata/html_en_files/oldcommission_html/fcreport/tenthreport.htm.

Government of India, Ministry of Health and Family Welfare (MOHFW). 2018a. *Ayushman Bharat – National Health Protection Mission: Guidelines for Release of Premium.* New Delhi: National Health Agency. https://www.abnhpm.gov.in/sites/default/files/2018-07/Final%20Release%20of%20Premium%20and%20Escrow%20%20Account%20Guidelines%20under%20AB%20-%20NHPM%20-%2018-07-2018.pdf.

MOHFW. 2018b. *Ayushman Bharat Pradhan Mantri Jan Arogya Yojana* (PM-JAY) *Branding Guidelines.* National Health Agency. New Delhi.

—————.2017. *National Health Policy 2017*. New Delhi. https://www.nhp.gov.in/nhpfiles/national_health_policy_2017.pdf.

Government of India, Ministry of Human Resource Development (MHRD). 2016. *School Education in India U-DISE 2015–16*. New Delhi: National University of Educational Planning and Administration. Department of School Education and Literacy. http://www.dise.in/Downloads/Publications/Documents/U-DISE-SchoolEducationInIndia-2015-16.pdf.

MHRD. 1998. National Policy on Education (as modified in 1992). New Delhi: Department of Education. https://mhrd.gov.in/sites/upload_files/mhrd/files/document-reports/NPE86-mod92.pdf.

Government of Indonesia, Ministry of Health, Government of Australia, Department of Foreign Affairs and Trade, and Center for Health Economics and Policy Studies. 2013. *Indonesia National Health Accounts 2013: Initial Results*. Jakarta.

Government of the Republic of Korea, Ministry of Strategy and Finance (MOSF). 2014. *Budget System of Korea*. http://english.moef.go.kr/images/TheBudgetSystemofKorea.pdf.

I. Gupta et al. 2014. *Essential Health Package for India: Approach and Costing*. New Delhi: Institute of Economic Growth. https://papers.ssrn.com/sol3/papers.cfm?abstract_id=2858723.

N. Habibi et al. 2003. Decentralization and Human Development in Argentina. *Journal of Human Development*. 4 (1). pp. 73–101. https://www.researchgate.net/publication/227620301_Decentralization_and_Human_Development_in_Argentina.

K. Harada. 2009. Local Taxation in Japan. *Papers on the Local Governance System and its Implementation in Selected Fields in Japan*. No. 10. http://www.clair.or.jp/j/forum/honyaku/hikaku/pdf/BunyabetsuNo10en.pdf.

M. Harjowiryono. 2012. *Development of Indonesia's Intergovernmental Financing System. Fiscal Decentralization in Indonesia a Decade after the Big Bang*. Jakarta: Ministry of Finance.

D. Hauner. 2007. Benchmarking the Efficiency of Public Expenditure in the Russian Federation. *International Monetary Fund Working Paper*. WP/07/246. https://www.imf.org/en/Publications/WP/Issues/2016/12/31/Benchmarking-the-Efficiency-of-Public-Expenditure-in-the-Russian-Federation-21380.

P. Heywood and Y. Choi. 2010. *Health System Performance at the District Level in Indonesia after Decentralization*. BMC International Health and Human Rights. 10 (3). https://bmcinthealthhumrights.biomedcentral.com/articles/10.1186/1472-698X-10-3.

Hickling Corporation. 2008. Two Case Studies on Implementing the Indonesian Conditional Cash Transfer Program. The Pro-Poor Planning and Budgeting Project. Program Keluarga Harapan—PKH. *Working Paper No. 5*. Jakarta. https://www.bappenas.go.id/files/1913/5462/9599/wp-5-pkh-two-case-studies-hjalte-final-16-sept-2008__20090217143243__1850__2.pdf.

B. Hofman et al. 2006. Evaluating Fiscal Equalization in Indonesia. *Policy Research Working Paper 3911*. May. World Bank. http://www1.worldbank.org/publicsector/decentralization/decentralizationcorecourse2006/OtherReadings/HofmanEtAl.pdf.

M. H. Hur. 2013. *Korea's Government Performance Evaluation System and Operating Experience*. Ministry of Strategy and Finance. Republic of Korea. https://www.kdi.re.kr/kdi_eng/publications/publication_view.jsp?pub_no=13347.

Z. Husain et al. 2012. Opportunities and Challenges of Health Management Information System in India: A Case Study of Uttarakhand. *MPRA (Munich Personal RePEc Archive) Paper* No. 40014. New Delhi: Institute of Economic Growth. https://mpra.ub.uni-muenchen.de/40014/1/MPRA_paper_40014.pdf.

S. Ichimura and R. Bahl. 2009. *Decentralization Policies in Asian Development*. Singapore: World Scientific Press. https://books.google.com.ph/books?id=FS_C2RSKLPIC&pg=PA57&lpg=PA57&dq=%22Local+Finance+Law%22+Japan&source=bl&ots=XrgclyJWUV&sig=78PjwsQRc-00WxVLQBudfKZOceQ&hl=en&sa=X&ved=2ahUKEwiezeiq8_rdAhXH6Y8KHY4gCh0Q6AEwB3oECAEQAQ#v=onepage&q=%22Local%20Finance%20La.

Indian Council of Medical Research (ICMR), Public Health Foundation of India, Institute for Health Metrics and Evaluation and Ministry of Health and Family Welfare. 2017. *India: Health of the Nation's States. The India State-Level Disease Burden Initiative*. New Delhi. https://www.healthdata.org/sites/default/files/files/policy_report/2017/India_Health_of_the_Nation%27s_States_Report_2017.pdf.

P. Jain and R. Dholakia. 2009. Feasibility of Implementation of Right to Education Act. *Economic & Political Weekly*. 44 (25). pp. 38–43. http://re.indiaenvironmentportal.org.in/files/Right%20to%20Education%20Act.pdf.

A. Jaitley. 2018. Reconciling Fiscal Federalism and Accountability: Is there a Low Equilibrium Trap? In *Economic Survey 2017: Volume I, Chapter 4*. Government of India. https://ideas.repec.org/p/ess/wpaper/id12443.html.

D. Jimenez-Rubio. 2011a. The Impact of Decentralization of Health Services on Health Outcomes: Evidence from Canada. *Applied Economics*. 43 (26). pp. 3907–3917. https://www.tandfonline.com/doi/abs/10.1080/00036841003742579.

D. Jimenez-Rubio. 2011b. The Impact of Fiscal Decentralization on Infant Mortality Rates: Evidence from OECD Countries. *Social Science & Medicine*. 73 (9). pp. 1401–1407. https://www.sciencedirect.com/science/article/pii/S0277953611005016.

Y. Jin and R. Sun. 2011. Does Fiscal Decentralization Improve Healthcare Outcomes? Empirical Evidence from China. *Public Finance and Management*. 11 (3). pp. 234–261.

W. Juswanto and S. Nugroho. 2017. Promoting Disaster Risk Financing in Asia and the Pacific. ADBI Policy Brief. No. 2017-1. https://www.adb.org/publications/promoting-disaster-risk-financing-asia-and-pacific.

P. Khaleghian. 2004. Decentralization and Public Services: The Case of Immunization. *Social Science & Medicine*. 59 (1). pp. 163–183.

H. Kim. 2018. Fiscal Decentralization and Inclusive Growth: Considering Education. In J. Kim and S. Dougherty, eds. *Fiscal Decentralization and Inclusive Growth*. Chapter 6. pp. 127–151. OECD and Korean Institute of Public Finance. http://www.oecd.org/tax/federalism/fiscal-decentralisation-and-inclusive-growth.pdf.

J. Kim. 2015. Fiscal Illusion over National Mandates. In J. Kim, J. Lotz, and N. Jørgen Mau, eds. *Interaction Between Local Expenditure Responsibilities and Local Tax Policy: The Copenhagen Workshop 2013*. Chapter 7. Copenhagen, Denmark: Korea Institute of Public Finance and Danish Ministry for Economic Affairs and the Interior. http://www.kipf.re.kr/CopenhagenWorkshop/TheCopenhagenWorkshop2013.pdf.

K. Kis-Katos and B. Suharnoko Sjahrir. 2017. The Impact of Fiscal and Political Decentralization on Local Public Investment in Indonesia. *Journal of Comparative Economics*. 45 (2). pp. 344–365. http://ftp.iza.org/dp7884.pdf.

A. Kumar et al. undated. *Social Sector Expenditure of States Pre & Post Fourteenth Finance*

Commission (2014-15 & 2015-16). NITI Aayog. http://www.niti.gov.in/writereaddata/files/document_publication/Social%20Sector%20Expenditure%20of%20States_%20Paper.pdf.

S. Kumar. 2015. Private Sector in Healthcare Delivery Market in India: Structure, Growth and Implications. *Working Paper 185*. New Delhi: Institute for Studies in Industrial Development. http://isid.org.in/pdf/WP185.pdf.

C. Lahariya. 2018. Ayushman Bharat Program and Universal Health Coverage in India. *Indian Pediatrics*. 55 (6). pp. 495–506. https://link.springer.com/article/10.1007/s13312-018-1341-1.

B. Lewis. 2017. Local Government Spending and Service Delivery in Indonesia: The Perverse Effects of Substantial Fiscal Resources. *Regional Studies*. 51 (11). pp. 1695–1707. https://www.tandfonline.com/doi/abs/10.1080/00343404.2016.1216957?journalCode=cres20.

B. Lewis and P. Smoke. 2017. Intergovernmental Fiscal Transfers and Local Incentives and Responses: The Case of Indonesia. *Fiscal Studies*. https://www.researchgate.net/publication/286539749_Intergovernmental_Fiscal_Transfers_and_Local_Incentives_and_Responses_The_Case_of_Indonesia.

Y. Liu and J. Zhao. 2011. Intergovernmental Fiscal Transfers and Local Tax Efforts: Evidence from Provinces in China. *Journal of Economic Policy Reform*. 14 (4). pp. 295–300. https://www.tandfonline.com/doi/abs/10.1080/17487870.2011.591175.

J. Ma. 1997. Intergovernmental Fiscal Transfers in Nine Countries: Lessons for Developing Countries. *Policy Research Working Paper 1822*. The World Bank, Economic Development Institute, Macroeconomic Management and Policy Division. http://www1.worldbank.org/publicsector/LearningProgram/Decentralization/ITFNineCountries.pdf.

K. Mackay. 2011. The Performance Framework of the Australian Government, 1987 to 2011. *OECD Journal on Budgeting*. 2011/3. https://www.oecd.org/gov/budgeting/49042370.pdf.

A. Mahal et al. 2000. Decentralization and Public Delivery of Health and Education Services in India. In J-J. Dethier, ed. *Governance, Decentralization and Reform in China, India, and Russia*. Kluwer Academic Publishers.

A. Maharani. 2015. *Decentralisation, Performance of Health Providers and Health Outcomes in Indonesia*. Thesis Submitted to the University of Manchester for the Degree of Doctor of Philosophy in the Faculty of Humanities. https://www.research.manchester.ac.uk/portal/files/54575246/FULL_TEXT.PDF.

J. Martínez-Vázquez. 2011a. *The Impact of Fiscal Decentralization: Issues in Theory and Challenges in Practice*. Manila: ADB. https://www.adb.org/sites/default/files/publication/28927/impact-fiscal-decentralization.pdf.

J. Martínez-Vázquez. 2011b. *Fiscal Decentralization in Asia: Challenges and Opportunities*. Manila: ADB. https://www.adb.org/sites/default/files/publication/28805/fiscal-decentralization.pdf.

J. Martínez-Vázquez et al. 2017. The Impact of Fiscal Decentralization: A Survey. *Journal of Economic Surveys*. 31 (4). pp. 1095–1129. https://ideas.repec.org/a/bla/jecsur/v31y2017i4p1095-1129.html.

J. Martínez-Vázquez et al. 2006. Local Public Finance in China: Intergovernmental Transfers. *CEMA Working Papers 552*. China Economics and Management Academy, Central University of Finance and Economics. http://down.aefweb.net/WorkingPapers/w552.pdf.

M. Matsuura et al. 2010. Overview of Public Sector Performance Assessment Processes in Japan. *Global Expert Team (GET) Note*. Washington, DC: World Bank. https://openknowledge.worldbank.org/

bitstream/handle/10986/10477/600930
BRI0GetN10BOX358310B01PUBLIC1.
pdf?sequence=1&isAllowed=y.

B. Meessen. 2009. *An Institutional Economic Analysis
of Public Health Care Organisations in Low-Income
Countries*. Doctoral Dissertation. Louvain-
la-Neuve: Université Catholique de Louvain,
Département des Sciences Economiques,
Facultés des Sciences Economiques, Sociales et
Politiques.

B. Meessen et al. 2011. Performance-Based Financing:
Just a Donor Fad or a Catalyst towards
Comprehensive Health-Care Reform? *Bulletin of
the World Health Organization*. 89 (2). pp. 153–
156. https://www.ncbi.nlm.nih.gov/pmc/articles/
PMC3040374/.

M. Mehta and D. Mehta. 2013. *Performance
Based Grants for Urban Local Bodies: Suggestions
for the Third State Finance Commission,
Gujarat*. Ahmedabad: CEPT University. https://
www.pas.org.in/Portal/document/ResourcesFiles/
pdfs/PBGS%20for%20Gujarat%20SFC.pdf.

N. Mochida. 2001. *Taxes and Transfers in
Japan's Local Public Finances*. World Bank
Institute. http://documents1.worldbank.
org/curated/en/291691468774913337/
pdf/330430JP0wbi37171.pdf.

R. K. Mohanty and N. R. Bhanumurthy. 2018.
Assessing Public Expenditure Efficiency in Indian
States. *National Institute of Public Finance and
Policy Working Paper*. No. 225. https://www.
nipfp.org.in/media/medialibrary/2018/03/
WP_2018_225.pdf.

A. Mukherjee. 2016. Fiscal Devolution and Health
Financing Reform: Lessons for India from Brazil,
China and Mexico. *CGD Policy Paper 97*. December.
Washington, DC: Center for Global Development.
https://www.cgdev.org/sites/default/files/fiscal-
devolution-health-financing-reform.pdf.

E. Murniasih. 2005. *Is the New Intergovernmental
Equalisation Grant in Indonesia Equalising?*
Institute for Public Finance Reform. Moscow.
http://www.ipfr.ru/filemanager/files/ind_2_
transferts_indonesia.pdf.

C. Murray. 1996. Rethinking DALYs. In C. J. L.
Murray and A. D. Lopez, eds.
*The Global Burden of Disease:
A Comprehensive Assessment of Mortality
and Disability from Diseases, Injuries,
and Risk Factors in 1990 and Projected
to 2020*. pp. 1–98 Cambridge, MA:
Harvard School of Public Health.
http://apps.who.int/iris/bitstream/
handle/10665/41864/0965546608_eng.
pdf?sequence=1&isAllowed=y.

T. Muttaqin et al. 2016. *The Impact of Decentralization
on Educational Attainment in Indonesia.
Decentralization and Governance in Indonesia*.
Springer. pp. 79–103.

A. Nasution. 2016. Government Decentralization
Program in Indonesia. *ADBI Working Paper*.
No. 601. October. Tokyo: ADBI Institute.
https://www.adb.org/sites/default/files/
publication/201116/adbi-wp601.pdf.

National Assembly Budget Office (NABO). 2013.
National Finance of Korea at a Glance 2013. http://
korea.nabo.go.kr/adm/bbs/down.php?code=publ
ications&idx=5681&no=1.

NITI Aayog. 2019a. *The Success of Our Schools: School
Education Quality Index (SEQI)*. New Delhi.
https://niti.gov.in/sites/default/files/2019-09/
seqi_document.pdf.

—————. 2019b. Healthy States, Progressive India:
Report on the Ranks of States and Union
Territories. *Health Index June 2019*. New Delhi:
Ministry of Health and Family Welfare and World
Bank. http://social.niti.gov.in/uploads/sample/
health_index_report.pdf.

————. 2018a. *Healthy States, Progressive India: Report on Ranks of States and Union Territories in India*. Ministry of Health and Family Welfare and World Bank. http://niti.gov.in/writereaddata/files/Healthy-States-Progressive-India-Report.pdf.

————. 2018b. *Strategy for New India @75*. New Delhi. http://niti.gov.in/writereaddata/files/Strategy_for_New_India.pdf.

————. 2017. *Performance on Health Outcomes: A Reference Guidebook December 2016*. New Delhi. http://social.niti.gov.in/uploads/sample/Guidebook_SHI.pdf.

National Sample Survey Office (NSSO). 2015. *Key Indicators of Social Consumption in India: Health*. New Delhi: Ministry of Statistics and Program Implementation. https://www.thehinducentre.com/multimedia/archive/02460/nss_71st_ki_health_2460766a.pdf.

R. Nussbaum. 2015. Involving Public Private Partnerships as Building Blocks for Integrated Natural Catastrophes Country Risk Management—Sharing on the French National Experiences of Economic Instruments Integrated with Information and Knowledge Management Tools. *Journal of Integrated Disaster Risk Management*. 5 (2). pp. 82–100.

Organisation for Economic Co-operation and Development (OECD). 2017. *Multi-level Governance Reforms: Overview of OECD Country Experiences*. OECD Multi-level Governance Studies. Paris: OECD Publishing. https://www.oecd-ilibrary.org/docserver/9789264272866-en.pdf?expires=1543989108&id=id&accname=ocid177207&checksum=349FDD348CBE3A233F928554B24E34A1.

OECD. 2016. *OECD Economic Surveys: Indonesia 2016*. Paris. https://www.oecd-ilibrary.org/docserver/eco_surveys-idn-2016-en.pdf?expires=1576066264&id=id&accname=ocid177207&checksum=62876CA1FABBBAD74C0BA36FC73AFFA7.

————. 2012. *International Budget Practices and Procedures Database*. Paris. http://www.oecd.org/gov/budgeting/internationalbudgetpracticesandproceduresdatabase.htm.

B. Olken et al. 2017. *Project Generasi: Conditional Community Block Grants in Indonesia*. The Abdul Latif Jameel Poverty Action Lab. https://www.povertyactionlab.org/evaluation/project-generasi-conditional-community-block-grants-indonesia.

K. R. Panta. 2017. *Study on Intergovernmental Fiscal Transfers for Federal Nepal*. Government of Nepal, Ministry of Federal Affairs and Local Development. Local Body Fiscal Commission. http://lbfc.gov.np/sites/default/files/Study%20on%20Intergovernmental%20Fiscal%20transfer%20for%20federal%20Nepal_0.pdf.

N. Park. 2017. *Current Issues of PFM Reforms in Korea*. Center for Performance Evaluation & Management (CPEM), Korea Institute of Public Finance. https://www.unescap.org/sites/default/files/Panel%201-2.%20KIPF_Dr.%20Nowook%20Park.pdf.

P. Prakash. 2013. Property Taxes Across G20 Countries: Can India Get It Right? OXFAM *India Working Paper Series OIWPS-XV*. New Delhi. http://www.cbgaindia.org/wp-content/uploads/2016/03/Property-Tax-paper-1.pdf.

Public Affairs Index, Governance in the States of India. Public Affairs Index. Bengaluru: Public Affairs (Years: 2016, 2017, and 2018). http://pai.pacindia.org/#/2016/public-affairs-index; http://pai.pacindia.org/#/2017/public-affairs-index; and http://pai.pacindia.org/#/2018.

I. Rajaraman and M. Gupta. 2016. Preserving the Incentive Properties of Statutory Grants. *Economic & Political Weekly*. 9. pp. 79–84. https://www.researchgate.net/publication/296235351_Preserving_the_Incentive_Properties_of_Statutory_Grants.

I. Rajaraman and G. Vasishtha. 2000. Impact of Grants on Tax Effort of Local Government. *National Institute of Public Finance and Policy Working Paper*. No. 176. https://www.nipfp.org.in/media/pdf/working_papers/WP_2000_176.pdf.

A. S. Rajkumar and V. Swaroop. 2008. Public Spending and Outcomes: Does Governance Matter? *Journal of Development Economics*. 86. pp. 96–111. https://web.archive.org/web/20170810204200/https://www.unicef.org/socialpolicy/files/Public_spending_and_outcomes_governance.pdf.

M. G. Rao. 2018. The Effect of Intergovernmental Transfers on Public Services in India. In J. Kim and S. Dougherty, eds. *Fiscal Decentralization and Inclusive Growth*. Chapter 4. pp. 71–98. OECD and Korean Institute of Public Finance. http://www.oecd.org/tax/federalism/fiscal-decentralisation-and-inclusive-growth.pdf.

M. G. Rao. 2017. *Central Transfers to States in India: Rewarding Performance while Ensuring Equity*. Final Report of a Study Submitted to NITI Aayog. New Delhi: National Institute of Public Finance. http://niti.gov.in/writereaddata/files/document_publication/Report%20on%20CENTRAL%20TRANSFERS%20TO%20STATES%20IN%20INDIA.pdf.

N. Rao. 2018. *Demand for Grants 2018-19 Analysis Human Resource Development*. PRS Legislative Research. https://www.prsindia.org/sites/default/files/budget_files/DFG-%20HRD%202018-19.pdf.

D. Reidpath and P. Allotey. 2003. Infant Mortality Rate as an Indicator of Population Health. *J Epidemiol Community Health*. 57 (5). pp. 344–346. https://jech.bmj.com/content/jech/57/5/344.full.pdf.

Reserve Bank of India (RBI). 2018. *State Finances: A Study of Budgets of 2017-18 and 2018-19*. Mumbai. https://www.rbi.org.in/Scripts/AnnualPublications.aspx?head=State%20Finances%20:%20A%20Study%20of%20Budgets.

D. A. Robalino et al. 2001. Does Fiscal Decentralization Improve Health Outcomes? Evidence from a Cross-country Analysis. *Policy Research Working Paper Series*. No. 2565. World Bank. http://documents.worldbank.org/curated/en/832091468739534469/pdf/multi0page.pdf.

R. Ryan and R. Woods. 2015. Decentralisation and Subsidiarity: Concepts and Frameworks for Emerging Economies. *Occasional Paper Series No. 15*. Forum of Federations. The Global Network on Federalism and Devolved Governance. https://www.uts.edu.au/sites/default/files/Decentralisation_Subsidiarity.pdf.

A. H. Samadi et al. 2013. The Effect of Fiscal Decentralization on under Five Mortality in Iran: A Panel Data Analysis. *International Journal of Health Policy and Management*. 1 (4). pp. 301–306. http://www.ijhpm.com/article_2795_4d03 6a6cb3b76cc8130c4c250fc580f0.pdf.

V. Sari. 2018. Educational Assistance and Education Quality in Indonesia: The Role of Decentralization. *WIDER Working Paper Series 037*. World Institute for Development Economic Research (UNU-WIDER). https://www.wider.unu.edu/sites/default/files/Publications/Working-paper/PDF/wp2018-37.pdf.

S. Schiavo-Campo and D. Tommasi. 1999. *Managing Government Expenditure*. Manila: ADB. https://www.adb.org/sites/default/files/publication/27901/managing-government-expenditure.pdf.

T. K. Sen et al. 2014. *Intergovernmental Finance in Five Emerging Markets*. National Institute of Public Finance and Policy Study undertaken for the 14th Finance Commission. http://fincomindia.nic.in/writereaddata%5Chtml_en_files%5Cfincom14/others/31.pdf.

A. Shah. 2012. *Lessons from Worldwide Practices of Intergovernmental Fiscal Transfers.* Presentation at Seminar on Fiscal Federalism. Azores. 5–6 July 2012.

A. Shah. 2006. A Practitioner's Guide to Intergovernmental Fiscal Transfers. *World Bank Policy Research Working Paper.* No. 4039. World Bank. https://openknowledge.worldbank. org/bitstream/handle/10986/9013/wps4039. pdf?sequence=1&isAllowed=y.

C. Shen et al. 2012. Fiscal Decentralization in China: History, Impact, Challenges and Next Steps. *Annals of Economics and Finance.* 13-1. pp. 1–51. http://www.aeconf.com/Articles/May2012/ aef130101.pdf.

D. Simandjuntak. 2018. A Special Law for Archipelagic Provinces: Is It Necessary for Kepri? *ISEAS— Yusof Ishak Institute Perspective Working Paper.* No. 10. https://www.iseas.edu.sg/images/pdf/ ISEAS_Perspective_2018_10@50.pdf.

P. Smoke. 2016. Looking Behind Conventional Intergovernmental Fiscal Frameworks: Principles, Realities and Neglected Issues. *ADBI Working Paper Series.* No. 606. Tokyo: ADBI. https://www.adb. org/sites/default/files/publication/203921/adbi- wp606.pdf.

P. Smoke and Y. Kim. 2002. *Intergovernmental Fiscal Transfers in Asia: Current Practice and Challenges for the Future.* Manila: ADB. https:// think-asia.org/bitstream/handle/11540/4965/ Intergovernmental%20Fiscal%20 Transfers%20in%20Asia%20Current%20 Practice%20and%20Challenges%20for%20 the%20Future%20%28Dec02%29%20. pdf?sequence=1.

A. Soejoto et al. 2015. Fiscal Decentralization Policy in Promoting Indonesia Human Development. *International Journal of Economics and Financial Issues.* 5 (3). pp. 763–771. http://www.econjournals.com/index.php/ijefi/ article/view/1314/pdf.

V. Soto et al. 2012. Fiscal Decentralisation and Infant Mortality Rate: The Colombian Case. *Social Science & Medicine.* 74 (9), pp. 1426–1434. https://www.sciencedirect.com/science/article/ pii/S0277953612001153.

M. Sow and I. Razafimahefa. 2018. Fiscal Decentralization and the Efficiency of Public Service Delivery. In J. Kim and S. Dougherty, eds. *Fiscal Decentralization and Inclusive Growth.* Chapter 9. pp. 213–240. OECD and Korean Institute of Public Finance. http://www.oecd. org/tax/federalism/fiscal-decentralisation-and- inclusive-growth.pdf.

D. K. Srivastava and B. C. Rao. 2009. *Review of Trends in Fiscal Transfers in India.* Madras School of Economics. https://fincomindia.nic.in/ writereaddata/html_en_files/oldcommission_ html/fincom13/discussion/report02.pdf.

Steering Committee for the Review of Government Service Provision. 2013. *National Agreement Performance Information 2012-13: National Healthcare Agreement.* Canberra: Productivity Commission, Commonwealth of Australia. https://www. pc.gov.au/research/supporting/national- agreements/healthcare/healthcare- agreement-2012-13.pdf.

A. Tandon et al. 2016. Indonesia—Health Financing System Assessment: Spend More, Right and Better. World Bank. http://documents.worldbank. org/curated/en/453091479269158106/ pdf/110298-REVISED-PUBLIC-HFSA-Nov17- LowRes.pdf.

D. Tirtosuharto. 2017. Does Fiscal Decentralization Help Indonesia Avoid the Middle-income Trap? *ADBI Working Paper Series.* No. 729. https://www.adb.org/sites/default/files/ publication/297151/adbi-wp729.pdf.

H. Uchimura and J. Jütting. 2009. Fiscal Decentralization, Chinese Style: Good for Health Outcomes? *World Development.* 37 (12).

pp. 1926–1934. https://doi.org/10.1016/j.
worlddev.2009.06.007.

N. Uda. 2015. Japan: Fiscal Discipline of Local
Governments. *Fiscal Policy for Long-Term Growth
and Sustainability in Aging Societies*. https://www.
mof.go.jp/pri/research/seminar/fy2015/tff2015_
s5_03.pdf.

UK Essays. 2013. Fiscal Federalism in India:
Intergovernmental Transfers Explored. *Economics
Essay*. November. https://www.ukessays.
com/essays/economics/fiscal-fedaralism-in-
india-intergovernmental-transfers-explored-
economics-essay.php#citethis.

United Nations Capital Development Fund (UNCDF).
2010. *Performance-based Grant Systems: Concept
and International Experience*. New York. https://
europa.eu/capacity4dev/public-pub.sector-
reform-decentralisation/document/uncdf-2010-
performance-based-grant-systems-concept-
and-international-experience.

United Nations (UN) Habitat. 2012. Fiscal
Decentralization in Japan. *The Global Urban
Economic Dialogue Series*. Nairobi. https://web.
archive.org/web/20170222131206/http://
unhabitat.org/books/91686/#.

P. Vergeer et al. 2011. *In Schematics: Argentina
Performance Based Financing Plan Nacer*. https://
www.rbfhealth.org/sites/rbf/files/Argentina%20
schematic.pdf.

P. Vujanovic. 2017. Decentralisation to Promote
Regional Development in Indonesia. *OECD
Economics Department Working Papers*.
No. 1380. Paris: OECD Publishing. https://www.
oecd-ilibrary.org/economics/oecd-economic-
surveys-indonesia-2016/decentralisation-to-
promote-regional-development_eco_surveys-
idn-2016-7-en.

H. Wibowo. 2015. Measuring Fiscal Decentralization
in Indonesia. http://www.anggaran.kemenkeu.

go.id/api/Medias/1e01d82c-861a-47fe-8ccc-
f0999e7687b9.

C. Wong. 2013. Reforming China's Public Finances
for Long-Term Growth. In R. Garnaut, C. Fang,
and L. Song, eds. *China: A New Model for Growth
and Development*. Chapter 10. pp. 199–219.
Canberra: Australian National University Press.
http://press-files.anu.edu.au/downloads/press/
p244991/pdf/book.pdf?referer=131.

World Bank. 2019. Making Decentralization
Work. *South Asia Economic Focus*. Fall 2019.
Washington, DC. https://openknowledge.
worldbank.org/handle/10986/32515.

—————. 2018. *Indonesia: Public Expenditure
and Financial Accountability (PEFA)
Assessment Report 2017*. Washington, DC.
http://documents.worldbank.org/curated/
en/681171529941208881/pdf/PEFA-Report.pdf.

—————. 2016. Do Fiscal Transfers Generate Results?
Cross-sectoral Debate on Results-Based Fiscal
Transfers. *Results-Based Financing Operational
Notes*. The Results in Education for All Children
(REACH) Trust Fund. http://pubdocs.worldbank.
org/en/827381525113694676/QD-Notes-No1-
Fiscal-Transfers-Final-PROOFREAD.pdf.

—————. 2013. *Argentina: Plan Nacer Improves Birth
Outcomes and Decreases Neonatal Mortality
among Beneficiaries*. Press release. 18 September.
Washington, DC. http://www.worldbank.org/en/
news/press-release/2013/09/18/argentina-plan-
nacer-birth-outcomes-decreases-neonatal-
mortality-beneficiaries.

—————. 2012. *Indonesia: A Healthy and Smart
Generation (PNPM Generasi)*. Washington,
DC. http://www.worldbank.org/en/
results/2012/07/03/indonesia-healthy-and-
smart-generation-pnpm-generasi.

—————. 2003. *World Development Report
2004: Making Services Work for Poor People*.

Washington, DC. http://documents.worldbank.
org/curated/en/527371468166770790/pdf/
multi0page.pdf.

——————. 1998. Linking Policy, Planning, and
Budgeting in a Medium Term Framework. In
Public Expenditure Management Handbook.
Chapter 3. pp. 31–52. Washington, DC. http://
www1.worldbank.org/publicsector/pe/handbook/
pem98.pdf.

World Health Organization (WHO). 2018. *World
Health Statistics 2018: Monitoring Health
for the SDGs.* Geneva. https://www.who.int/
gho/publications/world_health_statistics/
2018/en/.

World Observatory of Subnational Finance and
Investment. 2019. *SNG-WOFI Database.*
http://www.sng-wofi.org/.

A. Yamini et al. 2015. *Power to the States. Making
Fiscal Transfer Work for Better Health.* Final
Report of the Intergovernmental Fiscal
Transfers for the Health Working Group.
Centre for Global Development and
Accountability Initiative, Centre for Policy
Research. Washington, DC. https://www.cgdev.
org/sites/default/files/India-fiscal-transfers-
CGD-working-group-report.pdf.

E. Yee. 2001. The Effects of Fiscal Decentralization
on Health Care in China. *University Avenue
Undergraduate Journal of Economics.* 5 (1).
Article 5. https://digitalcommons.iwu.edu/cgi/
viewcontent.cgi?article=1053&context=uauje.

A. Young. 2015. *Local Autonomy and Local Finance
in Korea.* Korea Research Institute for Local
Administration. http://oecdkorea.org/
common/attachfile/attachfileDownload.
do?attachNo=00003369.

S. Yusifov. 2018. Regional Development Policies of
Korea and Policy Suggestions for Azerbaijan.
*KIEP Research Paper, World Economy Brief
18-16.* https://papers.ssrn.com/sol3/papers.
cfm?abstract_id=3181779.